A Polish Son in the Motherland

LEONARD KNIFFEL

A Polish Son
in the
Motherland

An American's Journey Home

TEXAS A&M UNIVERSITY PRESS
College Station

The paper used in this book meets the minimum requirements of the American
National Standard for Permanence of Paper for Printed Library Materials,
z39.48–1984. Binding materials have been chosen for durability.
∞

LIBRARY OF CONGRESS CATALOGING-IN-PUBLICATION DATA

Kniffel, Leonard.

A Polish son in the motherland : an American's journey home /
Leonard Kniffel.—1st ed.

p.   cm.

Includes index.

ISBN 1-58544-420-0 (cloth : alk. paper) — ISBN 1-58544-441-3 (pbk. : alk. paper)

1. Poland—Description and travel.   2. Kniffel, Leonard—Travel—Poland.   I. Title.

DK4081.K6 2005

914.3804'57'092—dc22

2004016545

An earlier version of "Back in the Old Country" was first published in
New Horizon: Polish American Cultural Review 26, no. 5 (May 2001): 6–7.

In memory of my mother and my grandmother

Contents

Acknowledgments

Immeasurable thanks to the Kopiczyński family for opening their homes and their lives to a stranger; to Pani Urszula Wituchowska for her warmth and affection; to Ryszard Ulatowski and Grażyna Jonowska, who never let me miss a moment; to my relatives in Poland, who welcomed me with open arms and open hearts; and to my cousins and aunts and uncles in America, who are always with me. Special thanks to Maria Śliwińska for her faith and persistence, to Danuta Brodacka for not hanging up on me, to Carlon Walker for his loyalty and assistance, and to the American Library Association for the sabbatical leave that made writing this book possible.

A Polish Son in the Motherland

Back in the Old Country

I brought my mother here to Poland in 1988 to see the motherland, the place where her parents were born. We rented a taxi in Warsaw. In those days you could hire a cab for an entire day for twenty American dollars. The grateful driver chauffeured us to Nowe Miasto Lubawskie and then to Boleszyn, towns I remembered from the little cedar box my grandmother kept in her dresser. The box held letters from family, letters that stopped coming after her husband died in 1950. It was a quick tour, and we marveled at being on the same land where my grandmother was born, where she had run as a little girl. That was before I learned that her village was Sugajno, a couple kilometers down the road.

It had been three-quarters of a century since my grandmother's feet had touched this ground and sixteen years since she had died. My mother surprised both of us with the Polish that came automatically from her lips, welling up from some floppy disk in her brain, the file corrupted with English and bad grammar. But for the most part we were strangers in a foreign land, connected to it only by some idea of Polishness that relied largely on *kiełbasa,* vodka, and the sound of accordion music.

We walked through the cemetery in Boleszyn, even found a Bryszkiewski grave. Two old women tending flowers told us they believed there were still some relatives with that name living "somewhere far off in that direction." And then we went back to Warsaw and the next day back to the United States.

Before we left, however, I vowed to come back. I want to know what I missed by being born in America, to understand what it means to lose two thousand years of history in the time it takes to buy a ticket on a ship leaving "the old country" for the new.

So I have returned to Poland, this time not to pass through but to live here, where my grandmother lived, to see if any threads of Polishness still dangle from that severed connection. What happened to the people in the few old pictures and letters I have packed in my suitcase? And why did they stop writing fifty years ago? Little mysteries. Every family has them.

To escape the chilly winter drizzle, I duck into the underground passages near my hotel on Jerozolimskie Avenue and follow them to Warsaw's central train station. Below the streets, dozens of stalls bulge with merchandise—not at all the way they looked the first time I came to Poland—in 1981. The colors of fruit and vegetables, compact disks, and videocassettes announce themselves against the gray concrete walls and floors: "This is the new Poland of plenty, where American marketing is king." The old women selling flowers will give you a special rate on roses if you buy more than a dozen, and the brassiere stand advertises its abundance with an ambiguous two-for-one sale.

At the ticket counter shuffles the characteristic Polish queue, a funnel of bodies elbowing their way to a crabby cashier behind a window, through which it is impossible to hear and with an opening too low for anyone but a ten-year-old. This part of being in Poland has not changed since my first trip here, when the shops were stagnant but the air was electric with change.

My destination isn't posted, so before I get to the window I tear a little piece of paper out of my notebook and write down in Polish that I want to buy a ticket to Nowe Miasto Lubawskie for tomorrow at midday, and I ask the woman behind the glass to write down what she is telling me and from what platform the train will leave. But she is impatient. I am stuttering, trying to remember the right words, and a man in a dirty sweater is leaning his face into my *złoty*. The cashier passes the paper back with my ticket and tells me I must catch the train for Gdańsk and get off at Iława. "Next," she barks, and the man in the sweater has already lowered his face to the hole in the glass.

Oh well, I rationalize, this aggravation is part of what I came here for, and it is merely a taste of what it must have been like for my grandmother when she arrived in America in 1913, a strange land with people babbling impatiently in a different language.

Dusk arrives just past five o'clock, and I head back to the hotel to settle in for the night. From somewhere comes the unmistakable smell of cooking cabbage. I make up Polish sentences in my head, for practice. A young woman lets rip with a laugh that could curdle milk, as if she can hear my mistakes. Up and down Jerozolimskie Avenue wafts the inexplicable sound of Peruvian pipe music from some source at the Metro stop near the Palace of Culture and Science. This edifice, Stalin's gift to Poland, stands like a grotesque reminder of the big ideas, the big plans Russia had for the pigheaded Poles, who seem able to wear down the biggest of them, complicating everything—even the purchase of a train ticket—with persistent disorganization.

The next day I begin my journey to Nowe Miasto, regretting that I did not listen more closely and ask more questions when I lived with my grandmother and she talked about her life in Poland. On the train I share a compartment with a man named Cezary, a former shipyard worker from Gdańsk, who is traveling with his daughter, Katarzyna, and just happens to be reading *Moll Flanders* in English. He hands me his card. They both speak my language fluently. "You are going to be considered quite exotic in Nowe Miasto," Katarzyna advises.

I am caught up in their predictions and questions and suddenly realize we have stopped for Iława, and my three enormous bags are still on the shelves above our seats. Cezary heaves the largest to the floor. Katarzyna rushes into the corridor, yelling "Wait! Wait!" out the window to the conductor. She and her father jump off the train as I hand luggage down to them and follow. But the train won't wait and starts to roll away without them. "Stop! Stop!" demands Cezary, and the wheels screech and scrape to a halt while they hop back on.

"Come and see us in Gdańsk," Cezary yells. "We'll go sailing!"

The hotel in Nowe Miasto has sent a man named Marek to meet me, and he is waiting inside the train station. He looks like Tadeusz Kościuszko, Polish hero of the American Revolution, in a jogging suit. He eyes me for a moment, then welcomes me enthusiastically, grabs my heaviest bag—now handleless from being dragged through the train station—and leads me to his little Polish pickup. Marek inquires politely about what I am doing here. I tell him my grandmother was born in Sugajno. Helena Bryszkiewska. "Don't know the name," he says.

The hills and lakes around Nowe Miasto are dusted with snow as if someone had sprinkled powdered sugar over them like *chruściki,* the delicate egg confections you see in every Polish American bakery. The river is overflowing with the early spring thaw, and water sits along the banks in half-frozen pockets visible through the birch and linden trees.

Beyond the town, over the bridge, a cheery blue, modern building appears down a long gravel driveway, now mud packed from the thaw. Behind an old brick building that clings to the road like a piece of burned pie crust is a sports complex, complete with a stadium and a soccer field, where loud young men are grunting in huddles. My "hotel" is a camp for high-school athletes.

Ewa at the front desk smiles and welcomes me and assures me every time I open my mouth and begin to sputter that I speak wonderful Polish. Marek shows me to my room. "Everything works," he says, nodding at the crude holes cut into the walls and floors for pipes and wires. There is no phone, no television. A painting of some unidentifiable tourist destination hangs high on the wall. The door between the tiny vestibule and the bedroom won't close completely. In the halls, young men giggle and chatter about girls and games, their speech casually peppered with variations on the word *kurwa*—whore.

Ewa directs me to the Ratuszowa restaurant on the Rynek, the town square, for dinner. It's cold outside. I put on two coats and wonder why I expected Poland to be warm in March. A short walk up the road, a bridge crosses the river Drwęca. Beyond stands the town, where it has stood for hundreds of years, through one hundred fifty years of partitioned Poland, through two world wars, and through the loss of so many people to America. To get to the square I must walk past an old brick tower, five or six stories tall, part of a medieval wall that once surrounded the town. This square must have once hosted a market. It's easy to imagine the stalls and horse-drawn carts that carried produce to town from Sugajno and the little farm where my grandmother was born. Nearly a hundred years ago she walked the streets of Nowe Miasto. I remember her telling me about the wonders to be found in "such a big town." Each building makes me ask: Was it here then? Did she see this? Her nationality was officially German; it said so on the ship's manifest when she came to America. Poland was no longer a nation; it was an idea, a memory that lived only in the minds of its people.

Twice around the square and I give up and stop at a store to ask where the Ratuszowa restaurant is. "In the center," I'm told by a friendly woman in a *delikatesy*. The building in the center of the square is not a church, as it appears, nor the town hall, as its name says. It is a cinema through the front entrance and a restaurant through the side door.

Snow is falling now like tiny crystalline doilies that disappear into my dark green coat, and early darkness has left the entrance in shadows. Three men in suits pace outside, chatting and smoking. I excuse myself and pass them to swing open the heavy wooden door. The bright lights blind me for a second, but then I see that every head in the place—and there are at least fifty of them—is turned toward me. I see flowers, more men in suits, women in evening clothes, tables arranged in long communal seating. There are twelve thousand people in Nowe Miasto, I have been told, and one restaurant. The evening I arrive, it's booked for a *wesele,* and I blunder into a Polish wedding reception at an apparently crucial moment. Everyone is staring at me as if to say, "And who are you?" before I realize my mistake and gently shut the door.

I trudge back to the delicatessen and the smell of sausages and dairy. I buy a small package of *pumpernikiel* bread and another of *morski* cheese and a jar of *musztarda.* At the counter I ask for a little ham, and she says something I don't understand except that it has to do with weight. I agree, and she starts to wrap a huge stack of slices. I try to tell her that it's too much, to give me half, and she looks perplexed, as if thinking, "He looks Polish. Why can't this man talk right?"

In the morning, heavy footsteps and young voices in the hall remind me of where I am. More snow has fallen in the night, and frost decorates the window wall. Outside, a cluster of buildings sits stiff and gray across the lawn and beyond a shabby concrete fence. Here an overturned wheelbarrow, there a wire clothesline, clothespins stuck to it like tiny sleeping birds. There is no early spring here, as I had hoped. I will have to buy a hat.

The sun tries to break through the clouds, and a determined crow waddles across the tilled yard behind a cement house. I make my way out of my room, and two blonde young women, smiling behind the glass reception area, seem to know already that I am here. They show no surprise, but I see curiosity in their faces. The strange American has emerged, they seem to be thinking, the man of whom we were warned. He'll need a lot of help.

"Proszę," they sing out, which means everything: "What can I do for you?" "Please take this." "I need your answer." I reply by asking if I can have coffee. "And what about breakfast?" one says.

Minutes later I have a hot cup of coffee in my room and food on a white plastic plate with matching white plastic fork and knife, a tiny, tissue-paper square, three slices of rye bread, packets of Danish butter and plum jam, and a tublet of *kurczak w galarecie,* cold chicken and vegetables congealed in gelatin. Also on the plate is a shot glass containing a bitter-smelling liquid. Vodka at eight o'clock in the morning? Well, this is Poland, so I take a sip. If it's vodka, it's the worst I have ever tasted.

I carry the little glass out to the reception desk and ask the young woman, "Co to jest?" What is this? To drink? I make drinking motions. Both the women laugh with alarm. "Nie, nie, ocet." I find the word in my dictionary: vinegar. "To pour on your *galareta,*" the blonde explains.

In my room I flip the plastic container upside down on the plate, and the galareta slides out with a smack. It looks like chicken soup that has been in the

Back in the Old Country
—

refrigerator overnight. I pour the vinegar over it and poke it with a plastic fork. Peas and pieces of corn and carrot tumble out. In the center a sliced egg sits captured amid pieces of its mother. I try, but I am not hungry enough to eat it. So as not to seem ungrateful, I throw the galareta into the toilet, where it sits on the peculiar ledge that Polish toilets have where water should be. After several flushes it remains, like a clump of rubber, impervious to the water slushing around it. Finally I must force it down the drain with a stick.

A wave of homesickness passes over me as I contemplate my next move— to mass, drawn by the clanging of bells that persists for twenty minutes.

Sunday morning finds what looks like the entire town walking to church in a gentle snowfall—stylishly dressed women, self-conscious teens, obedient children, trickling in from sidewalks and around corners in every direction. Small groups feed into larger streams, past the Rynek, and around the corner, now hundreds strong, all flowing into the enormous stack of bricks and stucco bathed in sunlight made brighter by the new snow.

Inside the church, giant baroque and rococo constructions of wood and metal hang on the columns that brace the arched ceiling, possibly sixty feet high. The stained-glass windows let in only enough light to emphasize that the chandeliers are not lit and to give hazy illumination to the dozens of altar statues. Elaborate frescoes on the walls and paintings on the altars depict the lives of saints and the Blessed Mother.

From my seat at the back I watch as the church fills to capacity. It is like St. Florian's in Hamtramck, Michigan, where my mother was born, only much older. The people look the same—modern, dressed in fur-trimmed coats and woolly hats. But the differences soon show themselves. The kneeler in my pew is worm eaten and half broken away. The church is freezing cold, yet no one seems to mind. As they enter, the faithful do not merely genuflect, they kneel firmly on the stone floor for many minutes, young and old, meditating. All the while the priest at the front altar quizzes a row of children about how best to serve God. They recite with sincerity:"I will help the poor and those who have nothing," one little girl's voice resounds through the hall over a microphone.

The mass proceeds to the spot where a mandatory handshake and "Peace be with you" make for awkward touching and smiling in American churches. But here it is different. The congregation mutters something about "to all" into the air. The man on my right and the woman on my left nod suspiciously at me, their hands at their sides; then they turn their eyes heavenward.

For dinner I brave the Ratuszowa restaurant again. This time it is open for business, with its fake flowers, aluminum foil wrapped around the old church columns, flimsy salmon-colored paneling. It is all somehow familiar, like Polish restaurants on Milwaukee Avenue in Chicago. I order at the counter, where a polite and pretty young woman with a child playing at her feet recommends a schnitzel. I ask for a salad, and she assures me that something that sounds like "white cabbage" is quite *smaczna,* delicious. I find a table and listen to the grease sizzle as another, older woman scampers about behind a pass-through. From loudspeakers above, the BeeGees sing "To Love Somebody."

At the next table a quiet young couple wearing wedding rings gulp their hamburgers, cheeks bulging, even as they open wide for another chomp. When they get up to leave, the young man has turned his cap rim to the back, like my cousin in New Jersey. Except this cap is tweed and of the old-fashioned golf variety.

Three more young men stumble in from the cold. Every one reminds me of a cousin in America.

The woman behind the counter cheerfully delivers a plate of steaming schnitzel and boiled potatoes to my table, along with a big bowl of slaw, a bottle of beer, and bread and butter. When I tell her yes, I do want a glass, she looks perplexed, as if to say, "Where are you from?" But she never asks and then smiles and seems glad to see me. "Smacznego," she says, Polish for "bon appétit." Every morsel is delicious, and it all costs about three dollars.

On the way back to my room, I stand on the bridge looking at the swollen banks of the Drwęca. For all its distance from Michigan, it looks exactly like the Coon Creek of my childhood, where I heard my grandmother's voice call loud and sweet, "Lenuś! Lenuś!" And I knew it was time to put on my shoes and come home for lunch. Our farm must have seemed to her a remote outpost in a distant land without a past.

CHAPTER 2

Her Father's Child

The calico cat that screamed through the night outside my hotel window sits licking its paw on one of the joining posts of the buckling stucco wall around the next property. Beat up but proud, the old tom seems to be saying, "It couldn't have been me making all that noise last night."

Beyond the dozen or so tarpaper and tile roofs framed by my window, the brick-and-mortar Brodnica Tower stands waiting, its sturdy, four-sided roof poking up above the town, calling me to explore. Two of these medieval towers stand guard over Nowe Miasto, scarred but sturdy, like the old cat.

Eighteen years was all my grandmother had in Poland, but she never forgot Nowe Miasto. It was the destination for which she put on her best clothes, a place that made her smile just to think of it. She told me she was her father's *sprytna* child, the clever one, who was ready to go before he had finished asking her to put her coat on, and it was he who saw her off to America at the train station in Nowe Miasto.

The *Prinz Friedrich Wilhelm* sailed from Bremen on July 12, 1913, with my grandmother on it, and arrived in New York on July 21. Nine nights at sea, during which everyone was seasick except her. She once told me the part of the trip she loved best was being able to eat all the *śledź*, herring, she wanted, while her sister ran for the basin.

I pull a copy of the ship's manifest out of my suitcase. The passenger log lists her place of birth as Sugajno, Germany. I remember asking her if she could speak German. "Eins, zwei, drei," she counted, laughing, and then she waved me off, saying, "I no German." And I would tease her, "Well, if you 'know German,' why don't you speak it?"

Her Uncle Stanisław Jurkiewicz, her sister Wanda, and my grandmother are the first three entries in the manifest, written in a careful, readable hand. Uncle Jurkiewicz's wife, Weronika, awaited them at 580 Ferry Street in Detroit, the log says. Scrawled across his nationality in the ship's record is "U.S. Citizen." Among the others who sailed with them were Arno Dunkler, a German grocery clerk headed for Cleveland; the brothers Bohdan and Jaroslau Pelechowycz, students from Austria headed for Minersville, Pennsylvania; August Pezulis, a Lithuanian farm laborer on his way to Hoboken; Albert Prill, another farm laborer, off to Reading, Pennsylvania; and Mendel Reiser, a "Hebrew" bartender headed for New York from Galicia.

Near the medieval towers, the cemetery in Nowe Miasto is on the main thoroughfare, cars zooming past a sign that says, "May they rest in peace." The headstones—thousands—are too numerous to count. It seems they all died at once in the 1980s and 1990s, taking their memories with them, just after my first trip to Poland. I scan names: Many are the familiar surnames of friends and people I have worked with, but there are no Bryszkiewskis. My grandmother's life here is nearly a hundred years—lifetimes—away.

The paths in the cemetery are muddy, the air freezing, so I find my way to the post office, a hulk of an old, German-style brick building on Działyńskich Street, then head for a wine store I spotted on the Rynek. "Wines from around the world," says a little sandwich board on the sidewalk.

Beyond the heavy, wooden double doors, through maroon velvet draped from metal shower tubing to buffer the cold air, behind a dark wooden counter sits an imperious old woman wearing a brown dress, a delicate floral, silk scarf around her neck, and pearly button earrings on either side of her stern face. Her hair is carefully colored brown, and her skin dusted with powder. She is gazing out the window through lace curtains and past the small display of wines to the Rynek. As if awakened by the sound of my accent, she smiles and listens as I explain that I would like to buy a French wine. Her face lights up, and she gestures toward a shelf of bottles, five to ten in a cluster, a single bottle of each wine.

"This one is very dry, this one a little sweet," she explains. "Will you be drinking this wine with meat or fish?" she asks, moving on to the wines from Italy and California.

I don't have the heart—or the words—to tell her that I'll be drinking it with potato chips and slices of ham, alone in my little stadium room, in front of my laptop, from a plastic galareta container that I washed out with a dab of shampoo.

Patiently she explains that there is no good Polish wine because Poland has neither the soil nor the weather nor the history nor the expertise to grow the necessary grapes. She shows me something from Australia.

I ask her to tell me about the town's history. It's like turning on a faucet. "So many things were destroyed at the end of the last war by our good friends, the Russians," she accuses slyly. "And they were not rebuilt as carefully as they should have been." She darts to one end of the L-shaped counter, where she keeps handy a grainy photograph of the town square as it looked in 1915, shadowy figures in dark clothes floating down the sidewalks.

"I wanted to live where my grandmother was born," I answer when she asks what I am doing here.

"Your father's mother?"

"No, my mother's. She raised me, my *babcia*. Busia, I call her. She was born in Sugajno." She nods and waves vaguely to the south and then wants to know all about me. Formal Polish requires that I address her as "Pani"—madam—and never as "you." Pani Urszula Wituchowska. I show her my old pictures, but she recognizes no one.

"They were poor," she says, gazing at the threadbare cloth coat and felt hat of one of these unknown relatives. "Yes, that is what they wore after the war."

Not many people in Nowe Miasto are buying wine today; we talk for fifteen minutes without interruption. Pani Wituchowska shows me more photographs. One is of this store, "B. Jaranowski," her father's store, in 1924. The second is of the shop today, looking the same at it did then. Even the sign has been repainted in the same style, above the entrance and display window, as it was three-quarters of a century ago. She pulls out a picture of her uncle, who was once the parish priest, Father Alfons Mechlin. "He would have known your family. He knew everyone," she boasts, "but he died ten years ago."

Pani Wituchowska takes me to the window and parts the lace curtains. "Look at what the thieves did," she says. Splattered with white, stick-on stars that seem to be holding it together, the window has been cracked by several heavy blows. "You can see where their fists landed. They wanted to steal wine," she explains, but they were caught in the act and confessed. "Now I have a big price to pay for a new window, and they have all they can eat and drink in jail," she adds with disgust. "They even bragged about it."

Her son, she tells me, lives in Toruń, and "Michał does everything for me."

CHAPTER 2

—

12

He makes the hour's drive to Nowe Miasto a couple times every week. "You must meet him," she decides.

"There was another man here once," Pani Wituchowska warns me, "looking for his family from the 1860s, but all the documents were burned in the war. I don't think he ever found much of anything. It's all gone, even the church records. All burned." And of Sugajno, she advises, there will be nothing much left from 1913.

The Rynek was built in the eighteenth and nineteenth centuries, says Pani Wituchowska, and what I see now was poorly reconstructed after World War II and then "neglected for fifty years" under Russian rule. "They were worse than the Nazis," she hisses. "We were well-to-do before the communists came, you understand."

I leave the wine store with my Baron de France, a bottle of red table wine from Montreuil-Bellay, fifteen złoty—a little over four dollars.

"Come back again soon. I will tell you everything you need to know," Pani Wituchowska promises with a wave good-bye.

Outside, it's drizzle instead of snow today, even bleaker than yesterday, but people scurry about the Rynek, red and tough as beetroot. I spot the public library, situated next to a park in a gully near the western tower, in what might once have been part of the town moat. The door is open, and I walk past dingy stacks of books and tables of young people who seem to be doing homework.

The librarian sits behind a trench of file cards, elegant in a long gray skirt and turtleneck sweater. Her shiny brown hair flips forward below her ears, and with a wry smile she listens to my explanation of what I'm doing here. Respectfully she brings me three books about the town, one to lend, one a gift, and one for sale. Then she leads me downstairs to another librarian, this one equally friendly, with her yellow hair and white frilly blouse. She seats me at a table; they both chatter beyond my comprehension and offer me the use of the copier. She piles before me scrapbooks of the library's history since it was built in 1968, newspaper clippings, and a collection of publications ranging from a commemorative brochure on the occasion of the one-hundredth anniversary of the local volunteer fire brigade to a history of the Norwid lyceum—the high school, which I passed this morning on my way to the post office.

I peruse a 1963 history of the region, looking for names. Sugajno, it seems, is known for nothing and does not even have an entry in the index. Boleszyn is listed for its late-baroque church dating from 1721; I recognize it as the wooden church my mother and I visited in 1988. The book tells of Nowe Miasto's beginnings in 1325. Its transition into Neumark reflects the German

Her Father's Child

—

influence in this area. Then come chapters about the glorious social achievements of postwar Poland.

There is virtually nothing in the library about Nowe Miasto published before the library itself was built. For that, "you must ask Andrzej Korecki," both librarians agree. "You'll find him at the Papirus Bookstore on Third of May Street."

At closing, five o'clock, the blonde librarian invites me to come back tomorrow even though the library will be closed. "I will be here," she says, laughing when I tell her it will take me an hour a page to read the three books I am taking with me.

Drizzle envelopes the town like clammy hands, and I shuffle with the rest down slick pavement. Errands take on new urgency in the rain. A car splashes to a halt in front of a tiny women's shop; a thin blonde in clingy black slacks dashes in front of me. I can see her inside, breathlessly imploring a clerk for special service.

Stalin, it is said, understood, even as he triumphed at Yalta, that "fitting communism onto Poland is like putting a saddle on a cow." It's all around me now, this thick-headed cow of a country—the first nation in Europe to break free of communism, the first in the world to establish religious freedom constitutionally (nearly five hundred years ago) for Eastern Orthodoxy, Islam, and Judaism, as well as Roman Catholicism. Even Lutherans, Calvinists, and Unitarians were tolerated! Is there anything of that history left in this town, in my family, in the millions of Poles who live un-Polish lives all over the world?

The word "pole" means "field," the dust from which we came, the land that gave birth to my grandparents and sent living pieces of itself across the world to settle in a language that turns even the name of the country into a redundancy: Poland, Fieldland, Land of Land.

I backtrack to a pizza sign and duck into an entry down a driveway at the side of a cement-block building on Kazimierza Wielkiego Street. Two clusters of young men at tables barely look up as I cross the room to a small bar, where two young women chatter vigorously, then flip their shoulders toward their duties. One deposits napkin holders on tables; the other fetches a pizza for a father-son duo. The barmaid points to a menu sign, the only thing in the place that is brightly lit. I order beer and she hands it to me. We play dueling "Proszę" to see who can sneak in the last thanks. I ask for vegetarian pizza, pay, and find my place.

The men grumble about the weather in low voices. The father indulges his son with questions and quiet answers. Beyond the plate-glass window, the paving stones glisten as the rain pelts them. The scene is pure communist

Poland as I glimpsed it years ago. A dark and chilly room with American music throbbing in the background, the indiscernible mutterings of groups of men whose heads turn only slightly as two young girls enter.

The pizza comes with pickled red peppers and soggy asparagus, sprinkled with peas and corn. But the crust is perfect, bubbly and crunchy, and under the cheese fresh onion slices and every now and then a pungent olive—with pit.

Relentless rain and melting snow have swollen the Drwęca to the top of its banks and beyond, into the yards of houses near its edge, the garden plots now mud, with dried remnants of last year's corn jutting from pools of river. As I make my way back to the hotel, a horse-drawn wagon hauling scrap metal and broken boards makes its way down the main drag, holding up a dozen trucks and cars. They wait patiently as the driver sits huddled against the drizzle, one hand juggling the reins and an umbrella, the other cradling a cell phone.

The sun is setting. A street lamp sends down its grainy glow, and I spot a woman wearing a babushka and a nappy cloth coat much like one I remember my grandmother wearing, with boots above her ankles and that space between the top of her boots and the bottom of her coat showing her legs in thick winter stockings. As I pass, she stares straight into my face, and I see the face of my grandmother, and in that face my uncles, my aunts, all of them in that confused expression that seems to be asking, "Do I know you?"

I look into her eyes. "No, you don't know me," I think—and walk on. Across the street I glance back, and she is looking back at me.

After the First People in the World

———◆———

Several days have gone by when I return to a computer-appliance-telephone store on Grunwaldzka Street, where a patient couple has explained telephone service in Poland, with advice on the side about how to find a place to live in Nowe Miasto.

"The boss," a man as thin as a string, with dark curly hair, appears, shakes my hand, then invites me to follow him to his office. Adam Kopiczyński is his name, and he explains that he has a very large house, his wife has left him and taken their two children, and he wouldn't mind if I came to live with him. Surprised, I manage two questions in Polish: "Can I see it?" and "How much will it cost?"

The Polish equivalents of "Sure you can" and "Gosh, I really don't know" are his answers, but he seems to expect me to grab my bags and move in.

Adam and I speed off in a Mercedes. "It's not my car; it belongs to my brother," he says. Soon I'm getting a tour of Adam's house, a twenty-year-old, modern cement cube up the street from the Lubawa Tower. "My grandparents' wedding furniture," he says of a Victorian settee, chairs, and china cabinet in the living room. Bounding upstairs to his children's bedrooms, he says, "You can have this room or this one. My two sons live with their mother," he explains. "The house was renovated two years ago. She had to have everything just so. Me, I don't care."

After the house tour, Adam says he must return to another one of his stores on the Rynek. He owns four: the computer-appliance-telephone store, a clothing shop, a shoe store, and a cosmetics emporium, plus a jam factory in Lubawa. "Interesująca kombinacja," I quip, getting the Polish almost exactly right: interesting combination. Adam laughs quietly and gives me another sideways glance. He drops me off at the Ratuszowa and offers to pick me up at eight for more talk. "It'll be better for my health if I walk," I counter, beginning to feel indebted.

At eight I return to Adam's house. He serves tea, and later we head upstairs to what is to be my room and fiddle with my laptop computer, trying to establish an Internet connection. His friend Mieczysław Łydziński stops by, and we fiddle some more, but the connection won't happen. Finally we give up and go downstairs, and Adam pours tiny glasses of the sweet Polish wine I bought in the delikatesy on the Rynek. It's like muscatel. Pani Wituchowska was right.

Patiently they listen to my feeble attempts at conversation, looking at me as if to say, "My God, how is it possible for anyone to make a mistake on every single word?" Still, I manage to learn much about Nowe Miasto. Both had grandmothers who once left for the United States, Adam's in 1910 and Mieczysław's in 1937. Both came back. "Mine just in time for World War II," says Mieczysław, because "she didn't like Baltimore." Adam remembers less about his grandmother's aborted immigration but says she went to stay with relatives in Detroit. "Perhaps our grandmother's were neighbors there," I suggest. "Wouldn't that be a fine one," he quips.

They are both full of information about the town and show me copies of a newsletter that Mieczysław—a librarian-turned-bookseller because "in library work there was not enough money to live on"—edits and for which Adam now and then writes, *Gazeta Drwęca,* named for the river. Perhaps Sunday, says Adam, you will let us drive you to Sugajno.

It seems I have stumbled upon a nest of local history buffs. "We all know each other," Adam says encouragingly. "Maybe you will find family." It seems to me I already have. They seem to understand, to know that but for the grace of God they would be me—an American, made so by a wandering grandmother. I return to my hotel room elated.

The next day I want to hear what Pani Wituchowska has to say about my new friends. Perhaps some would see her as the town gossip; better to say that she excels in oral history, and it is time for another visit to her wine shop.

She greets me with a big smile, asks me where I have been, as she does every visit. "I hope you haven't been looking for a woman," she quips, smiling devilishly and pointing to my bare ring finger. "You'll never find one suitable for you here," she flatters.

After the First People in the World

—

I assure her that I am not wife hunting and divert the conversation to my question of the day: "Do you know Adam Kopiczyński?"

"Of course, of course," she says. "A good man, but he doesn't have a wife anymore."

"Yes, I know, and he has a big house and lives there alone and says he will rent me a room. Would that be a good idea?"

"Oh yes, yes, a very good idea. You would be doing well to have such a fine place to live. He doesn't have a wife anymore—but of course he has a girlfriend," she asserts.

"And two children," I offer, to assure her I've gathered some oral history of my own.

"Yes, yes, and two children," she confirms. "And stores in the town center." She leans forward over the counter and clasps my bare hands gently. "He comes from a very good family, you understand, a very good family."

I ask her for a bottle of wine to take to Adam's house. She reaches for another bottle of the red wine I bought yesterday and wants to know if I liked it. I pull out a fifty-złoty bill this time. Yesterday it was a hundred, and I had to go to the bank for change. "Always the big bills," she says, digging through her small stash and making negative little grunts.

"I'll just buy an extra bottle of wine," I offer.

"Oh, but then you won't have the occasion to come by and practice your Polish with me," she protests.

"I'll pay for the wine now and pick it up on Monday," I offer.

She bows and laughs. "Prepaid. Now there's a smart idea."

Snow has begun to fall, and I decide to take another route to the hotel, over the bridge behind the church. From there, the view of St. Thomas's is splendid through the soft blur of white. The swollen Drwęca swirls by and grows ever larger. Trees and bushes around it soak in its excess, and their dark bark balances new wet snow and offers it to the wind.

"They said it wasn't supposed to snow today," says Ewa, the receptionist at the hotel, as I run past her to get my camera.

"But it's beautiful. I'm going to take a picture," I explain. She shrugs her shoulders.

On the town square a little girl breaks from her family and runs up to me. "Mister, why are you taking pictures in the snow?" she inquires.

"Never mind, little one," her father calls her back. "He does what he does because he likes to do it."

"I like snow," I tell her, and smiling she runs away.

Can it be that only a week has gone by? With no car, no phone, no Inter-

CHAPTER 3
—

18

net, already I sense that America is a million miles away; even Warsaw seems like another world. How good it feels.

In the evening I settle into my reading and learn that in August, 1914, czarist troops entered many towns in the Lubawa district, including Boleszyn. People were chased from their homes in surrounding towns and came to Nowe Miasto. Furniture was strewn everywhere, bedclothes, food. Terrified cattle roamed in the fields, and German soldiers were also concentrated here. This, just as my grandmother told me, was what lay in store for the family she had left behind.

I close my eyes and wish for their stories to come to me in a vision, a revelation like the ecstasy of Saint Theresa on the holy cards the nuns gave us in catechism class. I imagine climbing to the top of one of those computer-generated DNA ladders to a time before the wars and reaching my family that lived here a hundred years ago. But that is not the way things happen.

The Four Corners of Sugajno

It wasn't supposed to be so easy. I've been in Nowe Miasto for just eight days when Adam Kopiczyński and Mieczysław Łydziński arrive in Mieczysław's little Fiat at eleven in the morning to take me to Sugajno. Even though this village is just a few miles down the road, they carry a map, which Adam reads. We take the first left off the main drag, drive a couple miles, keeping left until the asphalt disappears, and we seem to be entering a dirt lane drifted over with snow.

"Step on the gas," Adam urges, and we barrel through the drifts for another mile or so. The sun is so bright I have to squint to see the rolling fields before me, a placid lake to my right and straight ahead a sign that says "Sugajno."

The village is really just a crossroads, with one store that is shut tight for Sunday. Several houses nearby are quite old, others obviously built after World War II, only about a dozen of them clustered together, and then you can see farmhouses in the distance. Straight ahead is a building that both of my new friends assure me was a school and has stood here for at least a hundred years, the school my grandmother no doubt attended. "Built by the Germans," says Adam. We walk around it, then knock at the first door. It seems that it has been divided into three apartments. A man comes to the door and within a minute has explained that, yes, indeed, the Bryszkiewskis live up the road—Jan Bryszkiewski, the same name as my great grandfather. He points to the house.

Eighty-seven years it's been since Helena Bryszkiewska and her sister Wanda took off for America with their uncle Stanisław. Now I am walking back up the same road, one sunny day, to see what remains of those who stayed behind. Two wars later, the fields covered with snow, my breath hangs in the air, and we are about to intrude on somebody's Sunday dinner.

"I am looking for my family" is the only way I know how to put it. The young man at the door seems perplexed and moves aside to reveal Jan, a portly, gray-haired man with two hairy moles on the left side of his chin. (My grandmother had an identical one on her upper lip.) His ragged shirt and striped pants look like they've been worn for fifty years.

"Yes, I am Jan Bryszkiewski," he says, eyeing me expectantly as if I were from Publishers Clearinghouse. He seems stunned, but he and a woman he introduces as his wife—they appear to be in their mid-sixties—and the young man and woman with him are very gracious. But Jan seems to need time to think, and then he apologizes. "We were about to eat."

It's noon, the table is set with four plates heaped with boiled potatoes and roasted chicken. We are ushered into the living room, where Tom Jones shouts "It's Not Unusual" from a television. It all seems *very* unusual to me, but their home is immediately familiar in odd ways; the dining table in the kitchen, where we entered, is one of those chrome and vinyl numbers from the fifties. The living room furniture reminds me of the last matching, overstuffed sofa and chair my mother bought for her house in Hamtramck. The television blares in a corner below a wooden crucifix. At the same time it's as if this cannot really be happening; I've lost every word of Polish I ever knew. My new friends rescue me with explanations, which are, of course, the same explanations I somehow managed to convey to them in Polish the day before.

The family finish their meal in seconds and then rush tea and coffee and a yellow pound cake to the coffee table before us. It's good coffee, but too late I realize it's the kind that needs time for the grounds to settle to the bottom of the cup.

Gagging on coffee grounds, I try to explain who my grandmother was. It's clear that Jan's family history is not one of his priorities. I show him my old photographs. He is sure that one of them is Franciszek, my grandmother's brother, whose letter to his sister in America I carry with me. Jan's father was named Izydor, and Franciszek was his first cousin, which means that Wincenty, his grandfather, and my great-grandfather were brothers.

Jan's wife, smiling and calm in her floral dress and apron, offers to bring out photographs. Jan is working hard now to remember. His wife brings an Adidas box, and he begins to shuffle through the photos inside. "Jak groch z kapustą," he chuckles, the same words my grandmother used to describe a mess. "Mixed up like peas with cabbage."

The Four Corners of Sugajno
—

The school is way over a hundred years old, Jan assures us. "It's for sure where your grandmother went to school. I went there myself. They just closed it a few years ago." Abruptly he announces, "I'll call the teacher, Pani Ostrowska." Into the kitchen he shuffles and moments later announces, "It was built in 1858 by the Germans."

I was so self-conscious about my intrusion that I didn't immediately see how nervous Jan is as well. He has forgotten to introduce me to his son and daughter-in-law. "This is Piotr and Grażyna." He apologizes for his manners, his tongue whirling like a propeller around missing teeth, which also reminds me of my grandmother. I swear there is even something familiar about the homey smell of him.

His father's house is no longer standing, Jan says. Soon we are looking through a pile of old photographs. I mention again my grandmother's name, Helena. I know he has been taken aback by my arrival, for he looks astonished, really hearing it for the first time. "That's my wife's name, Helena Bryszkiewska. Here she is," he laughs. His wife smiles demurely. "My father always said we had an aunt—or was it a cousin?—who went to America," Jan marvels. But he remembers nothing about any other great aunts or uncles. He, like me, is an only child, so there is no one else to ask.

Next we are looking at their wedding picture, a beautiful, blonde young couple in 1958. And there is a picture of his grandmother's funeral, during the war, he says, a somber group of men in overcoats and women in dark hats behind an ornate coffin being carried to a wagon filled with straw. Behind them is a timber house of wide, rough-hewn boards, children peering through the one visible window. They would be almost seventy years old now, those children; Jan is among them. And there is a picture of the old woman in death.

He finds a duplicate of the funeral picture and casually, sixty years after it was taken, gives it to this relative from America, this distant cousin. "Perhaps one day I'll go to America," he chuckles.

"That was the Bryszkiewski family home," he says. "It could very well be where your grandmother lived. Take the picture, go ahead."

By now my head is spinning, and we've been here for over an hour, so I ask if I can come back another day. "Of course," Jan and Helena say, smiling, still bewildered. They offer their phone number.

In the car on the way back to Nowe Miasto, I stare out at the snow-covered fields. Adam and Mieczysław seem proud that they, the best local historians, have been able to make short work of finding my family.

But my grandmother left many brothers and sisters in Poland; she told me so. Can they really all have disappeared without a trace, without children?

CHAPTER 4
—

My new friends sweep me off on a tour of the town's oldest sites. We park on the Rynek and walk to the church. Emboldened by their success in Sugajno, they urge me to follow them as they sneak up the dark side steps that seem to lead to the choir. Dumbly I follow, but the stairs lead instead into a winding brick tower and to another set of stairs and then another until we are walking on planks that bisect the length of the church over the buttresses on its side.

Giddy, Adam runs to the tiny window at the end and urges me to have a view of the town. I step cautiously past three dust-caked angels frozen on their sides in the rafters. On either side of me are the plaster domes of the chapels below.

There is no stopping Adam now, and Mieczysław and I follow as if we've come too far to turn back. We ascend yet another narrow set of steps and another—without banisters—until I look up and see that we are in the belfry, and around me are dozens of hand-hewn beams at every angle reaching to the very top of the church. I lift my head, and above me hangs the tongue of an enormous bell. Adam is checking the rope and pulley.

"It's not going to ring," I plead.

"No, this one doesn't work, I think," Adam assures me.

But above this bell is another, and when we reach the top of the tower, Adam throws open the shutters to reveal a splendid view over the town, the river, the hills beyond.

"We've never been up here before either," he says, and just then a rope beside the bell seems to have been pulled and begins to descend. The bell is less than three feet away and more than five feet high, and there is nothing to do now but hear it. I put my hands over my ears, but the clang of the ringer against a ton of metal starts my head vibrating. It rings and rings, fifty clangs and more, until I'm convinced it will not stop until we are driven out. Adam darts around the bell, smiling, looking out the window, like Quasimodo. The bell goes on until I feel foolish holding my hands over my ears, so I drop them and let the noise reverberate through me.

This same bell that rang out on Sunday mornings when my grandmother was a little girl and for generations of little girls before her now dazzles her grandson with its uncompromising clang. Don't hold back, it proclaims, for you are here for a reason.

Back on the street dusk is in the air. We head up Działyńskich Street, and Adam tells me to look left at Kazimierza Wielkiego Street. "That was the Jewish section. There was the synagogue." To my right is a severe, geometrically correct building. "Gestapo headquarters," he says, right at the end, "like a tombstone."

The Four Corners of Sugajno
—

"There is not a single Jew left in Nowe Miasto," Adam tells me, although, as I study the faces of the townspeople, they all look Jewish to me, including Adam, with his bony face and dark curly hair, his tentative half-smile.

I ask Adam if he has given any more thought to my moving in. "Of course," he replies. "When will you be ready to do so?" To money, he has given no more thought, he says.

"I don't use the kitchen," he announces. "You can use it all you want. Just tell me what you need. There is more stuff in the attic."

The next morning one of the men who gather in the hotel vestibule to drink beer and socialize tells me there are no apartments available on the Rynek or anywhere else in town, for that matter. It seems the fates are conspiring to make me live with Adam.

A procession, involving a priest and altar boys elevating purple banners, and a long line of people, a hundred or more, head through the Rynek and up Third of May Street. Then I notice a white hearse that looks like a sport-utility vehicle, but in the windowed cab is a casket, looking very much like the one in the old photo of Jan Bryszkiewski's grandmother. People are carrying bouquets wrapped in shiny cellophane. A delivery truck follows. Too impatient to park and wait, the driver creeps on the heels of the last mourners as they stubbornly make their way to the cemetery beyond the Lubawa Tower and Grunwaldzka street.

As the funeral passes, I think of the heavy wooden crucifix my grandmother kept in the top drawer of her dresser. She never seemed to mind when I poked through her things. It was almost as though she wanted someone to know her secrets. I must have been six or seven when I found it. I remember that the top of the crucifix rotated to reveal a hollow chamber in which she kept a half-burned candle and a flat, round bottle of holy water capped with a crownlike cork top, saved from my grandfather's extreme unction.

Extreme unction, as I had learned for my First Holy Communion, was the last sacrament I would receive as a good Catholic. And timing was of the essence. God forbid that extreme unction be administered too soon and the sick person recover—or too late and the deceased be deprived of swift entry into heaven.

My grandfather's extreme unction was timed right, and his funeral was the last held in our farmhouse, where he was laid out in the parlor. I can still see myself standing eagerly on the davenport, for I was merely three, peering into the parlor and asking, "When is grandpa going to get up?" After a moment of silence someone said he wouldn't be getting up, and then my mother cried, and her sister Mary put her arms around her.

There was a large picture of Jesus with a flaming heart pierced by a dagger above the davenport and another of the Blessed Virgin with her heart aglow. There was a ceramic Last Supper that hung in our kitchen. Near the arch between the kitchen and dining room was a porcelain holy water font, Christ on the cross, with a small basin at his feet, as if to remind us of the drink he had been denied as he hung dying. Pani Wituchowska has one like it in her store.

By the time my grandmother died, our rituals of candle and holy water had been abandoned, and the idea of taking them to the hospital where she lay comatose seemed somehow superstitious. Dying had already become more the unacceptable consequence of unhealthy living than the logical outcome of life. She was, after all, only seventy-seven. Twenty-four years later my mother, at seventy-seven, lay waiting for death to take her, with no holy water, no cross, not even a rosary.

The Sign of the Cross

Outside my room, the hotel staff slams doors and prepares for another day. Boys are yelling and running. Marek's wife tries to convince me not to move out of the hotel. "You can cook right here," she pleads, directing me to the tiny closet from which she has magically pulled my breakfast every day. There is a small stove and refrigerator inside, a sink, and cupboards. "Yes, I suppose I could," I tell her. But I have big Polish meals in mind, with somebody's babcia showing me how to cook them.

This morning, the church in Nowe Miasto is freezing, colder than outdoors; the gold leaf looks tarnished and dusty. The weekday faithful—about a dozen, mostly women—are scattered about the church on their knees in the wooden pews. In the section of pews parallel to the aisle near the front altar, about twenty ten-year-olds are being led in silent meditation by a middle-aged teacherly woman in glasses. She kneels on the stone floor, and the children in the front row follow. Then they all break into memorized prayers, delivered in the soft, sibilant whispers of Polish aimed at God's ear. When the prayer is finished, the children stare at nothing in particular, waiting. It's Lent now, and it seems there is never a time when the church is empty. I wonder if these children are learning to say "prayers for a happy death," as the nuns taught me.

When I was a child, nuns seemed to me to be holy women, usually hidden away but brought out to deliver the truth direct from God to us Catholic children unfortunately enrolled in the public school. I remember only one nun—

although she was no doubt really several—with a scrubbed, pious face, infinitely patient, and equally determined to make good Catholic children of us. I remember a pale holy face asking, "Where is God?" and instructing that the proper reply was "God is everywhere."

I leave the church and walk to Adam's house, but he's not there, so I sit on a bench in his yard and write a note with occasional help from my dictionary: "I was here, but you weren't home. Do you have time to see me later? I've had enough of living in a hotel. If you're not busy this weekend, perhaps it's time to make the move. What am I waiting for?"

I met Adam's father earlier today, a man with the same reserve and quiet seriousness as Adam. I showed him my old photos, but he recognized no one. The day before, Adam and I spied on him through the front window when he was busy with customers in his film-processing store. "He looks just like you, only older," I said. "But I have hair," Adam smirked.

I leave the note in Adam's mailbox and head back to the hotel. Soon the receptionist knocks on my door to tell me I have a call. Adam is hollering from his cell phone that he will meet me at the Ratuszowa at three.

So I wait for him at the restaurant and formulate questions to ask over beer. When he hurries in and sits down at the table, I am ready. "How many Jewish people lived here before the war?" I ask.

"There were perhaps three hundred here before World War II," Adam responds. "Before World War I perhaps six or seven hundred. Before the first war the street where the synagogue stood was named Synagogen Strasse."

"And Gypsies? I saw men outside the church this morning on their knees in the dirt, begging, with children at their sides. Were they Gypsies?"

"Yes, from Romania," Adam says. "There are perhaps a hundred living here, but they don't live the traditional Gypsy lifestyle."

"What do ambitious people in Nowe Miasto want?"

"Ambitious people want to leave," he smiles.

"But you are ambitious," I argue, and he counters that he was ambitious ten years ago, when he went through Romania and Bulgaria to Greece and bought contraband goods and brought them back to Nowe Miasto to sell. "We made a lot of money, and when communism fell, we invested, and now I have four stores and a factory. It has not been so for everyone. Thousands of people in this small town alone are unemployed. That's the biggest change in the last ten years, this unemployment."

Later we go to Mieczysław's for tea. His wife, Urszula, loosens up and begins to grouse about how little money she makes, how inadequate their apartment is, how if she had it to do over again she would learn English and move

The Sign of the Cross

—

to Canada. She works as a nursing assistant and earns about two hundred dollars a month. She has an endearing, at times cloying, way of demanding sympathy with a pout and a half cross-eyed glare.

Except for the language, I could be sitting in any living room in America, talking with any family worried about why young people are so rude, why in school they even put their feet up on the desk. What's to be done about unemployment? How do you make more money when the skills you have don't pay off?

Mieczysław wants to show off his computer and scanner and digital camera. I wonder how he has the money for all of this, but it is none of my business. Tonight the Internet connection is swift, and soon we are all reading a facetious e-mail message from a friend, in which she attempts to identify the major Polish food groups: *pączki, jabłka, kiełbasa*—doughnuts, apples, and sausage.

"Tomorrow I'll have a new address," I tell them as we say good night, "and Adam will have a new maid." They laugh and promise me I will learn more than three Polish food groups.

More than religion or politics, it is language that separates people, and after two weeks of struggling as a semiliterate I am beginning to speak English to myself now and then just to hear the sound of it.

Today I learned the right way to say "camera." You can say "kamera" here and be understood, but in this place it means video camera. The correct way to say "camera" is "aparat fotograficzny," a "photographic apparatus."

Polish is a coy language; its objective, to say things in as indirect a way as possible. Polish writers had a field day with obtuse communist ideologues around whom they wrote rings in the years between Yalta and Solidarity.

My grandmother never truly left Poland. The tree-lined roads to Sugajno, the tilled fields, the lake, the chickens pecking in the yard—these are scenes straight from her life in Michigan. She brought Poland with her to America, as if a farm in Michigan were merely a farm in a distant province, a place so far away that there was no possibility of leaving.

In the morning Adam comes for me in his white Honda. We heave all my belongings into the trunk. I pay my bill and say good-bye. Equally quickly we heave my things into my bedroom. Adam tosses aside his sons' books and games to make room on the shelves for my books.

"Make yourself at home. I have to go back to work," he says and is gone, and I am in my new home. Now I will have a Polish kitchen of my own, but not like my grandmother's, rather a modern kitchen in a Soviet-style block house. I'll be living in a real Polish home, a broken one no less.

CHAPTER 5

—

Each store in Nowe Miasto has its own flavor. The next day I go to my favorite for a chicken to roast in my new home. A self-confident blonde in her thirties inquires about my language, then assures me that I speak just fine. She grabs one of the headless plucked birds off the meat counter and unceremoniously wraps it in paper. She begins to sense the vacancy in my eyes when she launches into a complicated assessment of its size and quality. "Will there be anything else?" she says abruptly.

In another shop a gaggle of young women near the front cash register ask if they can help me. I need egg noodles for my chicken soup, so I tell them I'm looking for the *makaron* section. Then out comes the boss Pani, and she wants to be the one to lead me to just the right package. She is charming and curious, and before long I have told her why I'm here and where I live and my relatives names, all the while she is recommending noodles but apologizing because she does not sell colanders, although I will need one to drain the noodles. Instead she offers bathroom cleaner and napkins.

I have brought with me my faithful string bag, the kind that stretches like a hammock with every addition to its net. I bought it in the United States when overcome one day with a sentimental longing to stroll through European markets. I am the only person in Nowe Miasto with such a bag. The rest carry plastic, or so it seemed for days, until today I noticed two women coming home from market carrying sturdy willow baskets that reminded me of the ones my grandfather wove from willows he had planted down the lane on our farm in Michigan.

The women employees close in as I talk to the Pani. At times they smile, at times stare blankly as if in wonder that someone has come from so far away. At times they giggle at my attempts at Polish. I realize I must sound like the man my mother laughed about for years, who came into the New Palace Bakery in Hamtramck and demanded every time, "Give me bread!" She said at first she thought him rude and mean, but she broke through his shell, only to find a frightened man who had learned three words in English, and not one of them was "please." It's a mistake I don't plan to make. "Proszę," I repeat all the way out the door.

CHAPTER 6

Mothers and Sons

A dam has gone to work, and I sit in the bathtub, fairly sure that before long I will hear his mother clomping around downstairs. The bathroom walls and floors are made of ceramic tiles, and the house has enough hot water to supply a steam bath—further proof of Adam's success as an entrepreneur in the new Poland. This is a palace compared to the tiny closet of a bathroom in the stadium hotel, compared to the bathrooms I knew as a child in Michigan. We didn't *have* a bathroom until I was seven years old.

Adam's wife moved out less than a year ago, but her presence lingers—her perfume on the bathroom counter, her sponge in a corner of the bathtub. The curtains she picked out hang on every window; jars of sour pickles she canned ferment in the cellar. And the kitchen wall is full of holes where she ripped out cupboards and took them to her new apartment in town.

Adam's mother, Pani Jadwiga Kopiczyńska, is everything a son could love. She comes into the house carrying stuffed cabbages and shredded beets. The best of both I've ever tasted. "Polish cooking does not have to be unhealthy," she announces, singing the virtues of fresh ingredients. "Meat a couple times a week won't hurt you, although it's not really necessary to eat meat at all." Within an hour of meeting me she says she wishes her son were more like me, that he cared about the curtains and the dishes. She invites me to hike in the woods with her and her big homely bulldog named Puma, and, yes, she'd be happy to show me which mushrooms are edible and to teach me how to stuff a cabbage. She moves through the house efficiently, with one hand scooping up everything that's out of place and with the other depositing it where it belongs. "It's really such a pretty house, isn't it," she sighs, sad to see that it no longer holds her son's family. She talks to me as if my inadequacy in Polish were a minor inconvenience. She tells me she'll bring me a kettle and serving dishes and anything else I need if I want to cook in her son's kitchen.

Today Adam waits with me in the bank as my traveler's checks are changed into cash so I can buy a car. While tellers stamp ferociously and scurry into the backrooms, he concludes that "everything here is still far too complicated."

Later, in a city office, we ask what I must do to buy a car. Then we walk down the hall to the next office and present a form that we were given at the first. There we are told that I can expect a two-day wait just to get an answer from someone who knows whether what we have been given in the first office will suffice.

We drive to a used-car lot at the edge of town near the monastery ruins, where a red-faced salesman in his early thirties assures me that cash is all I need to buy a car in Poland. The phrase "Would you buy a used car from this man?" occurs to me as he strains to hold a fake smile.

We'll make it simple, Adam proposes to me, as we pull away from the lot in his Honda. "You'll give me the money, I'll buy the car, register it in my name, add it to my insurance, and you'll have a car."

A simple plan it is, but a lot to expect from someone you barely know. It can all wait until I buy a bottle of wine from Pani Wituchowska.

When I enter her shop, she's chatting with someone else but makes an efficient switch to me, with a smile and cheerful scolding. "So why have you taken so long to return?" The other woman says "Good day" and sheepishly makes her way out the door.

Pani Wituchowska is dressed, as always, to the nines, this time in a wool suit with a silk scarf around her neck. She has prepared for my return and pulls an envelope full of pictures from a shelf under the counter.

Two years ago she and her son had a private audience with Pope John Paul II. She presents two color, eight-by-ten glossies to prove it. In one she is sitting with John Paul II in a small chapel in Rome. In the other she and her son are in his private library. She is shaking his hand. I cannot make out (and don't know how to ask) why the pope has granted them this moment, but if I were the pope I'm sure I'd do the same for this lady.

"My son is very religious," she says. "He wants me to go to Jerusalem this year, but I don't know. . . ." I tell her that I intend to go to Jerusalem in August.

"August is when he wants to go," she says, surprised. "My son says it's the best time of year to be in the Holy City."

Then she shows me a picture of herself as a baby in a lace dress, others of her as a young woman, looking like Princess Elizabeth just before she became the Queen of England. In a series of studio portraits, she is wearing a floor-length gown and holding a bouquet of lilies, a small pearl tiara nestled in her brown hair. It is her *cywilny ślub,* civil marriage ceremony, she tells me.

"A girl one could love, isn't she?" Pani Wituchowska observes, like a proud artist commenting on her creation. "I learned to play the piano; my brother, the violin. That's how it was then. No discos," she wiggles playfully and laughs. "Sometimes in the evening my father would sit down with his cigar, and I would play for him. That was what we did. There was no television."

More pictures. In one she looks like Mary Astor in *The Maltese Falcon.* Now and then Pani Wituchowska reaches over the counter and places her hand gently on my arm. "The pearls were real, the flowers flown in from Italy," she remembers. "We were wealthy then." All of this she tells me not with regret but with pride that such a life was possible—before the war, before the communists. She shows me elegant pictures of her mother and father, startlingly sharp studio photographs, the kind that seem to have stopped being taken some time not long after the war.

"My husband was thirty years older than I," she confides, "but he was such an elegant man, always so beautifully dressed, and how he carried himself." She makes it clear that she was a virgin when she married him in 1946 at the age of twenty-three. "It wasn't like this new business of going around with this one and then that one before you are married." Her husband is a distinguished, gray-haired gentleman who gazes at her adoringly in each photograph.

She brings out later pictures: her son in short pants at his First Holy Communion; her brother, the *kawaler,* bachelor, who died young of kidney failure. And there are pictures of her life without her husband and father, her diminished family gathered around a dining table.

"I have a big home upstairs filled with old furniture," she announces proudly. "I like to keep it to myself," she says. "My home is big, lots of room, and after the shop closes, I go upstairs and have a little bit to eat, and this is all mine. Even when I go to Toruń to concerts with my son, I want to get home to sleep in my own bed with my own pillow in my own room. Do you know what I mean?" She says that, after her husband died, many men pursued her, but she didn't want them, not even the ardent doctor who never gave up until he died just a few years ago.

What Pani Wituchowska misses most in this town is high style and romance, neither of which seems to exist in Nowe Miasto or in little villages like Sugajno. For that, her son takes her to Toruń, to Warsaw, or to Rome.

"I've been walking everywhere," I tell her.

"Yes," she says, "you were in the cemetery Sunday. Then you went walking in the woods. This is a small town. Everybody watches and talks." She pauses. "You must have dinner with us the next time my son comes to Nowe Miasto, in my home above the store."

"Our home," Pani Wituchowska remembers. "The Germans came in September of 1939. They took everything they wanted. They emptied our store and trashed it. They broke the piano to pieces."

"Did you flee?" I ask.

"No, we stayed and lived above the store," she replies. "But my father couldn't bear to look at it all. Two years into the war he had a heart attack and died."

"My son doesn't have many people in his life. His wife and child, of course, but no aunts, uncles, or cousins, as you do. Maybe it would have been better if I'd had more than one child. You are an only child, too," she remembers.

"I don't miss what I never had," I tell her.

Then Pani Wituchowska gives me the lowdown on Adam. His wife will never come back to him. He has girlfriends somewhere, she is sure. He lacks *namiętność,* she says. It's a difficult word, but I am pretty sure I know what she means. I check my dictionary under the English word "passion." Exactly, she confirms. "You knew what I meant, didn't you?"

It's nine in the morning the next day. I brush my teeth and go downstairs to the kitchen for my cup of instant cappuccino. Adam is at the kitchen table, talking on his cell phone. I can already tell by the obedient tone that it is his mother. She has found a car for me to buy, a better deal than the used-car lot.

Into the yard a half hour later barrels a yellow Polski Fiat holding two young men and a middle-aged blonde, a *blondynka* of the excessively yellow-haired sort. She works for Adam's father. They race through their sales pitch, and I get the general idea. The car is eleven years old, has a radio, is badly rusted, and the engine shakes under the hood so violently that it looks as if it will fly loose. But it is one-third the price of the one at the used-car lot with no radio. I must decide.

When faced with a similar decision I generally conclude that neither is the right choice, and Adam happily agrees, so we decline the rattletrap and begin looking through the newspaper. A phone call and an afternoon later I am the

Mothers and Sons

—

proud owner of a green, 1989 Polski Fiat, a "Maluch," as Poles have dubbed these glorified lawn mowers, for 2,500 złoty—$625—sold by a young man about to enter obligatory military service.

As we close the deal a couple miles away at the young man's house in Kurzętnik, Adam is still in contraband mode, a holdover from his days of duping the communists with merchandise smuggled in from Greece and Turkey. He fusses over the sales receipt for several minutes, and then the young man, who looks like my cousin in New Jersey, offers us coffee and signs where Adam tells him to sign. Then Adam speeds off to work, and the young man hands me the car keys. He chuckles and shakes his head as I pull away, the car lunging forward, then jerking to a halt repeatedly as I get used to the clutch.

After work Adam returns home to watch the news. We learn that today in Łódź, Marek Edelman, the last surviving leader of the Warsaw ghetto uprising of 1943, found a swastika painted on his house. He was among the outnumbered and virtually unarmed Jews who had been prisoners of the city's ghetto and fought bravely for nearly a month against Nazi forces. We shake our heads in dismay. Outside, a train rumbles over the nearby trestle.

Pani Kopiczyńska arrives to prepare lunch, her hair freshly hennaed. She brings food in little plastic containers or tightly sealed plastic bags. One container is "very expensive, but worth it," she says. To close it so the food stays fresh, you have to use an apparatus that sucks out all the air. Today she has brought a raw chicken breast, vegetables, and seasonings to show me how to prepare a nutritious, tasty meal from fresh ingredients in a matter of minutes.

She moves in firm, efficient steps, back and forth from stove to table. First she shreds carrots and celery root into a bowl, then chops garlic and a leek and adds them. She shows me how to slice the chicken into the proper-sized pieces, then heats up a little olive oil (which she has noticed I bought and of which she approves). She browns the chicken with a few quick stirs and pats. Into another pan she pours a little water, adds *vegeta* (the magic convenience spice I ignore in Chicago because it seems to be largely salt), soy sauce, curry powder, and water. The vegetables boil for a few minutes, in goes the chicken, and smacznego—Polish stir fry. Bon appétit!

Pani Kopiczyńska has also brought little bags of snacks—soy products and seeds—which she stashes away in the cupboard for Adam. She compliments me on the new dish drainer I bought yesterday and on my sense of color, then takes my big bowl of chicken soup out of the refrigerator, spoons out a few pieces of meat for the cat, and shows me where such garbage is to be dumped behind the garage. "Too old," she says and marches out as swiftly as she came.

It's snowing again, my third Sunday in Nowe Miasto Lubawskie. Spring does not want to come. In my new home I can no longer hear the bells of St. Thomas the Apostle very well. Across the street is the stonecutter's lot, full of headstones, a hundred or more, crosses and slices of granite, all blank, waiting for the chisel. Next door, says Adam, they don't have much money and still heat their home with wood because it's cheap. The house beyond is a dilapidated, brick two-story decorated with rotting prewar gingerbread, divided into apartments by the communists.

To get to the Rynek now I must pass under the railroad viaduct. As I walked under it yesterday with Adam, I asked him if these are the same rails that carried the Jews of Nowe Miasto away during the war. "They are a hundred years old; certainly they are the same," he said. Yesterday, to get to the shoe repair shop and the CD store, we walked across the parking lot where the synagogue had stood until the Nazis burned it.

"I have never seen a picture of the synagogue," Adam says. "I don't know if one exists."

My list of questions grows. Are the names of the people taken from Nowe Miasto during the war nowhere written? When were they taken? What were the names of the people who took them? How can no one know these pieces of information? Is the same true of the hundreds of villages all over Poland, all over Europe? Daily life is what matters here, yet the record of our daily lives is nowhere to be found; it's left only as stories older people tell of relatives packing up and leaving for America. The town library here has no records of daily life. My family, too, is among the missing.

I've grown fond of walking in the little woods across the street from my new home. Pani Kopiczyńska, however, assures me that this clump of trees by the railroad tracks is not a proper woods. She promises that one day soon I will see the real thing. But I like the way this messy cluster of birches and lindens rises behind a roadside shrine—"Our Lady of Concrete" I call her, a simpering cement virgin with her hands folded, her eyes lifted heavenward. The inscription says "Matko nie opuszczaj nas, 1938–1946"—"Mother, do not abandon us." At her base are bunches of fake flowers, orange chrysanthemums and pink daisies, the same faded flowers that pepper the old cemetery just beyond the viaduct.

At the top of the mound behind the virgin is a deserted, concrete gazebo covered with graffiti. As I walk up the path to the woods, an old man casts me a long look as he sails by on his bicycle. Ahead are two sets of railroad tracks, one seemingly in disuse, both made with concrete ties on a bed of crushed rock. On the other side of the tracks stands a three-story, gabled mansion with a tile roof. With its Alpine porch and slatted stucco, a matching carriage house nearby, it looks like the home of some important German official. Soon, however, I can see that it is now a hospital.

The fence between me and the tracks ends, and for a while a moss-covered cement base continues, with holes that had once held fence posts. A mossy set of concrete stairs leads to a cement floor near a boulder with a memorial tablet embedded in its side. I learn later that the floor was an ill-conceived attempt to build a music stage—right outside a hospital—and it was abandoned. "Another bad communist idea," says Adam.

High in the trees above, dozens of rooks caw in agitation. Their nests, more than a hundred of them, look like clumps of beard in the branches. Now and then their droppings descend like snow. Their merciless croaking is angry and irritable, rising to a chorus of squawks as dog walkers pass by. I see a crumbling concrete outhouse and then cement bench bases sinking into the ground, the forest reclaiming them. A handleless shovel dissolves into the earth it once moved.

Here you can see how it happened. You can see how a few soldiers could load three hundred, frightened people on a train to nowhere. The trees stand black and bare in the cold, a white stripe up their north sides. One tree has a hole in it and a tapping sound coming from within. At the end of the woods are open fields and behind a fence a new cemetery with just a few fresh graves, acres of new land waiting.

A skittish fox looks up from beyond the fence, and behind me rises the endless scolding of the rooks.

I turn to walk back and see a young couple hand in hand. He runs away from her laughing, then turns back, and she urges him on. Then they freeze, lean on one another, and stare out at the tracks as if planning an escape.

Like Grandma in the Back Seat

⊸————⊸

O ne senses that this new Poland is something many people have waited for—a time to succeed and to relish day-to-day freedoms, especially the triumph of the Catholic Church over communism. The conflicts of the entire last century can be seen through people's daily routines—having them taken away, struggling to maintain or regain them, and then settling in to enjoy them while they last.

It's a good day to drive on, with nowhere in particular to go. I decide to head for St. Martin's in Boleszyn. I'm meditating on the seriousness of religion in Poland, lost in reverie, when I notice alongside the road ahead a figure near a tree. As I get closer I see that it is a man in work clothes and a brimmed cap. He is squatting, and as I pass I can see that he has his pants pulled down to his knees. In the rear-view mirror I see his bare white behind aimed at the ditch, and he is unabashedly defecating, oblivious to passing cars.

In one village a group of middle-aged men, at least two of them staggering drunk, loiter outside a church. In another village a group of very young men stand solemnly in front of the general store, holding liquor bottles and killing time, as if preparing to become the staggering drunks of the future.

Like a ribbon threading through crushed velvet, the road to Sugajno winds around hills where crops of wheat are sprouting and fields are already plowed, ready for spring planting. The path flows under an archway of trees, their trunks now and then posted with memorial crosses where a motorist has died.

The hills are almost terraced in some places, patches of woods here and there. Many of the old houses are brick, in the style of my grandmother's schoolhouse, all built by the Germans before World War I with a decorative row of reddish-brown bricks between the first and second floors. They now sit in little clusters along the road, with the newer, plainer buildings overtaking them.

At the entrance to every village is a roadside chapel. In Sugajno people have left plastic flowers for a ceramic Virgin Mary encased in glass. A woman cleans the dirt off the streets with a shovel and heaves it into a wheelbarrow.

The combination of Polish and German that colors every part of this area makes sense of so many of my grandmother's attitudes. I used to wonder why she didn't hate the Germans in a way that I could clearly understand. Instead she would Polishize my name to Kniffelski. Of her seven children, my mother and three others married Americans with German names. Two of her three daughters married Polish boys. It must have been familiar to her, this Polish-German mix, and she effortlessly converted everything to Polish. When it came time to send her sons back to Europe to fight the Germans, that too was familiar.

St. Martin's in Boleszyn is the parish to which Sugajno belongs. It's a long walk or a short buggy ride away. The wooden church there was built in 1721 and 1722, only a few years after the so-called Silent Sejm of 1717, in which Peter the Great of Russia imposed a protectorate over Poland, leading to the first partition, in 1772, when portions of the country were annexed by Russia, Austria, and Prussia.

The church doors are open this morning, and a telltale pail sits at the entrance. I'm in luck. It will be an old cleaning woman, I imagine, who will know all the people in town and love to talk.

I peer in and instead see a young woman, perhaps still in her twenties, with a mop, giving the floors a speedy scrub. It is the cleanest church I've yet seen in Poland, I tell her. In its simple, rustic style it's beautiful—the freshly painted white ceiling, the brightly colored statues, and stations of the cross.

"These parts are very old," she says, smiling and pointing to the timbers to the right and left of the entrance. The inside doors have been meticulously stripped and restored so as to show the damage the wood has endured and to reveal their construction, even the flat-head nails. Very old hinges have also been carefully retained. On the wall near the entrance is posted a list of all the parish priests, the first being Jakub Kowalkowski in 1644. It is a stunningly short list—only twenty-six lives leading from then to today.

"How old is the oldest member of the church," I ask. "A hundred years?"

"No, I am sure there is no one who is a hundred years old. I think the oldest woman in the parish is eighty-seven." That would make her born the year my grandmother left for America.

"Have you always lived in Boleszyn?" I ask. She is a handsome, stocky woman, unadorned, her dark hair cut in a feminine flip below her chin. Close up, she looks even younger.

"Oh, yes," she says with a confident grin. "I like it here very much. My mother has lived her whole life here, so has my grandmother. It's beautiful here, the lakes, the land. Beautiful."

I ask about family records. She gives me the rectory telephone number and tells me evening is the best time to telephone the priest, Father Brunon Jank. "What is your family name?" she asks.

Bryszkiewski, I tell her. "Oh, yes, in Sugajno. Jan, kind of a big guy." She waves her hand over her stomach.

"This is St. Martin's parish, Święty Marcin, but Święty Walenty is the patron saint of Boleszyn," she offers, St. Valentine. Every town has its patron saint.

"And who is the patron saint of Sugajno?"

She thinks for only a split second. "Święty Jakub."

Now I will be able to tell my mother's sister that it is perhaps no coincidence that her married name is Jakubicki—Jacobson in English—after her mother's patron saint.

The next day Adam and Mieczysław want to show me castles, and the ride from town to town gives me a chance to ask questions.

"What is the most important thing that ever happened in Nowe Miasto?"

Adam says sarcastically, "Nothing important ever happened in Nowe Miasto." Mieczysław says the most important thing happened more than five hundred years ago, when Poles took the region in 1466 after the disbanding of the Teutonic order.

"Who was the most important person from Nowe Miasto?"

Neither of them can think of anyone. I break their silence. "Come on, guys, that's an easy one. It's my grandmother."

"Does Nowe Miasto produce priests?" I ask.

"Oh, yes," they both nod their heads, but they cannot name one. "There are seminaries in Pelplin, Toruń, and Olsztyn," Mieczysław offers. "There was one a hundred years ago in Łąki, just up the road. Maybe you noticed the ruin, near the used-car lot; just parts of the brick wall that surrounded it remain."

I want to hear all their stories about the tumultuous days of Solidarity, about what it was like to live through the dissident movement, but it's hard to understand what they are saying when it gets complicated.

Like Grandma in the Back Seat

—

Mieczysław says two men from Nowe Miasto were arrested in 1981 and held for a year without explanation. General Wojciech Jaruzelski, prime minister of Poland when martial law was imposed in 1981, was a puppet for Leonid Brezhnev, he says, who told him that if he didn't take care of Poland, Russia would do it for him.

I hear my own voice, sounding alarmingly like one of those frightened foreign voices you sometimes hear in Chicago when calling a home where babcia takes care of the children or a cleaning lady answers. My friends grow weary of my asking them to repeat everything they say, and they steer the conversation to more important things, such as what we will have for dinner tonight.

When I was a kid, my grandmother was the little lady in the babushka, sitting in the back seat, unable to rattle off trivia or gossip in English with the rest of the family, gazing out the window at the scenery while her grandchildren bantered and teased, at ease with English, the new family language. All her life she struggled for the words and often gave up with "To wystarczy." That will do. Or simply "Nie rozumiem." I don't understand.

Adam's eight-year-old son Filip is in the car, and I simply give up trying to keep up with his rapid-fire, slurred speech. We are on our way to Chełmno to see what is perhaps the most complete, medieval, fortified city walls in all of Poland. Chełmno is bleak, far too large for its population of twenty-two thousand. Its six enormous churches are in disrepair, some abandoned, with broken windows and graffiti.

More remarkable is the ruin at Radzyń Chełmiński, which leaps to our eyes as we round a curve into the town. Its former moat clearly defined around it, the castle sits elevated on a grassy plateau with a soccer field on its grounds. No guards, no admittance. It sits and crumbles.

The most remarkable sites are at Pokrzywno and Rogoźno, where we pull off the road and wander among the ruins. The Rogoźno site is now private property, but we beg for and are given a tour by one of the workers on this former collective farm now desperately trying to turn a profit.

The bridge from the farm's backyard has collapsed, but it leads to the gate and the castle tower, still intact. This was once one of the most immense of the Teutonic fortresses, with its vantage point at the fork of two rivers. It fell into ruin in 1626, and the Prussians pulled it down in the eighteenth century. The remnants are grown over with trees and brush, here and there an archway sticking up out of the ground, and everywhere loose bricks, still falling.

At lunch and then again in the car I am without words. Semiliterate, I sit relegated to the status of an eight-year-old, except that Filip can say quite ar-

CHAPTER 7

—

40

ticulately exactly what is on his plate or what we are passing on the road, and I cannot.

For a moment I am my grandmother, relegated to the fringes, entertaining but not essential. The older she got, the more she accepted that role until finally she let someone else make all her decisions for her. This is how it must have felt.

Last Train

———

The Nowe Miasto train station is closing. "Kocham Dawida Wiśniewskiego z Nowego Miasta," a proclamation of love for one David Wiśniewski, is the biggest of the messages scrawled on the walls around the refreshment stand, where a lone cashier stands with nothing to do amid bags of chips and bottles of pop. The dirty cement walls of the waiting room are fingerprinted with years of waiting.

No one is at the ticket window, and I must tap on the glass to get attention. A yellow-haired blondynka appears from behind a partition and sits down at a desk in front of a computer. At the bottom of the ticket window is another window, with a sliding frame, which she opens. I must bend down and twist my neck so I can face her and ask for the times from Iława to Gdańsk, Warsaw, Poznań, and Szczecin. It's a big order, for which the computer is useless, so she begins systematically checking her timetable and writing down the times for me. The station was empty when I entered, but as soon as the clerk came to the window, a mother with two children, an old man, and a young man all squeezed in behind me while I struggled to be understood. I let the others go ahead. "I have plenty of time," I tell her.

But when the others are finished, the blondynka begins filling out her cash report. The old man comes back and peers in at the woman's back. He shrugs his shoulders. "We just have to wait."

Four teenagers also wait on benches, their voices echoing even in this small station. The blondynka disappears. The old man gives up.

People gather themselves up and head for the boarding platform. I ask a young woman where the next train is headed. "To Brodnica," she says.

"And when is the last train back from Brodnica?"

"Immediately. You wouldn't have any time there. You would just have to turn around and come back." I'm sure she must be exaggerating. Surely there will be a few minutes to see the town. So I dash back into the station. While I can, I want to ride this train from Nowe Miasto, the last train.

The ticket window is closed, no blondynka. Then I see her out on the platform walking to the Brodnica train. I dash out the door and across the tracks and jump on. She is handing her cash over to the conductor along with the report she ignored me to finish.

"Can I buy a ticket to Brodnica?" I call to her as she makes her way past me to the door.

But she steps off the train as it chugs out of the station. "It's too late," she hollers, shrugging her shoulders on the platform.

I give the conductor my best I-don't-know-what-I'm-doing look, and he asks me where I am going.

"I want to go to Brodnica."

"Don't worry," he says, "proszę," and motions toward a seat. There are dozens to choose from.

As I pay him, I ask how old the train is. "At least fifty years," he says, resting his arms on his belly as he writes out a ticket, then stroking his graying goatee

"Why is the station closing?"

"This train doesn't pay. People have cars. The buses run."

"What will happen to the station?"

"Who knows? Maybe somebody will buy it. Everything in Poland is waiting now to be bought."

He takes my money and tells me not to worry that I didn't buy the ticket on time. The train picks up speed until it is moving about as fast as a bicycle over the old tracks.

My car is empty but for three men huddled in two seats facing one another. They all puff feverishly on cigarettes and gaze out the window at the fields and woods.

I wonder if these are the same tracks that took the Jews of Nowe Miasto to Auschwitz, if this is the last view they had—if they had a view at all—of their home. I can't stop thinking like this in Poland—thinking always about the war.

Last Train
—

I am in the first car behind the engine, and great puffs of dark smoke sail past my window.

The two-person red seat is comfortable, although its decorative white piping is yellow and cracked, and many seats are crudely reupholstered in something like the same color without the piping. We pass through pine woods and birch clusters, then to Kurzętnik for a brief stop. No one gets on. The car lurches and rattles and makes scraping noises like bear claws on a chalkboard. How handsome this car must have been in its day, how strong the sound of its powerful scraping and clanking.

"There should be something there. There should be something there," I keep hearing Janusz Laskowski say to the rhythm of the wheels. He is a car mechanic with his own shop on the main road just outside Nowe Miasto. I got to know him at a meeting of local historians, and we talked about the vanished Jewish cemetery, the disappearing railroad. He told me that some headstones had been pulled up from the street and are now stored in someone's backyard or shed.

The train stops at Szramowo. No one gets on.

We stop at Jajkowo. A man carrying a briefcase boards and begins chatting with the conductor. Outside the window a tractor is plowing for spring planting, adjacent fields already sprouting green. Only eighty-seven times has spring happened since my family became American. I can count to eighty-seven before the next stop, Tama Brodzka. No one gets on.

The smoking men have begun talking and grow aggressive, and I see my angry Uncle Joe in the irritation in one pair of eyes, the same disgust and frustration.

At Brodnica I cross the tracks to the ticket office and ask yet another blondynka when the last train leaves for Nowe Miasto.

"It's leaving now," she says, "just outside the station, on the other side."

So I buy my ticket, race back across the tracks, and jump onto the nearest train.

"To Nowe Miasto?" I ask a young woman. "No, no," she says, "next train."

I jump off and run to the next train, which is ready to chug off. "Train to Nowe Miasto?" I call to another woman as I grab the handrail. "Tak, Tak," she assures me, and I settle into a seat.

In the Brodnica train yard dozens of brown freight cars stand idle. Ancient wooden ones and gray passenger cars sit rotting and covered with graffiti, and with everything I see here I wonder, "Were they here then?"

There is no charm to these trains. The whistle blows briefly and without enthusiasm; the fluorescent light bulbs are yellowing in their sockets.

The lake outside the window is overflowing with spring rain, and two radiant swans glide slowly across its center, owning it and not caring if they reach the other side.

Along the road I see a man snapping photos of the oncoming train. He dives back into his car and takes off. Farther down the road he does it again.

At Jajkowo station graffiti is everywhere, the largest says in English, "Fuck the politics."

The stations at Szramowo, Kaługa, and Kurzętnik are in the German style, handsome brick buildings with slate roofs. What will become of them when no trains run on this line? A young woman at Szramowo walks down the road and waves at the engineer, her ponytail swinging behind her. To the building at Kurzętnik is attached a Soviet-style block from which a uniformed man motions the train on. Two children wave, smiling in their bright blue-and-green polyester coats, yellow caps, and crimson mittens.

We pull into Nowe Miasto. People jump out and scatter over the tracks. No one bothers to exit through the station. Each of us takes off—around the tracks, down the tracks, and over them toward the end of another day.

Last Train
—

Chiseled in Stone

I n the morning we head down Kopernika Street—Adam, Mieczysław, and I—alongside the swollen Drwęca, past the deserted brick slaughterhouse built by the Germans before the First World War, past three more stubborn brick houses standing despite neglect, past the new slaughterhouse with pig carcasses swinging from hooks beyond an open door, down a muddy driveway, and into the Sanibud, the department of sanitation, privatized six years ago, where men in blue uniforms carry pieces of metal and concrete from one place to another.

We ask at the administrative office if we can see the headstones from the old Jewish cemetery, which we have heard are here. "Yes, they are here, but I'll have to get the manager for you," says a fashionably dressed and coiffed woman in her thirties. She seems neither surprised nor annoyed that we are here.

The manager is a congenial man in a suit and overcoat, who is walking about outside. "Oh, yes, the stones are here," he tells us, "but, you know, I can't just let people in without the proper authorization." He seems rather glad that we are here, as if he knew someone would eventually show up.

Adam and Mieczysław have questions and want to see for themselves what is here. Back on the Rynek we find the director of the office for building permits, who is trying to convince a woman that her sewer will recover on its own. The red phone rings, and he tries to convince someone else that her sewer, too, will be fine. An assistant enters from an adjoining office, and she seems to be instrumental in making sure all sewers are given the appropriate attention.

At last the sanitation chief can see us. He speaks in such formal, official language that I can barely understand anything he is saying.

"It's a shame, so much time has passed. But what's to be done?" He tells the story of how these few headstones in the Sanibud surfaced while a sewer was being dug seven or eight years ago. They had been used as pavement and were brought to the department of sanitation to be stored until something proper could be done with them.

"But it would take a hundred thousand złoty for a proper memorial. And then, you know how it is, the hooligans come and desecrate the sites." He says the mayor once tried to get a foundation to help unearth all the headstones, but was turned down. The chief is a weary but congenial man, perhaps in his late sixties, who has been at his job a long time and wears the tired gray polyester suit of an office drone. On his wall is an enormous, yellowing map of Nowe Miasto with every home, every building plotted and numbered in fine ink lines.

He arranges for an assistant to take us back to the sanitation department, a thin smiling young man in glasses, who offers his hand. He walks with us back down Kopernika Street and around the administrative office, farther down the muddy driveway, and behind another shed, and opens a gate.

Twenty-four pieces of stone, most of them unrecognizable as tombstones, lay spread out on rotting wooden pallets. Adam recognizes that two pieces far from one another are part of the same stone and fits them together. The young assistant jumps to help him. The Hebrew writing matches. The inscription is in German: "Hier ruht in Gott mein geliebter Mann Jacob Brünn." Here lies in God my beloved husband Jacob Brünn, born 1858, died 1920.

We stare at the stones for a long time without saying anything.

"There must have been many more," Mieczysław says.

We head to Grunwaldzka Street to see the court building where the stones were recovered and to walk through the old graveyard, now an unkempt park. We pass the Catholic cemetery, with its tightly packed, shiny marble headstones and thousands of plastic flowers.

But there are no stones to be seen as we circle the courthouse. Did we think we would suddenly look down and there they would be? In sixty years Grunwaldzka has been repaved countless times, earth has moved, and stones have sunk. Between the wars it was called Łąkowska. It was renamed after World War II to honor a Polish Communist general, Karol Świerczewski, but renamed again by Adam and Mieczysław a few years ago when they were town councilors, to honor the Battle of Grunwald and the defeat of the Teutonic knights almost six hundred years ago.

There is nothing to be seen in the park but an old man pushing his little grandson on a swing. He tells us, "I know there was a Jewish cemetery here, but I didn't live here then. I don't know what happened to the stones. They are not here."

On the way back to town Mieczysław casually mentions that there was another, an older Jewish cemetery in Nowe Miasto. "I have always heard that there was one where the library now stands."

I leave my friends and make a quick left. It just so happens I have a book to return. The blondynka is there at her desk. "We thought you forgot about us," she says with a smile.

I hand her the book. "Somebody told me there was a Jewish cemetery on this site at one time. Is that true?" I ask casually.

"Oh yes, quite true. I was only a little girl when the library was built, but I remember my father telling me that there were graves here. There was also another small building, just down the street. I'm not sure what it was for; they went to pray there, I think."

"The synagogue?"

"No, not the synagogue. Another chapel sort of building."

"What became of the graves?"

"I don't know," she says, as if such a question had never crossed her mind.

"Is all of this written somewhere?"

"No, I think you would just have to talk to the old people in town who would remember. Or maybe Andrzej Korecki."

I asked only to visit the Jewish cemetery and found instead a park; I said my grandmother's name and no one remembered. As I walk home on this gray and again drizzly day, the faces coming toward me look different, less friendly, puffy, and determined to get where they are going today, no matter what.

The gravestones among the sewer pipes have not moved me as I thought they would. I think instead of my mother instructing me that she wanted a closed casket at her funeral. "I don't want nobody lookin' at me when I'm dead," she said many times. "Let 'em come see me when I'm livin'." She wanted her body cremated and her ashes scattered on Lake Superior. No monuments, no trace.

Castles in the Air

y little Maluch grinds its
way to Olsztyn this morning, radio blaring, and I wonder why I cannot follow
these newscasts the way I can follow Pani Wituchowska. Maybe it's the way
she uses her hands and arms, bringing an imagined something toward her or
pushing it away. Each conversation with her is like a little play in which she is
the leading lady with the best lines, and I am the wooden lead who needs only
to gesture, utter attentive uh-huhs, and be enthralled by her delivery.

In yesterday's performance the Russians had "liberated" Nowe Miasto in
1945 and were establishing a new order. The young Urszula Wituchowska
was conscripted for factory work in another town; she didn't quite remember
where she was taken, but she lasted one day.

"I fainted," she said flatly, as if to ask, "What more appropriate thing would
there be to do?" She was taken to a doctor, who discovered that she played the
piano and would be more useful doing that for the Russians than sorting nails.
She was sent back to Nowe Miasto, but as near as I can tell, the piano-playing
gig never materialized.

As we talked, a shabbily dressed man carrying a dirty brown bag entered
the shop and asked where he could get change. "At the bank," Pani Wituchowska snapped as she moved closer to me and showed me pictures of her trip to
Rome. The man persisted, his eyes flashing aimlessly from one side of the store

49

to the other. He mumbled inane questions I could not fully understand. Again she dismissed him and talked him out the door.

"Komuch!" she said after he left, spitting contemptuously at the floor and mingling the Polish word for "communist" with the word for "fly," as if to say "commie maggot."

"Now he doesn't know what to do with himself," she continued. "Comes in here and torments me with how good it was before—under communism. There are many who say that to me. I tell them go, go live in Russia if it was so great. I have no use for the man. And besides, he's crazy."

I asked her about the old Jewish cemetery where the library stands.

"Yes, yes, it was there. I remember very well. I didn't like the Jews very much, but it wasn't right what happened after the war. They knew there was a cemetery there. There was no respect shown to the dead."

To Pani Wituchowska they were all foreign. The Germans, the Jews, the Russians.

"On Saturday, the Jewish Sabbath day, you could see the men walking like this." She threw her arms behind her back and clasped a hand around a wrist and paced back and forth behind the counter, looking straight down with her head bent. "And they would not talk. All their stores were closed, and that is what they did—paced. But on Sunday, all their stores were open. I didn't like it."

"But who shopped in their stores on Sunday?" I asked.

"Ah. But that wasn't right either," she said. "I'm a good Catholic, and there aren't that many any more."

"But the church is full on Sunday," I sparred. And our conversation ended.

The road is sunlit today. I'm driving to Olsztyn and pass two men working a cultivator drawn by two brown horses. It looks like a photograph of my grandfather holding the reins of Tony, named after him, the horse my mother said he loved so much he cried when it died.

After talking to Pani Wituchowska yesterday, I went to Janusz Laskowski's home for tea. The television played all the while, but his children were more enthralled with me than with the local news. They smiled when I talked, bemused, as if for the first time realizing what skill they possessed when they spoke Polish.

Janusz and his wife have relatives in Chicago and compliment me on my willingness to embarrass myself in their language. Adam tells me later that Janusz doesn't make money because he closes his garage at three and hollers at his customers. But he makes his living in his own backyard, and he is king in his home. Smiling and eager in his blue jeans, half of his right index finger missing, smelling of lotion, and bragging about his interest in local history, he showed me pictures of the *klasztor,* the monastery that stood until a century ago in Łąki, outside Nowe Miasto.

As I head for Olsztyn, I pass the remains of the outer walls standing in what now looks like a typical farm field. This little chugging car of mine can deliver me to Olsztyn in an hour. In my grandmother's time it must have seemed like a major trip. It's doubtful, in fact, that she ever saw this city we now say is "just an hour away."

In Olsztyn, an enormous McDonald's greets me with its bright colors and big parking lot. I am not here for Big Macs, however, and I find a place to park in the old center.

The Rynek is bustling with construction, and the mortar is still fresh around new paving blocks. The city center was demolished in the war and reconstructed only in some semblance of what it once was.

The fourteenth-century castle is a museum of Warmia and Mazury regional history, but most of what is on display today is devoted to Copernicus, who spent time in Olsztyn working as a public official. His great contributions to the world in astronomy and science were, it seems, things he had to squeeze in as a hobby. There is a romantic painting by Jan Matejko of an ecstatic Copernicus against a night sky and displays of official town business in the master's own hand.

Outside in the sunshine children with sketchpads sit on park benches drawing the castle, while the river flows gently between them and the graffiti-covered, lower castle walls. "Ku Klux Klan" and a swastika dominate. I tell myself it is impossible to know how old those slogans are, but it is also impossible to understand why it bothers no one enough to remove them.

I move on to the museum inside the building that houses the offices of the local newspaper, *Gazeta Olsztyńska,* and then to the planetarium for a look at the Prussian museum, which is supposed to have a display of tombstones from old Jewish cemeteries. When I get there, however, I find that the exhibition consists of a few photographs and three tombstone replicas in Styrofoam.

Then it's time to return to Nowe Miasto and meet Ryszard Ulatowski, editor of *Gazeta Nowomiejska,* the local edition of the Olsztyn newspaper.

He greets me with broad smiles, a handshake, and the assumption that if he talks louder I will understand Polish better. By the end of our meeting he is almost shouting at me as if I were an irascible grandpa admitting only to what I wanted to hear. He also shouts into the next room where another editor, a younger woman named Grażyna Jonowska, translates some of his words into English.

Ryszard is about my age and wants so badly to talk to me, to make his handful of English words do a lot of work, but the only words he translates are those I already know and expressions like "country music," so I dive for my dictionary.

He has gathered his clips from twenty years as a reporter and his stash of historic photos of the town. Some I've never seen in books, and he's very proud of them. He shows me the pictures he took of the headstones from the Jewish cemetery the day they were dug out of the ground behind the courthouse. It was the Russians who made sidewalks out of them, he says.

One set of startling photos from the Second World War captures a firing squad as Nazi soldiers execute pairs of men standing bound against a wall. "These are from Lubawa," he says of three photos, "and this one is in Nowe Miasto." I have seen the memorial plaque on the site in town, the same wall in the background. I had been told that this happened, that fifteen men had been rounded up and shot in retribution for the burning of a German barn. These are photos that take your breath away, the faces of men staring death in the eye and not flinching. In one of the photos from Lubawa a priest is clearly one of those being shot.

"How can there be photos of this? Who took these photos?" I wonder.

Ryszard holds up an index finger. "The Germans photographed this. They documented everything." He tells how a relative who did the developing made extra copies and hid them away. He is full of stories. His uncle spent the war in the German army in Greece on a virtual vacation, while his father wore the uniform of Poland and his grandfather hid a fugitive priest in their house on the Rynek for the entire war. He even has a photo of the two brothers in their Polish and German uniforms with their father in the middle.

"My uncle to the German army," he says. "That was the trade for good treatment by the Germans. And it permitted my grandfather to hide the priest. People did what they had to."

In the 1950s American children were not interested in listening to our fathers' and uncles' stories of the war. I knew that my uncles had been in Italy, Germany, the Philippines. They might as well have been on the moon. They were just American boys fighting for America with cousins they didn't know they had—only miles away in the Polish and the German armies. My grandmother was a "three-star mother," entitled to display in her window a little gold flag with three deep blue stars representing her three sons overseas.

After I've met the efficient editor, the stores in Nowe Miasto today seem more irritating than curious in their Polishness and their antiquated systems— useless employees standing around to answer questions, then pointing instead of fetching. The fresh-vegetable section is so small it barely counts, but two women are stationed there selecting, measuring, weighing, writing prices. This little town has at least eight such markets. Meanwhile, on the road to Lubawa a mall rises, and in it a Lewiatan market as in Nowe Miasto, but this one is enormous, everything available to be touched and chosen by the shopper.

I grow impatient with the system today, after the third market, where a man with nothing to do tells me I must carry a shopping basket. He looks at my string bag full of groceries from other stores. So I hold the bag out to him and say, "Here, would you like to keep my bag while I shop?"

"Oh, no, no, no," he says, turning from officious to humble. "But you must carry a basket."

From my window at Adam's house I watch the woman next door walking home in a stylish trench coat, short hair, and gold-rimmed glasses, purposefully carrying a canvas bag through the open gates of the driveway, stopping to inspect the new green sprouts getting bolder in their yard. They have no use for grass, and their front yard is tilled and ready to become a vegetable garden.

Soon it's time for evening tea and questions for Adam. "I don't care much for them," he tells me as we watch the man next door strut like a rooster watching his hens. Every morning I see him plod to the hen house. "He's on disability," says Adam, "but I think he just doesn't want to work."

Meanwhile I see the fruits of Adam's labor piled in the attic, where I hang wet laundry on a clothesline. Toys the children no longer need, probably never needed, the electronics to which the neighbors aspire, abandoned.

I pick up the phone and call this new cousin of mine, Jan Bryszkiewski in Sugajno. "Oh, yah, yah, yah," he says, "good, fine, good" to my every suggestion.

"I'd like to stop by on Sunday."

"Good, yah, yah, yah."

"Perhaps we could talk some more."

"Good, yah, yah, yah."

"Are you sure it's okay? An hour or so? Four o'clock?"

"Good, yah, yah, yah."

The next morning I follow Pani Wituchowska's suggestions for making potato pancakes. Meanwhile, Pani Kopiczyńska has arrived to take me to a bridge in the woods where we can wave to Adam and his friends as they pass beneath in their kayaks.

The woods are starting to bloom. All along the banks of the Wel River, a tributary of the Drwęca a few miles from Nowe Miasto, tiny blue wildflowers are blossoming, in some places blanketing an entire embankment with six-petaled *przylaszczka pospolita*.

While we wait at the bridge for her son and his friends to appear in their kayaks, Pani Kopiczyńska points out the edible plants along the bank and plucks enough of them for a salad. She shows me how to squash the tiny nettle buds to stop them from burning your lips when you eat them. The wild sorrel is more to my liking, and she finds tender dandelions everywhere.

The forest is teeming with life. A tiny frog leaps out from a log into a trickle of water running to the river from the fields above. Everywhere there is evidence that the wild pigs have been here, digging for tubers. A woodpecker taps out a tune.

Another sort of wild pig has been here, I observe, to Pani Kopiczyńska's amusement, for litter is strewn about near the bridge. She hops over to the car and pulls a plastic bag out of the back seat. "For every person who throws garbage onto the ground, there must be a caring person who picks it up," she says.

Along the road someone is burning winter grass as I once burned it on our farm in Michigan. "A terrible waste," Pani Kopiczyńska observes. "They've done this for years, and they think they have to keep on doing it."

At last the kayakers appear, their voices echoing through the woods, but a log bars their way, so they disembark. Pani's faithful old Puma lumbers over to them sniffing and drooling. Adam introduces the members of the group to me and his mother—among them Iwona, a tall, tan woman in her thirties with whom Adam is clearly smitten, but he pretends she is just one of the gang.

This afternoon I am eager to get to Sugajno and meet again with my cousins, however many times removed they may be. This time I want to go alone. I imagine it will be less difficult without an entourage.

I pull in the driveway a half an hour early, swing around to the back of the house, and turn off the engine. In a moment Jan opens the door to greet me with a toothless smile, in another pair of baggy pants held up by old suspenders. But this time the family is expecting me. He and his wife have been sitting in the living room watching television, while off the kitchen his son and daughter-in-law are watching another TV in their living-room-bedroom combination.

"Come in, come in," he says, this time sure of himself. Helena smiles and urges me to sit. Daughter-in-law Grażyna appears and says, "Dzień dobry," good day, then attends to coffee on the kitchen wood stove. She brings a plate of chocolate cake cut in large squares.

"Baked in the wood stove?" I inquire.

"Of course," she replies. "Everything is cooked on the wood stove."

"And heat, too, from wood," says Jan, patting the huge ceramic stove in the living room.

This time I am bolder with my small talk, first about our family relationship: "I saw the graves of Jan and Anna Bryszkiewski in the cemetery in Boleszyn. Who are they?"

"They would be cousins to my father," Jan says doubtfully. "My father and mother are there, too, in that cemetery, in the older section."

"Do you have any other relatives, older relatives in other towns, that I might talk to?"

"No, no other relatives. Before the war, you know, one uncle went to France, another to England. And I'm the only child. I was only eight when the war ended, but I remember." He recollects how he bought the farm after the war, when it was *dla państwa,* public property, and less than twenty hectares, or almost fifty acres; therefore, it could be bought even under the communist system. "Fifty-one years I've lived here."

His son Piotr joins us and sits behind his wife on a sofa. The women joke about their men's pot bellies. Helena urges me to have another piece of chocolate cake.

Finally I suggest a walk around the farm, and everyone agrees that Jan and I should go together. So the two of us put on our coats and head down the driveway.

"It's still chilly, still the end of winter, but when everything is green it will be beautiful," Jan observes.

It's already beautiful, I assure him, as we look out over Lake Sugajno, nestled in the tilled fields. He points out the edges of his property. We walk down the road a bit, and he gestures toward a patch of pastureland, already with alfalfa sprouting and grass sending out green shoots.

"This is my land, too, all the way down to the water." He explains how the river flows from the lake to the Drwęca and then to the Wisła, the Vistula, which has already passed Kraków and Warsaw on its way to the Baltic Sea. "The lake is full of fish. I have always fished there." He tells me how inadequate his pension is but concludes that it doesn't matter. "I have everything I need here on the farm, no need to go elsewhere."

Jan and Helena smile indulgently as I blurt out my awkward good-byes and wave. They laugh with pity when my little Maluch jerks and sputters. I am happy to know them, yet I cannot help but wonder what happened to all those

Castles in the Air

—

brothers and sisters my grandmother had. Where are their children? I knew only her sister Wanda, with whom she crossed the ocean in 1913. I remember meeting her only once, some forty years later.

When my grandmother died, another twenty years after their last meeting on the farm, we made a phone call to Wanda in Detroit. Relatives said she was too ill to attend her sister's funeral. We made no more of it. An aunt in Detroit had become as distant as all those who were left behind in Poland, her fate as unknown to me as that of the relatives I seek here. Stanisław Jurkiewicz, the uncle who brought them to America, died before I was born, but his wife, Weronika, was alive when I was a child. I remember her only from a photograph.

I see them all now in Jan's face, in the way he holds his head and owns his world, in the laugh that comes from his belly, around and through bad and missing teeth as if somehow he carries inside him, in the details of his body, the long-forgotten history of this land and the people born of it.

CHAPTER 10

—

Pieces of Change

n Monday morning the painter arrives. Pani Kopiczyńska has decided the walls of her son's house are too dirty and must be repainted.

She explains, "It's not good to live like this. I told him: One, two, three, and this will all be clean again, and I won't have to be embarrassed."

The painter is a man in his sixties in paint-splattered, baggy blue jeans. He is ready to do what she tells him.

"And there will be cupboards in the kitchen now. Drill a couple holes, hang them up, it's done." She orders him to bring up the old cupboards from the basement, the ones that were in the kitchen before Adam's wife had new cupboards and fixtures installed, then ripped them out to take with her to her new home without him.

While Pani Kopiczyńska marches about, randomly rearranging and wiping, I slip out to buy the ingredients for stuffed cabbages. I visit six of the stores that sell meat on the Rynek. None have ground beef. None have beef at all. "Not on Monday, beef on Tuesday," one clerk tells me.

"The cow is still alive," I announce when I return to the house. Pani Kopiczyńska looks puzzled, then laughs when I explain that I could find no ground beef. I have the cabbage and rice and more of the odd packages of seasoning that line many shelves in every market. I bought hot pepper. "You should have asked me," she says, "no beef on Monday."

Not to be foiled, Pani Kopiczyńska dashes to her car and returns with a package of ground turkey from her freezer. "Are you ready to make *gołąbki?*" she asks proudly. I point out to her that ground turkey often contains a lot of fat. "Skin," she corrects.

So we get busy. I have clearly understood who is in charge, so I become the assistant.

We each chop an onion. Adam appears and brings down a cutting board from the attic, but Pani is already frying. She dumps the sautéed onions into the meat and tells me I may now mix it up with my hands, adding just enough of the rice I prepared yesterday so as not to dilute the *smak,* the taste. She dumps in her favorite flavor enhancer, the ubiquitous vegeta, and proudly pulls out an electric mixer she has brought down from the attic. She rams it into the meat-and-rice mixture and happily beats it for several minutes.

She calls for salt and pepper. I ask about the hot pepper. "Yes, put it in. You can put anything into stuffed cabbages—to your taste," she says.

"Yes, and they never taste the same twice," I observe.

"That's the beauty of them," she agrees.

By now I am convinced that these stuffed cabbages will be a disaster. My grandmother never owned an electric mixer and didn't know vegeta from schmegeta.

Pani tells me I may now sample the mixture to test the smak. I make a face and tell her I don't eat raw meat. She ignores me and pokes a finger into her creation, then licks off a big gob. "Good," she announces.

She tells me to boil the savoy cabbage, which she calls "Italian cabbage," too long, so it's soft and tears when we begin to roll it. She is undeterred but insists that the tougher, regular cabbage is simply better for stuffed cabbages.

She shows me that I am rolling them in the wrong direction, that I must leave the stem end outside and tuck the tender end inside, for the next step, she says, is to fry them.

"Fry them?" I exclaim, now certain that these cabbages are doomed. She pulls my bottle of popcorn-popping oil out of the cupboard. "Much better for frying than olive oil," she proclaims.

I'm thinking that it never occurred to me to fry a stuffed cabbage. "I usually put mine in the oven," I inform her.

"Oh, you can do that, too," she says and tells me to put my rolls directly into the sizzling frying pan.

When all two dozen or so cabbages have been sautéed for a few minutes, she packs them all into two covered pans, adds water, and says, "There. Everybody thinks it's a big job to make stuffed cabbages. Nothing to it." Twenty minutes have elapsed.

"Oh, what about mushrooms? I bought mushrooms," I remember.

"Bring them on," she says. So I dump them into the sink and wash them; she hacks them into irregular bits and scatters them on top of the simmering stuffed cabbages. "I believe they would have been better at the bottom of the pan," she says, "but no matter."

Adam returns and although she must hear the door closing, she begins divulging details of her son's financial situation, most of which I cannot understand.

Within minutes Adam is asking her to stop. "The painter doesn't need to know my business. It's not right for you to talk about these things in front of people."

Pani Kopiczyńska falls silent, shrugs her shoulders, and looks at me skeptically. Nobody but me wants any of the stuffed cabbages. They all take off—the painter, Adam, his mother. I help myself to a plateful and eat until I make myself sick—because they are delicious.

Later in the afternoon I join the historic preservation group on Grunwaldzka Street as they clean up the sight of the nineteenth-century monastery ruins that currently intrigue them so. When I arrive, Janusz is talking with the guys while his wife and kids rake up sticks and pick up garbage. They all smile and greet me cordially.

The mysterious Andrzej Korecki appears and explains where the walls of the chapel and other buildings once stood. The remains of the outer wall are all that is left. He's a gaunt man with a bony face and greasy brown hair. Everyone defers to him.

Janusz points to an enormous nest high atop a telephone pole, a pair of storks contentedly cooing within.

"We learned as children never to harm a stork. We still have many storks in Poland. In Germany they have driven them all away," Janusz says.

I notice that he is working with what looks like a child's rake. I offer him a bigger one that I have in the car. "No, no," he says. "I started with this one, I can finish with it."

"Are you sure?"

"Really, I'm sure. It's good for me."

"A Polish worker is not afraid of work," I joke, thinking he could probably cut an entire lawn with a weed whacker. They all treat me as if I have every business being here, fretting over the ruins of an old monastery.

Pieces of Change

—

When I return home, the painter is tired from an afternoon's work and ready to tell stories. It starts when I show him photographs of the Jewish cemetery in Kazimierz Dolny. The complete disappearance of Jewish history here is beginning to be an obsession with me.

"Do you know where the Jewish cemetery was in Nowe Miasto?" he asks.

I surprise him by telling him that the old one was by the library, the new one on Grunwaldzka Street.

"That's right. I remember the synagogue, too. It was beautiful. We bought our house from Jews," he recalls. "I can remember a woman named Mrs. Krieger; she paid us in candy to remove the weeds from her sidewalk." His father, he says, worked with documents during the war. "What he could tell you if he were alive."

He remembers that there were many Jewish headstones stacked in the Sanibud after the war. "Building materials and cement were in short supply. People went to the sanitation department and bought the headstones for next to nothing to use in foundations. There were masses of them at the time, I'm sure of that."

I have not seen Pani Wituchowska for more than a week. She beams when I enter her store the next morning. We talk for two hours. She repeats some of her stories, shows the same photographs. They are all worth at least two rounds.

She says she loves it when Adam spends time in the store chatting; then she loves to poke fun at him. "He told me he thought of himself as quite eligible, rich, handsome. I said, you? handsome?" She draws back in feigned scorn and leans toward me. "To me he simply has no sex appeal, and that's that. I insult him to his face, you know, but he still comes around." She is delighted with herself.

"Maybe he likes to hear the truth from someone," I offer.

"Maybe so. I hope so. It's good for him," she says.

She tells me her store makes no money, and she runs it only because she wants to. Her son, she says, makes sure she can.

The next stop on my rounds of the Rynek is the newspaper office, where Ryszard leaps up to greet me, smiling and rosy cheeked. He talks nonstop at the top of his lungs but seems genuinely enthusiastic about my presence. He wants to show me all at once everything he has done for the last thirty years, but duty calls, so I sit and observe the news grind. Then coffee is brought, and they are asking me "Three Questions" for a human-interest column by that name. I answer as best I can and ask them to clean up my Polish.

Ryszard's gal Friday, Grażyna, sits at her desk, a simple black chunk of wood with a good ergonomic chair, and works on a page dummy for next week; then she moves to editing stories as Ryszard and his assistant pass them to her. She remarks on the excellence of a quote that a reporter has obtained. These editors love their language; they are impatient with mistakes and euphemisms. They understand how to make a point. *Gazeta Nowomiejska* has been published for just five years.

"How long do you work every day?" I ask.

"Until it's done," Grażyna says smiling, and then she is off to take a picture of a kitchen somewhere for a reason I can't quite catch.

I'm not used to being on the other end of the interview, and I listen self-consciously as Ryszard dictates a literate version of what I'm trying to say as he plays my words back on the tape recorder. Then he says he has one more question: "What do you think of Nowe Miasto and the people who live here?"

"I see in the faces of everyone I meet the faces of family, cousins, uncles, aunts. It's like coming home." He seems pleased with that answer. He looks at the old family photographs I have brought along but recognizes no one.

Then Grażyna flies back into the office and edits my piece before my eyes, her pencil ticking off a series of marks and changes.

"Look how well I speak Polish now!" I note.

Spring is coming reluctantly to Nowe Miasto. Friends from home tell me Chicago is green, but last night, looking over the town from the castle ruins in Kurzętnik, there were no leaves to mar the early evening view of the fully lit town. The branches are still hibernating.

At Adam's house the eccentric next-door neighbors are already forcing their front yard into bloom with early vegetables under plastic sheets. Meanwhile, Adam's professionally landscaped flowerbeds are filled with early blooms, lining the stone sidewalk along the driveway. Every day the neighbor husband saunters out to the chicken coop to oversee the hens, hands on his hips, now and then waving a broom at the birds as they peck at the chicken-yard scapegoat. The sun shines bright today on his dirty chickens, the flowers, my little Maluch; the grass is green this morning, and the tree buds won't be far behind.

I remember the taxi driver who took my mother and me to Nowe Miasto in 1988. "I can tell that you are going to the right place," he told my mother. "You speak in the dialect of that region, you know."

We knew no such thing. Now it is happening to me. "Where did you learn those words? They are so old fashioned," Janusz's wife Anna said to me as I tried to make conversation while her husband inundated me with Polish accounts of Teutonic castle ruins and the story of that nineteenth-century monastery that was once the pride of nearby Łąki.

The Polish words I am best with, those that come without effort, are the ones I learned as a child. I mentioned a hoe and shovel, *graca* and *szpadel,* and called my clothes *łachy,* and I learned that these are dialect words, country speech, that have been replaced in common language with *motyka, łopata,* and *ubranie.*

Of course, Adam tells me later, "these words are *Polnische Ecke,* a dialect one of my grandmothers also spoke. It's endemic to this region, rural speech." Bernard Jacek Standara has documented it in a book called *Gawędy Klimka Dyb-zaka,* published in Lubawa in 1997; Adam brings me a copy. I poke through the book looking for more familiar words. *Chlać* appears, a variation of *pić,* to drink, that I heard my grandmother say a thousand times, usually disparagingly about someone who had overdone it. The same with the word *wiela,* which my grandmother often used instead of *duża* for "big."

I make up my own ungrammatical colloquial sentence: Ona miała wiela łachy do prania i on za wiela się nachlał i nie chce robić z szpadem. Which, as nearly as I can figure out, is tantamount to someone in the United States saying, "She had too dang many rags to wash, and he guzzled too much booze and don't want to work with no hoe and shovel."

What a strange thing, speaking another language. You open your mouth, make a bunch of funny sounds, and somebody hands you what you want.

The Land They Love

F rom my room, a gray drizzle blurs the view of the tombstone-maker's yard and the block houses across the street, the still-leafless woods rising behind like a tangle of barbed wire. It's Palm Sunday, perhaps a good day for mass in Boleszyn.

I arrive fifteen minutes early today and wonder if perhaps I have managed to miss mass, for there are just two or three cars parked near the church. But soon people begin to appear. A young couple with three children. Two old women. Two old men. Two young boys. Cars pull up. Women, children, men are carrying small bouquets of budding branches, pussy willows, and forsythias.

By the time I enter the church there is already standing room only, and a pack of dusty men in short jackets and dark slacks stands silently in the vestibule, settled in against the ancient timbers of St. Martin's.

More people enter until the church that can seat perhaps two hundred contains three hundred, each parishioner dipping a hand into the worn, stone baptismal font that must have stood here when my grandmother was born— over a hundred years ago. Two young women and several middle-aged men head through a corner door and up a set of worn steps to the choir loft; others continue to pile into the vestibule until we are shoulder to shoulder, boys with signs on their coats that say "Adidas," "Natural Cotton Project," and "Fila." One very old man with delicate wisps of white hair on his nearly bald head wears a black leather jacket with silver-buckled epaulettes like a biker.

A voice floats from a small, round speaker at the ceiling, a tired brave voice, then the voices of the choir, the loudest a man's uninhibited nasal whine. Father Brunon Jank's voice doesn't seem to be the same one I heard on the phone. This voice is a drone, perfected by repetition—the same readings, the same songs, the same penitents for ten years since he came in 1990 and added his name to the roster of only twenty-six since 1644. "I am a Kashub," he joked over the phone when I told him I do not speak Polish well. "We talk funny, too."

The Kashubian dialect, a sort of Germanized Polish thought to have derived from ancient Pomeranian, though dying out, is still spoken by some of the region's elders. I flash back to my grandmother again and can hear her speaking condescendingly of Kashubs as people to be tolerated despite their shortcomings.

The service begins with a sprinkling of holy water up and down the aisle to bless the little branches that lie in the pews as palms lay in the streets of Jerusalem when Jesus Christ entered the town nearly two thousand years ago. The priest's voice drones on, like the turning of a worn axle, into the readings from the Gospel, the story of the Last Supper and the denials of Christ by Peter, the agony, the casting of lots, and finally Jesus commending his soul to his father in heaven. At that moment the congregation kneels in silence. The men in the vestibule drop to their knees on the cold stone floor. Then we stand again and beat our hearts with our fists. These humble men with their pale drab bodies come here to be one heart, to relinquish for a time all identity but for the faith that life here will go on as it has for two thousand years and longer.

An hour of song, sermon, and prayer passes. I remember the hours I spent on my knees at my grandmother's side in St. Mary's Mystical Rose in Michigan, learning to repeat the prayers and responses until they lost all literal meaning and became instead a chant of faith. After Vatican II, I remember, she sometimes took her rosary to church and lost herself in the repetition of the Our Father, Hail Mary, and Apostle's Creed, unable to make heads or tails of the priest staring the parishioners in the face, the mass in English.

We were told that the mass in English would bring people together in love for one another, which is the will of God. Here in this tiny church in Boleszyn we are brought together by Polish, a gathering of the tribe, a tribe that has taught its members from birth to repeat the prayers of the church the way musicians learn to play the piano or athletes train for track, over and over again until the body and the mind do it automatically.

The mass ends, and the priest's vestments are removed. The altar boys line up beside him, and the tabernacle is opened to an adoration of the Eucharist, which permits them and the priest to turn their backs on the crowd. This is the Catholic Church I remember best. The congregation on its knees, the choir singing in another language, and the chime of bells being shaken by one of the altar boys, his pelvic thrusts the only evidence that he is the one holding them.

In this tiny church, clean and polished, statues brightly painted and shining, paintings of Mary and Jesus framed in wood and bright gold, however, is none of the sense of the big cities' cathedrals, even Nowe Miasto, where the vast Gothic vaults seem gloomy, damp, and dirty. The oversized grimy monoliths of Olsztyn, Toruń, and especially half-deserted Chełmno seem cold places, their dusty splendor a reminder of the futility of their purpose, the gilt and grandeur no longer a glimpse at what heaven must be but an omen of men's vanity.

People are leaving now; one by one the crowd weeds itself. A woman stops at the crucifix in the vestibule and casually kisses the feet of a Christ whose mournful face drops toward a muscular shoulder and sinewy armpit, her hand clutching branches blessed for Easter.

Back in Nowe Miasto I park the car and head down Narutowicza Street, into Third of May Street, past the Lubawa Tower, past Henryk Kopiczyński's Foto Express store and the hundred-year-old meat market of Pan Józef Świniarski, to the Rynek, ahead of me the former Evangelical church with its movie theater and restaurant Ratuszowa. In spite of the reconstruction of many buildings on the town square burned by the Russians in World War II, in spite of the ugly communist architecture one must pass to get there, Nowe Miasto is a beautiful town, its charm not to be measured in the amount of money expended on either historic preservation (nearly none, as far as I can determine) or attention to aesthetic details (mostly sacrificed for expedience and thrift) but in the mere fact that it exists and that the sun can shine down on the belfry of a Catholic church that is six hundred years old and remains standing-room-only for services.

Ever on duty, Ryszard has invited me on a tour of local sites. Grażyna is waiting, too, in their newspaper office in the *Dom Kultury*, a hodgepodge of offices related to music and education. The first time I met her she was wearing rugged, outdoor wear—hiking shoes, corduroy slacks, and a bulky knit sweater. Today she has on a short skirt with black hose and half-heel shoes—with another bulky sweater. Her blond hair is pulled back and clipped to her head. "Ryszard is nowhere around."

"Have a seat. He'll be right back." Grażyna putters, making small talk about the day's tasks, only about fifty percent of which I understand. She leans close to show me "Three Questions" in the latest edition. "You'll be there next week," she says with a crooked smile that seems to imply there is more to her every statement than the obvious. Suddenly she is describing where we might go and how good the sun is for photographs.

Ryszard arrives. Grażyna climbs into the back seat, and we are off to a dazzling array of Ulatowski's choices for the best local sites. He can barely control his excitement when he talks about the area. Even the trees and ditches inspire him to point with delight, and we dive into a dirt road in Bratian that leads to the remains of a castle from 1343, just a wall on someone's private property but clearly a ruin that has been there for centuries.

Next we stop at the church in Radomno, which Ryszard excitedly proclaims was built in 1903 with bricks from the *klasztor,* the monastery that Andrzej Korecki and Janusz Laskowski are intent on turning into a tourist destination.

To get the full effect of the footbridge on Radomno Lake to the island of Ostrów, we pile out of the car and take our time crossing it. Grażyna rushes to take a photograph of ducks just as they scuttle across the water with great flapping and splashing. Ryszard urges me to take a picture of everything he sees: an old wooden fence "from just this perspective."

I have told Ryszard and Grażyna that I love best the *chałupki,* the houses over a hundred years old, some with thatched roofs still, their windows clean, with white lace curtains carefully hung. In Lekarty they make sure I see the best of them.

"Better take a photograph today," Grażyna advises with a smile that makes the dimple in her chin deepen. "These may not be here next year." An old woman rides by on a bicycle. Storks have made a nest at the top of one of the chałupki that otherwise stands abandoned.

In Skarlin we see more of the nineteenth-century houses. They are all exactly as my grandmother described them, but the roofs now are dense with moss and gray with age. I think of how vivid that moment was to her when she and her family arrived back home from church in Boleszyn to find their thatched roof ablaze. Perhaps this was another reason it seemed sensible to send two daughters off to America. Perhaps that blazing roof was truly the last straw and made her father believe that his brother-in-law was right. The only hope for his girls was in America. Perhaps in the back of his mind he was sure that it was the best thing for the whole family and that soon they all would follow. Perhaps he knew in 1913 that the Polish hero Józef Piłsudski was grappling with the future of Poland as he watched Austria, Germany, and Russia maneuver themselves into war.

CHAPTER 12

—

To Market

◄━━━━━━►

Yesterday was the first real day of spring, the trees finally showing green buds against a sunny blue sky. Early in the morning Pani Kopiczyńska was already at work—spading, hoeing, raking, planting carrots, parsley, radishes. When I headed out to help her, she handed me packs of seeds and told me to take my pick: beans, basil, marjoram.

An hour of spading and my tender hands were ready to blister, but Pani Kopiczyńska was just beginning. She has taken it upon herself to get her son's house in order, to plant the trees and bushes his wife left from last year in plastic pots beside the garden, to clean out the garage.

Today, Pani Kopiczyńska has told me, is market day. Twice a week in warm weather, "and who knows what you'll find there." "Perhaps pirated CDs," Adam predicts. Perhaps prices not as cheap as they claim, says his mother.

I head down Narutowicza Street at eight o'clock, past the building site where the new hospital will be, past the cemetery and the house with chickens roaming in the yard where several old fruit trees have been cut down, left onto Grunwaldzka and down past the library. At the elementary school I make another left, onto a street I have not traveled. A shabby beaux-arts mansion with four columns gracing a recessed porch has been cut up into apartments.

People are beginning to fill the streets, and I see that I am going in the right direction. Some are already leaving the market, carrying their finds in yellow and black plastic bags.

Ahead I see blue-and-white-striped tents and awnings, tractors with trailers, and a mess of randomly parked cars. Beyond, a blanket thrown on the ground and scattered with tools and cheap electronic equipment, a calculator, a CD player, a rack of aprons.

There is the fish peddler with dirty containers full of ice-covered filets. In coolers sitting on the ground a few live carp tread water, while others float belly up.

In one stack of wire cages chickens are stuffed together mercilessly, brown-and-white feathered creatures, pressed against one another; here and there one has found its way out between the wires only to find itself trapped, and the endless poking of its head through the hole has worn the feathers off its neck.

In wagons covered with rope mesh, pink piglets oink and grunt in irritation. This little piggy went to market all right. But nobody seems to be in the market for him.

People who don't understand flea markets often ask me what I am looking for in them. I always say I don't know until I find it. Today is such a flea market. Beyond the brutalized chickens, an old man is selling baskets, and I can immediately see that they are the right shape and, as I get closer, that they are made of willow. I have not seen such a basket in nearly fifty years, but they are the same baskets my grandfather made on the farm in Michigan. We used them to carry newly picked potatoes or carrots in from the field or to gather walnuts. I wore them out, playing with the ones that remained in the garage after he died.

I pick one up cautiously. "Did you make these?" I inquire. Yes, the man says, with hints of a smile. How much he looks like my grandfather—the same dusty brown clothes, reddened unsmiling face, piercing eyes, like the angry man who hollered at me in Skarlin because I was taking a picture of his house. He is wearing the worn brown clothes that I have seen in photographs of my grandfather and a similar dark tweed hat. His mouth is clenched, and when I tell him my grandfather also made such baskets, he eyes me suspiciously as if to ask, "Your point?"

I buy two of his baskets, which does not seem to surprise him, and I examine one to try to find the mysterious spot where two willow branches must connect to form the perfect circles that are its basis. One branch is left half exposed as a handle; the other forms the basket's brim, from which the other branches are woven, forming a bowl. These are fresh willow branches; on some, the furry spring buds still show.

I am eyeing parsley when Pani Kopiczyńska appears beside me, but she has not seen me. "I'll take four," she says to the rugged man behind the makeshift table. "Dzień dobry," I say quietly, for she is at my elbow. "O, dzień dobry," she agrees in surprise. "I didn't see you here already."

"I'll take five," she says to the man and throws a sprig in my basket. "You bought a basket," she notes with a smile that says, "Nice for potato picking but hardly a decorator item." I explain their meaning to me, and she nods kindly.

"Are you going to take it back to the United States with you?" she asks.

Pani Kopiczyńska and I are still "Sir" and "Madam" to each other in the formal Polish style, and even though she sees me nearly every day now, often leaves meals for me on a plate in the kitchen, and tells me the most intimate details of her son's married life, we are not pals. She is the matriarch and I the foreign guest.

Pani passes through the market with me quickly, for she knows what she wants. We stop at a particular vendor, and she buys carrots and potatoes, tossing several of each into my baskets. I buy an enormous beetroot without the slightest idea what I'll do with it but because I want to cut into it and see how red it is. We stop at the fish vendor, and she buys a huge *tołpyga* filet, silver karp. "Easier this way," she says, "no bones."

On the way back home, another funeral procession passes, over a hundred people, carrying flowers and following the hearse to the cemetery. I wonder who it is today, how long I would have to live here before it would be someone I know and I would join the line of walkers.

Later in the evening a plate mysteriously appears on the kitchen table, filled with shredded cabbage slaw, peas, carrots, and a lightly breaded, ungreasy filet of freshly fried fish.

The next day something ornery is in the air from the start. Something too hot about the sun for April. "We don't have spring here in Poland. We go directly from winter to summer," a man says to me at Janusz Laskowski's car repair shop.

Today is the day my Maluch has to pass inspection, and I have come to Janusz for help. The system works like this: First you take the car to the inspector, who looks it over and tells you it'll never pass because the muffler is too loud. So you stop at the auto parts store and buy a new muffler, then you take it the repair shop and have it installed. Then you take the car back to the inspector, who looks it over again; this time he finds a problem with the brakes and the steering wheel.

The inspector tries to explain all of the necessary repairs to me, but my solution is to ask him to write it down and to promise that it will all be fixed. A good idea, he says. "I'll give you till Saturday."

To Market

—

Back in the car to Janusz. "Can you do all this by Saturday?"

"Oh sure," he says, "by tomorrow at two." Just when I think I'm off the hook, he hands me a slip of paper and tells me where to go to buy brakes, used or new.

I ignore the option of negotiating over used brakes and head straight to the store where I bought the muffler. The part costs fifty dollars.

On the way back I stop at home to apply some Plak rubber-and-vinyl cleaner to the bumpers and side strips, then decide to wash the whole car, which takes only one bucket of water. I remember my mother tenderly washing and painting the 1947 Chevy she bought in 1961. If she couldn't have a new car, by God she was going to have a clean one.

The sky has brightened; fruit trees are beginning to blossom, and grass is starting to cover the inevitable litter that mars every roadside and park.

It's time to visit Pan Świniarski in his hundred-year-old grocery store with the proud sign in the window proclaiming its centennial. The store is the size of a substantial broom closet, with a counter to the right and a counter straight ahead in the old style. No handling of the merchandise.

I casually ask for a couple of oranges and bananas. The woman behind the counter picks them out for me with a smile and curiosity over my accent. Out of the corner of my eye I see that the old man is listening.

"And what else?" the clerk asks. "Perhaps some of this macaroni," I say, reaching toward the exposed shelves to the left. "And beans and milk. Do you have nonfat?"

"Only one-and-a-half percent."

"I'll take it." Now the old man can resist no longer. He sees me looking at the top shelf above the dairy counter. "This is very good," he says, "but no, if you are looking for wine, none of these will do."

I tell him I'll take his recommended soda water, however, and he smiles. It seems he knows that I am in town and has perhaps been wondering why it has taken me so long to visit his store.

"Maybe you could have some coffee with me now," he offers, "for if you are looking for stories," he seems to be saying, "I want to add mine."

He shows me to the backroom behind a curtain, where a small assortment of shelves holds a collection of records and memories and virtually no merchandise. In one corner are two wall benches and an old table covered with an oilcloth. He sits on one side and I, on the other. The clerk makes coffee and asks me if I want cream and sugar. She smiles at me with approval. It looks as if the room has not changed in fifty years.

"Oh, yes, Pani Wituchowska is a good friend of mine," he tells me at the mention of her name. He pulls out a photograph of the young Pani in a white dress lying playfully in the grass with another well-dressed young lady, beaming at the camera.

"She was quite a girl, wasn't she," he muses. "Oh, yes, very beautiful." He shows me a woman with a round cheerful face in a dress with a buttoned lace collar. "This was my wife, gone ten years already."

Then, without preface, he announces to my surprise, "I thought you were a priest." Without much interest in my reaction, he continues, "You look like a priest."

Pan Świniarski is seventy-eight years old and has a full head of white hair. I can hear immediately that his missing teeth are going to make it rough going as he slurs his words. "I was seventeen when the Germans came," he says with a tone that suggests he has said it many times before.

"Bryszkiewski," he says, when I tell him why I am here. "I don't recognize the name."

The smiling clerk brings us chocolate cookies at his bidding. "These are really good," Pan Świniarski says, pointing to a round, crunchy-looking one. And they are.

He tells me of running away to Warsaw and of his father's store being taken over by the Russians after the war and the compensation he received and the decision to stay in the little store he now owns. But I cannot keep my eyes off the room, how unpleasant each portion of it is, but how together the pieces seem to create a comfortable space for him, one in which he is the most important person and can call a stranger in and offer him coffee and cookies.

Holy Days

O n sunny Holy Thursday morning, clearly this is not a town in Lenten self-denial. Perhaps there are some citizens tucked away in their homes, fasting and praying, but the streets are alive today with more people than ever. All of the small patches of falling stucco, the missing pavement blocks that trip you on the sidewalks, the untended garden in the park with its crumbling mosaic walls—they all blend today under the sun into one harmonious place.

Entering and exiting every store, streams of people flow through the town square as if programmed on invisible tracks. The flower vendors around the old Evangelical church have pulled their fake flowers inside in favor of bright-colored African violets, hydrangeas, azaleas, and cut roses. Adam's estranged wife struts along the square rhythmically in her stylish pantsuit, a bouquet of tulips swinging in her left hand. Pairs of animated old men gossip in front of every other store. Across from the ice cream window, a latter-day Lolita stands in a short black skirt and gigantic black boots with thick soles, unselfconsciously licking the white cream off the top of her cone.

Inside St. Thomas's, a few women are making preparations, moving aged carpets from side altars for cleaning, bringing in fresh flowers, even enormous calla lilies, and preparing the altars.

A merry worker smiles as I pass. "Beautiful, no? I'm supposed to make sure they are in the right place to look their best, but I'm not sure where to put the roses."

The right side altar has been transformed into a sepulcher with field stones built into a crypt, a path of sand lined with rocks leads to the representation of Christ's tomb. Scattered about the church three or four people kneel in private prayer. I spend a few minutes in a pew myself, but before long I'm distracted, thinking about what a caseload of Liquid Gold would do for these ancient wooden seats.

I stop for a beer at the Ratuszowa, beneath one of the three big beer umbrellas near the outdoor counter now open for business. The young woman who greeted me here on my first day greets me again with the same smile that praises my efforts in Polish. For entertainment there is another table crowded with four large men speaking German and two women with children running around them in every direction speaking Polish.

Back at Adam's house, the workman upstairs saws and stops, saws and stops, as he finishes the floor to the attic. Pani Kopiczyńska cannot bear to see a job unfinished. I offer him food, anything he wants from town, but he is content, goes home for lunch, and proudly tells me of his son, who works for a big import company, speaks English, and spends a lot of time in Florida.

Ryszard telephones to see if I want to go on another tour of local sights. "I'll be there in fifteen minutes," he says.

He arrives in overdrive, having commandeered Grażyna's car and hugging three loaves of bread. "These are fantastic. Fresh. Here, one for you." I take the bread to the house and then we speed away. He rattles off an itinerary, still yelling at me in the hope that somehow I will understand him better if he is loud. Grażyna appears and jumps into the car.

Down winding dirt roads and into the woods we drive, stopping to gape at two trees that grow separately for perhaps fifteen feet then merge into one tree. "Extraordinary, isn't it?" Ryszard says. "No one knows how it happened."

"They loved each other very much," I offer, and my companions are delighted with that explanation.

Next we must stop at two of the *kapliczki,* little chapels, that appear regularly along the road in towns all over Poland, shrines, usually incorporating a statue with flowers at its feet. First we stop at a grotto in Brzozie Lubawskie, where two barking dogs and a gaping little girl meet us in the driveway of a house next to the shrine. "Ask if we can open the doors," Ryszard yells to the girl, walking toward the house.

"Watch out for the dogs," Grażyna yells.

Holy Days
—

The little girl obeys, and soon a deep male voice yells out that it is fine to open the doors.

At the next shrine a woman and her young son are painting. She is gently applying white to the mortar between all the bricks of the kapliczka. Her little son has a bigger brush and dabs reddish-brown paint on the lower bricks. A checkered, flannel work shirt hangs loosely over her baggy brown trousers, her soft brown skin and long hair look fresh and unadorned. There's a look of serenity about her as she says, "My grandmother always kept this little chapel."

Next we stop in the woods where a large rock has been set upright at the edge of a field. On it a small metal tag designates it as something to stop and see. It, too, has a story—of a wealthy man who lived here in a beautiful house, until the war. He was a partisan, and the Russians made sure he was taken care of. "He dragged that rock out of the Drwęca with his horses," Ryszard says.

"And where is the house?" I ask.

"There, there," Ryszard indicates "You can see the ruin, the foundation."

Farther down the road we see a car coming toward us. Janusz Laskowski and his family have had the same idea and are spending the afternoon inspecting their country as well. We have stopped at a tree that also has a metal tag, but in this case no one is quite sure why.

"In the city you see monuments to Chopin and Mickiewicz. Here in the country we have our own monuments," Anna laughs.

At the end of our journey Ryszard and I are hungry. "The waitress at Ratuszowa is beautiful," he murmurs.

"What do you think about that?" Grażyna says to me. "Is she beautiful?"

Good Friday has always been for me the most difficult Catholic holy day to break away from. Christmas, after all, is a national holiday in the United States that has little to do with the birth of a savior. And Easter, wrapped up as it is in pagan fertility rituals, has always been easy to observe just for fun, as a celebration of the arrival of spring. But Good Friday is a tough one. As a child I always wondered what was "good" about it, and when I asked, I was told that it was good because of the goodness in what our Lord did for us by dying on the cross.

I remember the Good Friday trip to church. We would fast all morning, then Uncle Hank would come to pick us up in his Buick. It was a somber day, the trip to church quiet, perhaps because we knew that we were in for three hours on our knees for the stations of the cross and then the dreaded kissing of the feet of Jesus. It was Good Friday that turned all the other holy days into holidays.

When I arrive at St. Thomas's at noon, the stone floors have been washed and damp spots linger in the chill, but the church seems to have taken off its winter coat of grime and gloom, leaving only age, beautiful age. Even the baroque gilding around St. Joseph holding the baby Jesus has somehow been freshened. The tabernacle has been shrouded in purple to await the miracle on Easter Sunday, the miracle that all Catholics say they believe.

The church is not yet bulging with people. It's afternoon, and the floors are wet; a few women are still putting the final touches on the flowers—one arranging a starched, white linen runner on a side altar. A grandpa with his grandson genuflects and heads toward the exit. An old woman with a little girl saunters up the aisle, swinging from side to side on creaky hips.

Details of the interior seem to leap out today: The two wood pillars to the choir loft are cracked in such a way as to suggest they came from a single green log. Altar paintings of St. Helen, St. Lucy, St. Barbara. Three young men work at the main altar, one painting and two preparing for readings. The smell of fresh flowers has replaced the cold musty smell I remember from my first visit—lilies, daffodils, and roses.

Near me an old woman kneels on the stone floor and whispers a brief prayer to the side altar, where a huge white sign proclaims "Bóg jest miłością"—God is love. Another follows and kneels longer than the first, her hands clasped together, her wrinkled face gazing piously, devoutly upward.

At home Adam ignores the ritual preparations. Instead he takes me for a ride to see the new house his brother is building a few miles southwest of town. So I pile in the car with his parents, Filip, and Puma the dog, feeling like some senile uncle who babbles incoherently while the family tries to talk sense to him. When we arrive at the construction site, a wiry older man and his wife are finishing up for the day. They are apparently going to build the place double-handedly. Meanwhile we trek down to the river Drwęca, where Adam's brother Janusz and his wife, Wiesława, are waiting to greet us. He is hunkier, more athletic and outgoing than Adam. She is self-confident, quick, thin, and dark in a stylish white skirt and black shoes.

At the river's edge great pieces of earth have been bulldozed, and heavy rocks have been dumped into the river. Janusz shows Filip how to skip a stone across the water. Pani Kopiczyńska identifies plants and points out an anthill. Pan Kopiczyński, looking like an old version of Adam, nods and smiles.

"This is going to be our beach," Wiesława laughs.

When I take her seriously, she says, "Actually this is all going to be grass." Lovely, except for the *komary,* mosquitoes.

It is to be their home away from Brodnica, the nearby town where they work and keep an apartment. "Soon a fence will be going up here," says Janusz,

Holy Days

—

pointing to boards the man who greeted us has been painting green. He shows off the foundation of what will be the garage for his new Jeep. If we weren't speaking Polish, I would think they were American cousins, eager to tame the wild, to bulldoze the countryside, subdivide, and put up fences. But it is a beautiful setting, with a land bridge into the water, swans swimming nearby, and a pine forest all around the house-to-be.

When we return to Nowe Miasto, I decide to see what has happened at the church. It is now eight o'clock; it must be empty. However, I hear voices even before I get to the door, no organ for mournful Good Friday, just the plaintive prayers of the faithful. Inside, there is barely room to sit. The voices repeat "My Beloved Jesus" after every injustice, indignity, and cruelty of the crucifixion. Now the tomb at the side altar has been completed and lit in deathly blue, the ceramic figure of Christ pitiful in death behind glass.

Ryszard enters after me in matching denim cowboy clothes, nods, and shakes my hand. After an hour of prayer, people begin to leave, others to line up, so I join the line, as Ryszard has. We draw near, and the line breaks into two parts: those who want to kneel before the sepulcher and those who want to kiss the cross. I am in the line to kiss the cross, but as we draw nearer I switch lines. I cannot bring myself to do it, as I see the women lingering—no quick smacks to the feet, rather longing gazes and tender lips to legs, arms, face of the ceramic savior of Poland.

Followed by Water

——◆——

Easter begins in earnest with a Saturday afternoon walk in the woods with three ladies: Pani Kopiczyńska, her sister Irena, and a retired librarian from Bydgoszcz.

"Come, come," Pani urges. "You can't sit all day in front of a computer. It's not healthy." Her pleas are persuasive—a tinge of pout, quite a bit of guilt, and her patented look of concern. We climb into her Mercedes, her big, ugly Puma panting and drooling in the rear. Around corners and down a country road we zoom. She parks to let the dog out so it can run behind the car for a while. Then we park again, step out, and simultaneously inhale.

Every once in a while Pani Kopiczyńska stops and picks something and tells me whether it's good to eat and what vitamins it contains. Her sister and her friend indulge her but are not convinced. Her sister smokes a pack a day.

"Something bit me here," I complain, scratching a black-and-blue welt on my arm.

"Ah, use this," she says, bends over, and picks a flat round leaf. *Babka zwyczajna*. She rubs it on my arm. In a few minutes the itching stops.

We check the state of the family's little cabin by the water, which Pani says must be torn down and replaced with a stylish A-frame, "like in Zakopane." "But," she waves her arm, "something else Adam doesn't care about."

Pani Kopiczyńska trots down to the lake, pops her shoes off, and wades in the cold water. The rest of us follow dutifully, but the other ladies think it is too cold for wading. I compromise and take off my shoes to tickle the water while sitting on the little dock. The sun warms us all. Pani Irena refers briefly to her unhappy marriage that ended years ago. I ask the librarian what she was doing in 1981, when I first saw Poland.

"I painted signs for Solidarity," she says. "That was my specialty."

"What kinds of signs?"

"Calls to strike. Informational signs. You knew you couldn't learn anything from any official source. But we had other information in the library, hidden where it could be kept safely. We painted signs with gloves on, you know, so they couldn't figure out from one sign to the next who painted them. We had our ways."

Two crayfish pass by the bridge. They seem to be looking for one another. Pani Kopiczyńska says she has heard that it is customary to boil such animals alive in the United States. "Can't they at least hit them on the head first?"

"The mushrooms are coming," she promises me as we head for the car. "We'll be back for mushrooms," she tells her companions. "We'll be careful which ones," her sister says ruefully.

Evening comes slowly, but finally it is time for the late Saturday mass. I arrive at almost eight o'clock, and people are lingering around the church door; already it is full inside. Ryszard and Grażyna spot me right away.

Tonight seven priests in golden silk vestments celebrate the mass. They are attended by forty altar boys, sixteen of them dressed in long, white robes tied with a white cord. Out the front entrance they approach a small bonfire that has been lit on the sidewalk. From it they light a candle the length of one of Adam's kayaks, which will burn inside the church until next Easter "from start to finish, from alpha to omega," says a priest.

"May the light of Christ shine," says another priest over the microphone.

"How long has this tradition been going on in Nowe Miasto?" I ask Ryszard.

"Always," he replies without hesitation.

"A thousand years?" I persist.

"Yes," he says confidently.

The entourage heads into the church while an old man with a shovel attends to the embers. The two hundred people watching outside now try to squeeze inside.

Ryszard takes off. A minute later Grażyna whispers conspiratorially, "Follow me. We are going to the choir loft."

She leads me up the narrow side stairs, the same ones that go to the belfry, but this time we lift the latch on a worn, wooden door and pass a mechanism that pumps air for the organ. Grażyna opens another door, and suddenly we are suspended in midair over the congregation; their little candles, lit from the big candle, flicker in their hands below. From this perch we can see the choreography of the priests and altar boys. I look up, and the frescoes are so close I can almost touch them. In a corner where the wooden loft meets the stone I can even see an ancient, dusty spider web.

From the main floor one looks up to the choir loft to see Michael the Archangel guarding the congregation. Now I can see on his helmet the words "Goralski 1884." "The donor and the year," Ryszard whispers, suddenly returned from some mysterious escapade.

It is a bit like being back stage at an opera. The tenor voice of the man at the organ booms through the microphone, and his helping hand, standing beside him, initiates the congregation's response with an equal boom. He kibitzes with a short man in thick glasses standing next to me. The tenor rests his hands in his lap; there is no organ now, out of respect for the murdered Christ, who has not yet risen from the dead.

He enunciates each response to the priest with moist lips and extraordinary clarity, and then he breathes deeply to bring out the flawless tones. Beneath the three sets of enormous pipes that rise to the ceiling, his lungs and vocal chords now fill the church with sound.

The priest begins the story of the discovery that the body of Christ is not to be found in the tomb.

"He is not here. He is risen." Suddenly the organist lays his hands on the keyboard, and the magnificent sound of those ancient pipes resounds through the church, making stereophonic sound seem like mere static. The rejoicing begins, and the essence of Christianity is proclaimed: "He has risen."

To the sound of church bells I wake the next morning without an alarm clock. I told myself when I went to sleep at one in the morning that I would go to the early mass only if I awoke in time. It's ten minutes till six, and the memory of a dream about my mother's death is fresh in my head. My clothes are where I tossed them, and I put them on and head to town.

The morning procession has already begun, and I simply fall in line. Around the church we go, all seven priests again, one bearing the Eucharist under a canopy held by four attendants. To my surprise I spot Pan Kopiczyński alone, marching around the church, too.

What does this parade symbolize? No one seems to know for sure. "It's a demonstration of faith," says a priest.

Into the church we go, packed in tight rows. The service begins; everyone kneels. Those who have no pews kneel on the stone floor. The priest's voice seems to say, "This is all so clear. Only a fool would not believe." And then he explains that "life and death in this world would make no sense without the death and resurrection of Christ. Bez sensu."

The crowd is packed in so tightly no one can move, so the priests circulate, delivering the communion wafers as they pass. "The body of Christ," the priest says. "Amen," say the communicants as they open their mouths. I am in the middle. Everyone around me is receiving communion. I must decide in a moment what to do. When he looks at me and holds up the host, I, too, say "Amen."

On and on communion goes. I think it is long over when I see a priest coming back in through the front doors. He has just now finished with the crowd outside, many more than a thousand. The priest speaks again, urging people to turn off their televisions, to talk to one another, to go for walks in the fresh air, and to have a good Smigus Dyngus.

I look around at the crowd, all of us facing forward as if something were there that is not equally behind us. Each of us had to awaken this morning, pull on clothes. In some people I see the effort it took—matted hair in an uneven dye job, a skirt pulled on with the zipper in the wrong place.

At ten minutes to eight I'm back home and feeling grimy without my shower, tired and unprepared to face breakfast with the Kopiczyński family. I decide to start over. I undress and lie in bed again for an hour, thinking the simple truth: I miss my mother, my grandmother, only child that I am, with no children, no parents, no grandparents, no brothers or sisters. I begin to see that dark hole in which life has no meaning, no purpose. I hear my mother say, "We're born to die." I see my grandmother praying the rosary to keep the demons at bay, to keep from falling into that well of loneliness.

Then I am in the Kopiczyński family home with breakfast set on a long table that fills the front of the house on the second floor over Pan Kopiczyński's photo shop. When Adam and I arrived, everyone was waiting. His brother and sister-in-law and their son, his estranged wife and their two sons—all are seated around the table.

"How was church?" Pan Kopiczyński asks first thing.

"Ah, you saw me."

"Of course."

"It was long."

"Yes, it was long."

CHAPTER 15

—

So the conversation goes. Now and then it races away without me. Then it slows down and pulls me back in.

Wiesława brings it back with English comments, and suddenly we are talking about the difference between living with *innych ludzi*—many kinds of people—and living in Poland, where everyone is Polish.

"We have lots of kinds of people here," Pani Kopiczyńska protests.

"We have Polish people here," Wiesława counters. And soon she is telling us about her experience in Harlem when she went to hear a gospel choir. Then she tells Adam that it's the same for black people in the United States as it is for women. "You can't be equal to succeed. You have to be better," she says.

"Is that really true?" Adam turns to me.

"Yes, it is true," I tell him.

Disappointed, he says nothing.

A dish of eel in aspic is passed around the table. I work up the courage to eat it, but most everyone passes, and so do I. Wiesława laughs and describes what eels look like when you are skin-diving among them.

Out of the blue, Pani Kopiczyńska announces that I have "classic Slavic looks. Of everyone around the table you look the most Polish," she says, and that's that.

Pani Kopiczyńska smiles and passes food: A pan of "white sausage," *biała kiełbasa,* is her only concession to fat. "Tradycja," she says. Tradition This Easter meal consists of three or four meat rolls, turkey, chicken, ground meat, *pasztet z jajkiem,* plates of carp, and many more molds of vegetables and fish in aspic, sautéed vegetables, vegetable salads. Then there is coffee and with it Pani Kopiczyńska's poppy-seed torte—an enormous, double-layered cake with pineapple and coconut and frosting as light as air.

Pani Kopiczyńska modestly shows me the small, carefully arranged kitchen in which she created these delights. I am transported for a moment to Hamtramck, and I remember the apartment above the store on Conant Street, where my mother's boyfriend's mother ruled over her family and took my mother in as one of her own. What a strange world the city was to me then, a little boy from the country, and how easily my mother took to it. There I first tasted *czarnina,* soup made from duck's blood. Now, five thousand miles away, I sit in the second-story flat of a family in Poland. It is the same, only very different, and soon I must say good-bye for dinner in Toruń.

When I arrive, Maria Śliwińska and her mother are waiting for me, and her new apartment is lovely, but young boys loitering outside ask me for money. The apartments across the street are in shambles.

Followed by Water

—

Maria, a librarian at Copernicus University, and her mother seem a bit sad. It seems my duty to cheer them up, so I insist on Polish even though Maria's English is better than my Polish.

"I very much like Poland," I say immediately to Pani Śliwińska, establishing that I will speak Polish earnestly but not well. "I want know everything, not like tourist, like be live here."

"Do you have relatives here?" she asks in a world-weary voice, smiling behind large, plastic glasses at my Polish. She is a dignified, slender woman who keeps her hair brown and speaks in a quiet, monotonous plea.

I explain that my grandmother was born near Nowe Miasto, and I have not figured out what became of the seven brothers and sisters who were left behind when she and her sister went to America. I want to know how it is now for people to live here.

"It's not so good," she says bluntly.

"Was it so much better before when we had to stand in lines for food?" her daughter asks.

"No, but we didn't have people so poor they had to beg for food. Now there are people begging because they can't feed their children. Can you imagine?" she says to me. "It wasn't like that before."

"People don't have jobs?" I inquire.

"No, they don't have jobs, or they make very little money. It seems to me very hard now. People had jobs before. Nobody begged for food. Now the young ones don't know what to do. They paint graffiti on walls. I was never scared before, but now the young ones, they might just push an old person down instead of helping her."

"You can see we disagree on certain things," her daughter says to me. "We had to stand in line for an egg before. Everything was available only on ration cards. You don't remember?" she asks her mother.

"Yes, yes, I remember, but at least it was safe. I'm just afraid. People had money then, but there was nothing in the stores to buy. Now the stores are full, and people don't have money."

Almost without transition we are talking about the Second World War.

"It hurts me to hear the way people say Poles were as bad as the Germans, that Poles wouldn't help the Jews. I don't understand why people say this," Pani Śliwińska laments, her voice rising in irritation. "It's not true. What were we supposed to do? I remember when they came and took us away. We lived in a village not far from here. They put us on a train. I was thirteen. My brother was just a year old. He didn't have milk, they gave us nothing, told us nothing. Like animals they put us on a train, packed into the car, and this was July; it was so hot and we couldn't breathe. They were taking us to Owczary, a small village near Kraków, and they made us work there."

"Why did they force you to leave?"

"Germans were resettling here. They took our house, and we were relocated to work on a small farm. It was so small. And what were we supposed to do to help anyone? I can still remember that train, three days on that train, but mostly what I remember is the door opening. I remember the feeling of that outside air hitting us and breathing it in."

Pani Śliwińska is revealing this story so matter-of-factly that I have not detected until now how difficult it is for her to tell.

"You have to understand, there were old people on that train. They couldn't stand such treatment, couldn't live through such a trip. They died on the train; we were so pressed together on that train. Their hearts stopped, and they died standing because there was no room to fall down." With that recollection, her voice chokes only a little, and she shakes her head just a bit. Her hands are resting in her lap.

"For a while I had to work on a farm, and there was a family of Jews who were running from the SS. They came there to hide, and the SS asked me where they were, and I lied and told them I had not seen them. There were many people who hid Jews. Why do people think Poland was like that? It's not fair. It wasn't Poland; it was Poles dying, too. Sometimes I passed hand grenades to the partisans, to the home army, mixed into baskets of green tomatoes."

Maria says, "I can imagine why people in the United States couldn't understand what was happening here. People have their lives, they must go on living them. I do that now. I know of the terrible things happening to people now, let's say in China. What can I do about it? What could people do for us?"

Later Maria tells me that her mother witnessed the execution of a young man with whom she was in love.

The next morning I hear screams outside my window. When I swing it open, a group of teenagers are dousing one another with water. It's Smigus Dyngus, the Monday after Easter.

Long before anyone ever thought of having a wet T-shirt contest, long before there were T-shirts, the spring ritual of Smigus Dyngus took hold in Poland. It's as old as the nation as far as anyone can tell, and one of the only traditions my grandmother ever spoke about with something I could call delight, maybe even a little embarrassment.

But how interesting can it be, a glorified, squirt-gun fight? I jump on my bike to see what is going on in the Rynek. It seems quiet now, although Adam said this morning young people were dousing each other everywhere and flicking willow switches at one another's legs. Today it's the boys' turn to chase the girls, but tomorrow "is okay for girl to chase boy," as my grandmother said.

I round the corner to Kościelna Street toward the church, and the way is lined with boys, one pulling a screaming young girl while another throws a pail of water in her face. As I near the church, three young boys run toward me with plastic pop bottles, and they are aiming water at me! It's something of a free-for-all.

An older man rounds the corner from the church, where a large crowd is gathered because once again the church is full, and scolds the boys, but they know he doesn't really mean it. On my right a priest's voice rings out over the microphone; on my left three boys yelling and with delight aiming their Smigus Dyngus water pistols at this old *pan* on a bike.

I wheel past a well-dressed, middle-aged woman standing in her doorway with two younger people beside her smiling at her sopping-wet tank top. I speed by and laugh out loud at the astounded look on her face. She spots me. "Oh, look, and he is laughing at me," she hollers and chuckles as I pass, lifting her hands in a gesture of helplessness.

One theory has it that Smigus Dyngus is a reminder that the sinner has been washed in the blood of Christ, another that it represents the way in which early Christians in Jerusalem were dispersed when they gathered to talk about Christ's resurrection. But since the real origin is unknown, one is free to choose. My favorite explanation is that this is a pagan tradition handed down from the earliest settlers in Poland, a burst of spring energy and sexiness that is as refreshing as it is silly.

Easter ends as it began, in the woods with Pani Kopiczyńska, this time with Adam's ex-wife, Alina, and son Filip. The lake is warm enough to wade in. As I watch her frolicking with her son in the water, setting the table, and bringing out stuffed cabbages she made herself, I wonder at how effortlessly they have taken me in without demands or suspicions, seeing to it that one way or another I have a family in Poland.

Alina flirts one moment, the next she talks about her work as a dedicated educator. Then she runs a hand through her short blond curls, and we talk, as best I can, about what makes a marriage work. "It can't be just one person giving and giving; it has to be both, give and take. It has to be that balance," she says.

Pani brings out a magazine I spotted lying on the settee in the cabin, full of topless women in thongs. She laughs when I ask her if she isn't embarrassed.

"About what?" she replies.

CHAPTER 15

—

"American men go crazy when they see this in Europe, you know, because women don't go topless in the United States," she shrugs.

"In the land of sex and nudity," Alina snaps. "Americans are hypocrites about sex, you know."

"What is it that makes Polish mothers so determined?" I ask Adam later.

"Don't know," he shrugs and, in a few simple words, tells me his version of a marriage that just didn't work.

The Best Days Begin in Ordinary Ways

———◦———◦———

The twin sisters and their librarian friend are there to greet me when I return from a train ride to Warsaw. Pani Kopiczyńska has completed the redecorating with modular cupboard pieces brought up from the basement, which the house painter has repaired. She has carefully placed them so that the tallest piece conceals the ugly chipped fuse box on the window wall. It's good to be home.

When we are alone, watering the garden, she tells me the news that makes her want to cry. "I know now that Adam has another woman. We even met her that day we went to the river to watch him kayaking. She even petted my dog," she says sadly, with resignation.

I cannot respond intelligently to this news, so I only listen and shake my head as well. "He does what he must do," I offer.

"Come," she says, "let's water the front yard, too." While she waters, I weed, and she tells me to transplant the grass I pull up to a bare spot over an underground pipe. "Maybe it will grow, maybe it won't."

In the afternoon I stop at the curtain shop to buy lace curtains to send home to my mother's sister Mary in New Jersey. The middle-aged man and his daughter behind the counter are eager and hang on my every word in Polish. The daughter, a smiling teenager, says little but pulls out every bolt of cloth, every finished panel I eye.

I spot Pan Świniarski, and he talks faster than I can follow about his plans for tomorrow in his cottage. His tongue picks up speed, and he tilts from side to side as he talks, but he looks at me with such genuine interest and something that seems like admiration that I cannot bear to stop him and tell him he has lost me.

Pani Wituchowska is waiting behind the wine counter. "It's been a long time," I exclaim. "Such a long time, oh my God," she laughs, clasping her hands together.

"Tell me, so I can hear it from you and no one else. Where did your son take you?" I inquire.

"Oh, my God," she says reverently, "I didn't know until we got to the airport, otherwise I might not have gone. It was so far, so far, and so expensive."

"And where was it? Where was it?" I play along with her suspense.

"Jerusalem! I have been to Jerusalem!" she says, "and I swam in the Dead Sea!" She throws her head back and acts out for me what it was like to feel weightless in the water. "It was like a bed! People all around me were floating, and my son said, 'Just lie back,' and he held my head."

She takes me outside to show off the Polish flag hanging from her upstairs window. "Not so many people celebrate it, but I am Polish, and I celebrate the Third of May." The Third of May commemorates the constitution Poland adopted in 1921, which provided for equality under the law for all Polish citizens with respect to their economic, political, cultural, and religious interests, without regard to race, national origin, or creed. "Something to remember," she says.

On the way to the church I spot Alina Kopiczyńska closing her cosmetics shop, flashing a fresh smile my way. She tells me she knows that Adam was not home to greet me. "Adam is doing what Adam wants to do," she says, with a wise chuckle.

I already feel the distance starting, the separation that will come all too soon from these people who have opened their lives to me. I missed the Kopiczyńskis, Pani Wituchowska, Grażyna and Ryszard at *Gazeta Nowomiejska,* Mieczysław and Urszula, Janusz and Anna and their three good-natured children, wise and comfortable in their Polish lives. Going to Warsaw and returning reminds me that I am from another world and must soon go back.

As I head home from the Rynek at dusk, past the cemetery, and under the train trestle, a young man is staggering down the middle of Narutowicza Street toward me. Then he turns and shouts in the opposite direction. Seeing an oncoming car, he steps in front of it, waving his arms high above his head. The car stops, and he starts talking into it, but the driver wants only to find a route around this desperate fool. As the car turns in one direction to pass him,

The Best Days Begin in Ordinary Ways

—

he swings himself in front of it. The car turns again, and so does he. But finally he is too drunk to keep up with it, and the car passes. As I turn down the driveway to home, a police car pulls up, and two officers approach him, quiet now and back on the sidewalk, perhaps giving up.

The next day begins with sun beaming through the windows of my room in spite of the Venetian blinds that I keep closed so that my computer screen is not outshone by the sky. I head for the Rynek as another funeral procession makes its way down Third of May Street, its "Requiem" sign on the hood of the hearse. A morning of errands—at the bank, the cleaners, the Kopiczyńskis' photo shop, and two curtain stores (where I still have not been able to find just the right curtains for my Aunt Mary, in spite of my conversion of inches to centimeters)—ends at the Ratuszowa, where I indulge in the hamburger special, loaded with mayonnaise and cabbage slaw. The staff has become accustomed to me, but when I speak, the young male waiter still smiles as if hearing my mutilated Polish for the first time.

For a moment the disco music on the restaurant sound system and the church bells outside coincide, in a synchronized rhythm, tolling, it seems, just for me—one theme says live for today, the other for eternity—together for a moment their separate messages ring as one.

An old woman, thin as a twig, walks in and surveys the scene like a walking stick, with several curious glances my way, before settling at a table. Moments later an old man joins her, a man I've seen wandering about town in his Greek fisherman's cap. They slurp down bowls of soup, and then their food arrives—mountains of mashed potatoes and a cutlet. She shovels in her food two and three clumps at a time before chewing, knife in her left hand, fork in her right, and swallowing after two or three grinds.

I have not been in the Ratuszowa for a while, since Pani Kopiczyńska leaves meals on the kitchen table or I am experimenting with how best to prepare the fresh offerings from the open-air market. The little restaurant, so strange and silent in winter, has blossomed, with umbrellaed tables outside and an open door and ice cream window to the Rynek. The routines of life in Nowe Miasto are starting to seem familiar, prompting me to dream: Is this my real life? Are these my people?

"In 1902 the train lines were built, connecting Nowe Miasto to Iława," says Andrzej Korecki when I stop in the Papirus Bookstore for advice on how to retrace the route my grandmother took out of Nowe Miasto in 1913. He brings out a copy of *Nowe Miasto Lubawskie,* the 1992 history he coauthored. "Here on page 100, it tells you. The tracks to Iława meant Nowe Miasto was connected to the rest of the rail system, and those connections are very much the same now as then," he says with assurance. "To go to Bremen you would go from Nowe Miasto to Iława, then to Poznań. From there it is very fast to Berlin and then to Bremen."

"How long would it have taken?"

"It could be done in one day, two at the most. Of course they would have come in a horse cart from Sugajno to Nowe Miasto early in the morning, but I think they would have gone in one day so they would not have to pay for a hotel."

Pan Korecki ponders for a moment. "How short a hundred years is," he concludes. "For only a hundred years these trains ran, and now already the train to Nowe Miasto is no more. It's not a good thing. Now you must have a car or take a bus."

My Maluch performs well today, a minimum of sputtering and backtalk. Could it be I am learning how to drive the thing? The fields are green with new oats and wheat, cows graze, a boy on a bike stares back at me. "It is 1955 and I am you," I muse, a little blond boy on a country road, safe and ignorant in Michigan. A tractor cuts grass in the distance. In the bright sun another young man passes, in bib overalls like those I hated and never wanted to wear because they were not American enough, not what the other kids wore. While my grandmother lived in a remote outpost of Poland, her children and grandchildren became American all around her.

I pass through Boleszyn, where on the left side of the road a young drunk staggers toward town, his shirt flying open in the breeze, his brown hair dusty and matted.

As I round the bend I spy an old woman in a blue flowered dress, brown sweater, and babushka walking up the road. Ahead is a roadside crucifix with fresh flowers at its base, so I pull over to have a look. The woman is far more interesting than the cross, but I pretend to take an interest in the shrine while she draws slowly nearer.

"Dzień dobry," I call out when she is nearly beside me. "It's very beautiful."

"Oh, yes," she says sheepishly. "I bring flowers. I look after it." She rests on her cane and tilts her head toward me to hear better.

"You live here in Boleszyn?" I offer feebly.

"Oh, yes," she replies, "all my life."

"My grandmother was born here," I tell her. "In Sugajno."

"Oh?" she says with genuine curiosity. "And what was her name?"

"Bryszkiewski."

"Oh, Bryszkiewski, yes, there is a Bryszkiewski in Sugajno."

"Yes, I have already met him. He is my cousin, a distant cousin, but I don't know what happened to the rest of my grandmother's brothers and sisters. The wars, you know."

"Yes?" she calls out with an angelic lilt, her voice as soft and sweet as a violin. "And where do you live?"

"I live in the United States."

Her eyes widen, and every wrinkle in her face draws together into a smile. "Oh, and you are here now?" She seems perplexed, for surely this is the first time she has walked to the crucifix to find a man from another world waiting there.

"Yes, I wanted to see the place where my grandmother was born, so I am living in Nowe Miasto now."

"Oh, from the United States." She seems to be thinking carefully, trying to conjure up whatever she knows about this unknown place. "I have a sister in Mroczno. My sisters all have grandchildren now, and great-grandchildren. My sister-in-law went to the United States, or London, or was it Paris? I don't know, but you could ask her. What is your name?"

Momentarily she seems silenced by my German name. "My father's name," I tell her.

"You walk very well with your cane," I change the subject.

"I broke my leg—two times," she says, marking out the places with her hand, and she shuffles back toward her house, one of the brick German-style houses I love so much.

As I start the engine of my little Maluch, I see the young drunk I spotted on my way into Boleszyn. He staggers down the road and turns into the driveway of the old woman's house. He hesitates at the door, then turns the knob and goes inside, oblivious to the little babcia making her way home from an unlikely encounter with an American guy.

CHAPTER 16

—

Property

Another sunny day in Nowe Miasto, and our little garden grows dryer and dryer, clods of unhoed clay lie like misshapen bricks among the struggling wisps of carrot and beet. The neighbors water their neatly planted, front-yard garden daily, while our discrete plot behind the garage goes arid for days. Pani Kopiczyńska seems to have tired of her daily visits to tend the plants, clean the house, and deposit food on the kitchen table and has not been here for three days.

I have no time today for gardening, for I have been summoned before the *burmistrz*, the mayor, his honor Witold Lendzion, who has heard of this American gadding about town and would like to meet me.

The pair of large, white wooden doors to his office on the second floor of the town hall are closed, so I knock. Immediately a voice inside says, "Proszę," and I enter a quiet room with an L-shaped desk behind which two secretaries are conferring. The door to His Honor's office is open, and I catch a glimpse of a middle-aged man at a large wooden desk. A secretary ushers me into a conference room and asks me to have a seat at the end of a U-shaped wooden table for twelve. At the end of it is another desk. This is beginning to seem like work and probably leading to a tiresome conversation about finances and taxes. On the conference-room wall are a picture of the pope, a Polish eagle in red and white, and a large city crest.

The burmistrz enters smiling and grabs my hand. He is a handsome man, gray haired and carefully groomed, his belly bulging just a bit beneath a blue shirt and tie. His eyes sparkle with curiosity. He does not seat himself at the desk but rather in a chair straight across from me. He has a pile of gifts for me, books and brochures about Nowe Miasto, and we review them; some I own and some I do not.

"Will you have time to go to lunch?" I ask.

"Oh, no," he says. "The way we work is this: We come in at seven thirty, and we work till three in the office, on Tuesdays till four fifteen with no lunch break. We also work on the first Saturday of every month. That's the way it is in Poland. And when we need to, we work later. Coffee, tea, or mineral water?"

I explain that I rent a room from Adam Kopiczyński, and he begins finishing my sentences for me: ". . . and his wife has moved out . . . and he has a very big house all alone. Yes, yes, I know."

"So can we talk a little bit about what you think are the most important problems facing the town?" I ask.

"Housing," he says. "That is the number one problem. We have two hundred families waiting for housing now. But the town doesn't actually build it; we have no budget for that. We want private companies to do it. Last year a firm built the new housing units over the Lewiatan grocery store. But still we have people waiting. That housing was for people with money to spend. Meanwhile we have people still living six to a room. It's our biggest problem, and we can't solve it all at once. Then of course there is the problem of water and sewers. . . ."

Pan Lendzion smiles as he explains the way in which national tax rates are established by parliament and tax money is redistributed to municipalities, and I can see the charm that must be at least partly responsible for his station in life. He knows his stuff and explains it to me as if I were a hostile taxpayer in need of soothing. I am wondering how to get him to talk about himself. He sees my eyes glazing over, I suspect, so he summarizes, "The Polish tax system is very complicated."

"Like the Polish language," I add. He smiles and begins to try a little English on me. He knows his numbers and translates several of the words I have not understood in Polish.

"Do you think every child in Poland should be learning English?"

"Absolutely. It is the international language now."

"You speak it rather well yourself."

"No, unfortunately. I did study it for two years, and I am able to understand a little bit. I visited my son-in-law in New Haven last year."

"Connecticut?"

"Yes, he is there for five months working; my daughter is living with us. We got a tour of Yale University. Beautiful." He has seen Boston and New York. "Times Square. So big, so beautiful." His eyes glimmer again when he thinks about his visit to America.

He goes on a bit more about tax money and how it is used. A total budget of twelve million złoty, or about three million dollars, supports a school system with 150 employees, a preschool with 200 children, a social welfare office with 15 employees, the Dom Kultury cultural center, the public library, and the city offices with some 27 employees. "And what have I forgotten? Oh, yes, the sports stadium. It was just built last year for three million four hundred thousand złoty. But thirty percent of that came from Warsaw."

"The sports stadium by the Ośrodek Sportowy i Rekreacyjny?" I ask, explaining that I lived there when I first came to town.

"Oh, yes, and the OSIR hotel belongs to the city, too, and shop buildings like Adam Kopiczyński's shoe store on the Rynek. The city owns many shops and rents them out. The money goes for remodeling other buildings. One day we may sell them, but right now the city manages many such buildings. By the time the budget is distributed, we have only about one million złoty left to invest in new projects. The stadium was the last one."

"Is it true that I cannot buy property in Poland because I am not a citizen?"

"Hmm," he furrows his brow, "that depends."

"Depends?"

"You can't and you can."

I exaggerate my perplexed response with a raised eyebrow.

"You can. But only with special permission of the minister of internal affairs in Warsaw."

"Have you always lived in Nowe Miasto?"

"Yes," he beams. "I can trace my genealogy all the way through the nineteenth century in this city. My great-great-grandfather was born here in 1804."

"And my family? Bryszkiewski. My grandmother was born in Sugajno. Do you know the name? Nine brothers and sisters there were. Could it be they left no children?"

But the mayor shakes his head. "I'm afraid I can't help."

Disappointed and fairly sure I won't, I promise to call again and casually mention that I'll be stopping at *Gazeta Nowomiejska* for a beer with Ryszard and Grażyna at six. He seems not to have time, but at 6:30 Ryszard arrives at my house in a rush. "The burmistrz is waiting for you!" he gushes, and off we go for a couple of hours of talk.

Property
—

"I didn't think you had more time for me today," I explain feebly to His Honor, who has brought several bottles of beer and settled into one of the two waiting-room-style chairs in the *Gazeta* office. "It's fine, fine," he smiles, relaxed now, out of his business clothes and into a knit pullover that reveals a bit more of his ample belly. He wants to talk about literature and life in America and to tell me more about the hassles and responsibilities of being mayor.

During a lull in the conversation I mention again that it's hard to be an American in Poland without being curious about the fate of the Jews of Nowe Miasto. "Gone, gone," he shakes his head sadly.

"Gone, but where? I am told they were taken to Auschwitz."

"No, no, not to Auschwitz. They were among the first to be rounded up. The Germans came here early in the war, September 1939, and rounded them up. Auschwitz wasn't even built then. I don't know where they were taken. Perhaps to Stutthof. No one survived. Not one."

I am getting so many mixed messages. One person tells me they were taken to Auschwitz, another that Auschwitz has simply become a synonym for "concentration camp" in Poland. One person tells me to look in the history of Nowe Miasto published in 1992, but in the chapter on World War II it says only that Poles and Jews were rounded up and eventually killed, while Germans resettled here. Their fate unknown. No survivors upon whom the burden of memory could rest.

"In a hundred years there will be no Polish, according to an American Peace Corps volunteer I spoke to recently," I tease.

Grażyna and the mayor both look momentarily shocked, then Grażyna murmurs confidently, "There will be always be Polish." The mayor laughs and nods, "True, true always. That's a ridiculous idea. Well, of course there are recently dead languages, but from small cultures that disappeared. It's much different."

The phone rings. It's for the mayor. He slips into the next room; we can hear him saying the Polish equivalent of "Yes, dear, yes dear, I'll be right there, dear."

"The boss," Ryszard whispers with a wink. And the mayor hurries off.

After more beer Ryszard whisks me away for another drive into the woods to see another shrine, this one the "five-oaks cross."

The mosquitoes are biting, but the cross stands where a grateful soldier left a patriotic message written on a piece of paper. "But his patriotism was too much for the Russians," says Ryszard. "They had to come here and rip it up. So now we have the shrine of the grateful soldier, but his message is gone."

Before he will let me go home he decides I must see his workshop.

"This is what I used to do. Now my brother does this work. But I still love antiques." He leads me to an entrance on the back side of the town square, where he shows off rooms packed with tables, desks, sideboards, waiting to be refinished.

"My grandfather bought this in 1927 at the first flea market in Poznań," he says of a giant, German-made sander. He produces a picture of his grandfather in this very room, standing proud with his students.

"We still own a desk from Gestapo headquarters," he adds nonchalantly. "You have to come with us tomorrow to Olsztyn."

Here is a man who loves this land, who goes into overdrive at the suggestion of looking at a lake, a little chapel, or a castle ruin, a man who drives like a maniac at 80 kilometers down roads with signs posted at 40, who in Olsztyn was mortified when he made an illegal left turn and got honked at.

I meet my friends the next morning at the *Gazeta* office, and we are off for another harrowing ride. Ryszard calls Olsztyn a circus. I think of a joyride with him as a circus as well. From one site to another he shows off his land, and there seems to be no limit to his enthusiasm and willingness to play the guide.

Then he loads four loaves of bread into the trunk. "Łapówki," he jokes— bribes. "The bosses in Olzstyn love this bread, the best you can buy, only in Nowe Miasto. So I bring it to them. Maybe they do a little bit better job for us," he laughs, half serious.

He ignores the 30-kilometer speed limit and heads toward Olsztyn at 80. Grażyna sits in the back seat, smiling like the proverbial Cheshire cat as I try to make a point in Polish.

We whiz through Lubawa, where he points at the church. "It was Evangeli-cal." A few kilometers later he points to another. "A sanctuary, Our Lady appeared there; a marker says so." Ryszard is fascinated by miraculous tales. For two days in a private home in the town of Wyszków in a painting of the Blessed Mother she closed and opened her eyes. In Okonin a young farmer was rounding up his cows for the evening when he saw strange movement in the willows and then a brightness and the image of the Blessed Mother. There are too many occurrences to count, he says, books full of them, almost always of the Holy Mother.

To the right of the road, follow the line of old wire poles, the raised earth that winds through the trees, he says. "Railroad tracks. This area is full of abandoned railroad tracks, even old trestles, from the war. Hitler believed, you see, that once the Poles were removed from this rich land, it would become the center of food production for all of Germany, so he was making it ready with railroad lines to Berlin."

Property
—

Beyond Olsztyn, Ryszard says, is Wilczy Szaniec, with concrete bunkers from World War II still visible. Wolfsschanze in German—Wolf's Lair.

Movies and television have led us to believe that Hitler spent the war shouting from a pulpit in Berlin. In fact, he arrived in his lair in 1941, shortly after the invasion of Russia and stayed here in Poland until late 1944, with only occasional trips to the outside world. At Wolf's Lair an unsuccessful assassination attempt occurred on July 20, 1944. Claus von Stauffenberg, leader of the plot to kill Hitler, and some five thousand others were executed for their part in the failed coup.

Historians have speculated that had the assassination attempt succeeded, the course of the Second World War might have been very different. Hitler's death might have resulted in a peace treaty between Germany and the Allies and might well have saved the lives of five million people, including three million Jews, and it might have avoided the devastation of many parts of Poland and Germany. They have also dared to suggest that success at Wilczy Szaniec might have prevented a half-century of communism in many parts of eastern Europe.

In Olsztyn visits to the offices and printing plant of *Gazeta Olsztyńska* involve picking up a paltry box of supplies—pens, tape, cleaning liquid—that, it would seem, could have been purchased almost for the cost of the gas it took to drive here. "Once a month we do this," Grażyna says, then heads off to a computer with an older, red-faced man to debate layout solutions that will accommodate more and later advertisements.

The restaurant prices in Olsztyn make Ryszard blush. "We have all this available to us now," he shakes his head in disbelief, then wraps his hand around his neck like a noose. "This, this is how the Russians had us. I never want to go back to that. I would drive to Olsztyn for a piece of kiełbasa in those days or if we heard there was butter here. In Nowe Miasto we had lines from the main gate to the Rynek just for butter."

"And it was all on cards, anyway," Grażyna nods.

"Vinegar," says Ryszard. "That is what was on the shelves. Vinegar." He takes another gobble of *golonka,* a lump of skin-wrapped pork fat.

"We had to have ration cards for everything," Grażyna continues, "for tea, coffee, meat, sugar, even shoes."

"And there were łapówki for everything, too," Ryszard adds—always bribes. "People played little tricks with cards, trying to get more for their money, hoarding them, trading their vodka cards with drinkers to get more food cards. Kurcze," he says, one of his many inventive euphemisms for kurwa—whore. Like saying "shoot" instead of "shit."

The ride home is quieter, slower. We pass a little town called Ameryka, which Ryszard points to gleefully. Then we come to Grunwald, and this mysterious spot ignites his imagination like a spark plug. "The battle of Grunwald, July 15, 1410. It was supposed to happen at Kurzętnik but for the terrain. King Jagiełło and his troops had to choose another route." It is hard to imagine my favorite picnic ground as the sight of a great battle, but no doubt it, too, saw fighting. "This was the largest battle fought in medieval Europe," he says. "Nobody knows that. The defeat of the Teutonic knights."

Three monuments adorn the meadowlands where the battle had raged. "Take a picture, take a picture," he urges. I am more interested in the wild boar and bear skins for sale in the rustic little souvenir shop by the road. Grażyna loves the wildflowers that line the walkway.

We stop at a supermarket, where Ryszard stocks up on beer, juice, and milk. "This is the kind of store we will have in Nowe Miasto soon," he pronounces.

"And then all the little stores will close," he laments, resigned to the inevitability. Back to work they go.

I have not seen Pani Wituchowska in over a week. "Ah," she gasps, feigning shock as I enter her wine store. "I thought you disappeared." Then she clutches my arm, and her delicate eyes twinkle. "I am very angry with you, you know. Where have you been?"

I humble myself and recite the list of towns I've visited.

Pani is full of piss and vinegar today, ready to assess my latest acquaintances and all of the sites I have seen.

"What do you think of the burmistrz?" I ask. "I think he is a man who knows what to say."

"I think he is a phony. He says what he thinks you want to hear," she retorts. "And he was too much of a communist. Now, of course, he is not. But that is more of the same. Oh, he is all right, but he is neither here nor there to me. And besides, I say what I think. Before, we were not free to say what we think. Now we are, and I intend to say it.

"I have told you how it was then. Everyone with pockets open. Go to a store, and there is a clerk with her pocket open. 'Slip me a little something here,' she tells you. I was never that way. Can't stand bribes. But that is how it was with the communists."

I tell her that I intend to trace my grandmother's path out of Nowe Miasto to Bremen and the ship that took her to America. "Is it possible that people would go from here all the way to Bremen in one day?"

"Yes, yes, I suppose it's possible, but it would have been very hard for them. They didn't stay in hotels the way you can. They just didn't do that in those days."

Property
—

"I intend to make the same trip. No hotels."

"And so when will you be here? When am I going to get you to my house privately? You know, you are a client here in the store, but I want you to come to my home."

"And I would like that very much. . . ."

"My husband, you know, he was more than thirty years older than I when we married. He loved good cognac, French cognac. He dressed so beautifully. The head and the feet, he always said, you can judge a man by how well they are groomed. I still have a little Martell cognac upstairs, waiting for you."

I look into her romantic face, doting over me. She brushes against me and touches my arm now and then, smiling, lighting up when I entered the room, telling me what she saw this day that differed from the day before, telling me of her impatience with vulgarity and stupidity. I listen and agree as her husband must have, while he smoked a cigar and drank wine, while she arranged supper and made sure that it was served slowly and with flourish over each course.

"The doctor says I eat too much butter," she says, pulling out a piece of cardboard the size of a one-pound square of the stuff and telling me that this will last her two days.

Pani Wituchowska has more news for me today. She tells me again how much she deplores the rapid approach she sees so many young people take. Again she tells me that Adam is too skinny and passionless to be sexy.

"The girls, they throw themselves at the boys, they snuggle up so close to them when they dance it's as if they want to crawl inside them. Where is the romance in that? I don't understand. And I don't understand another thing: men going with men, women with women. I don't understand it. Why?"

To get her to continue I say only, "You know about everything that goes on in the world, don't you?"

Pani is proud.

"But this is a small town," I add.

"Oh, a small town. But we have two women here. I know them. They lived together, and the one told me, 'What do I need a man for? It's better with a woman.'" She lifts her shoulders and laughs, putting her hand to her mouth as if she had just said the naughtiest imaginable thing.

"Your wine is more popular now," she tells me proudly, pointing to a Côtes du Rhône I've taken a shine to. "Do you remember the woman, the doctor, who was in the store one day when you were here? You met her, do you remember?"

"I remember."

"She is a woman about your age, you know. She lives with her mother and sisters. Four women in one house, and they are all doctors. No thanks. She was here the other day, and someone asked her what wine she prefers. 'I always buy the Côtes du Rhône. It is very good, you know, it's what the American guy drinks.' That is what she said." Pani assures me it is all remarkably funny and terribly flattering.

Night falls, and I am at my computer. Adam knocks on my door for small talk, my questions for the day, to hear my observations.

"There is something interesting I can tell you," he says, looking grave and guilty but nervously eager. I am wondering what sort of trivia he has in mind. Something about kayaking? Perhaps a castle ruin I haven't seen? Before I can ask he says, "My great-grandfather was a Jew. Interesting, isn't it? Of course, my mother wouldn't like me to tell you."

"Why not?" I ask.

"This is a family secret. One of those things we aren't supposed to talk about to other people," he says flatly, flashing a nervous smile.

He looks for my reaction. Getting none, he continues. "During the First World War my mother's grandmother, who was just a young farm girl at the time, came to work for a Jewish family in Nowe Miasto. She got pregnant and was sent to Berlin to have the child. The child was my mother's father. Later she went to work in Westphalia, where she met a Polish man and married him, but she already had a son, my grandfather, Maksymilian, the same man who went to America for twelve years and lived in Toledo."

"The thing that is so odd to me," he says wistfully, "is that this great-grandfather of mine owned a store in Nowe Miasto on the Rynek. Now, a hundred years later, I own a store on the Rynek. Funny, isn't it?"

"Very. But sad, not to be able to talk about it because . . . ," I suggest, and he finishes my sentence, ". . . because people still are not favorably disposed to Jews."

"How can that be when our savior and his mother, the queen of Poland, were Jews?"

"It makes no sense," Adam concludes.

CHAPTER 18

The Priest and the Ledger

———◦———

The next day I force myself out of bed early in spite of a headache and a mouth like a blast furnace from a beer session with Ryszard and Grażyna. "How do I address a priest?" I asked them, certainly not with the familiar "you"—*ty*. Perhaps the formal *pan,* or should I call him *ojciec*—"father"? None of the above, Grażyna says. "Call him *ksiądz*." It seems an awkward solution to address someone as "priest" and to ask, "How is priest today?" or "What does priest think about this?"

However, Father Brunon Jank solves the problem for me by popping out of the rectory door in Boleszyn a moment after my car door slams. He is dressed in priestly black, his clerical collar tightly wrapped around his red neck.

"Good day!" he sings out cordially, taking charge of the conversation. As he talks happily about the weather, my little car, and how he understands my Polish completely, I hear traces of the chantlike tone he used at Sunday mass a few weeks ago, advising parishioners to lay off the bottle for Lent. Although it is a few minutes before our nine-o'clock appointment, he has been waiting for me and hurries me inside, then offers me a seat opposite him at a small wooden desk. "I think we are going to find you some things today," he promises as he pulls two books from a small bookcase. One is a large, leather-bound volume of parish obituaries from the beginning of the twentieth century to 1939, the other a ragged collection of birth and baptismal records, missing its cover and stuffed into an inadequate, black plastic binder.

The rectory in Boleszyn is another of the pre–World War I brick houses built, like the schoolhouse in Sugajno, by the Germans adjacent to and in no way complementing the seventeenth-century wooden church it now serves. The rooms are large; it feels like the Bryszkiewski home in Sugajno, the same sparse furnishings, tablecloths, and floral carpets. Someone is cooking in the kitchen. In the corner I see a rack of hooks, where Father Jank's vestments hang waiting for the next mass.

"We can just look through these. We will find something about your grandmother, I think," he assures me as he thumbs through the loose pages in the binder, dragging strings and bits of glue from the torn binding across the desk. "Now, when was she born?" he asks. I pull out the passenger list from the *Prinz Friedrich Wilhelm*.

"She was born in 1894 in Sugajno. She left for America in 1913."

"Hmm," he cautions. "These birth records begin in 1894, but they are not complete. As you see, some of these older pages are missing."

"How is it that they survived World War II at all? Do you know what happened here in Boleszyn?"

"The Germans came here and took over the church. They displaced many people and appropriated their farms."

"And what happened to the people?"

"They were taken to forced-labor camps in Germany."

"And after the war?"

"They came back. Many survived and came back to their homes. The Germans, of course, had all left town by then."

"And what happened to the church?"

"There was no Catholic priest here during the war. The Germans took all the documents away. They were never returned. What you see here was hidden in the attic. When the Germans left, this is what was found."

"What about the First World War?"

"People's lives were not as badly torn apart. Everything is still recorded in these books, as you'll see, so people, the church, were not displaced as they were in the Second World War."

We settle into silence as each of us combs through one of the books, he the births, I the deaths, all carefully recorded in clear, handwritten script under the subjects printed above each column in German. Father Jank's round jaw sets with determination; his smile turns into a thin, straight line, then a frown. After a while he says discouragingly, "It looks like 1894 will not be complete."

I want to grab the book from him and search it myself, but I continue looking at the obituaries.

The Priest and the Ledger
—

"I have something here," he says suddenly. "Born to a farmer, Jan Brysz-kiewski, and his wife, Franciszka Jurkiewicz, of Sugajno, a son, Teodor, April 21, 1897. Baptized April 22."

"That is no doubt my grandmother's brother, for Jan was her father and she had a brother by that name," I reply excitedly as he hands me the tattered page. I return to the passenger list. Frances Jurkiewicz, maiden name. So now I see that my grandmother and her sister went to America with their mother's brother, and I have in front of me—in writing—for the first time in my life, the names of my mother's grandparents.

"How long and far I have come for this," I nod in gratitude. It makes Father Jank more determined. "We will find more," he says and notes that sometimes the name is spelled "Brzyszkiewski." "It all depends on who's doing the spell-ing," he smiles.

We uncover sad events in the life of Wincenty Bryszkiewski, grandfather of my new distant-cousin Jan. He and his wife recorded here the death of their daughter, Leokadja, in 1906, at the age of fifteen months; the birth and death of a son in 1908, Bolesław, who lived only three and a half months; and the death of a second daughter, Anna, in 1910, after just five months of life. Father Jank finds the birth of another daughter, also named Anna, in 1911, and then the death of another son, Franciszek in 1928, at the age of twenty-six. I find the death record of Wincenty himself in 1931, with his living children listed, among them a son, Izydor, whose only child welcomed me into his home only a few weeks ago.

Although it does not say so anywhere the records seem to show that my great-grandfather and Wincenty were brothers. Uncles and often godfathers for each other's children, they both lived in Sugajno and were perhaps the sons of that robust babcia who ate salt pork and told my grandmother stories of life in a dugout house where the wolves howled and scratched at the door.

Soon Father Jank finds more. Born in 1903 to Jan and Franciszka Brysz-kiewski, a daughter, Nikodema. My great-grandfather is listed as a *chałupnik*—"builder of huts." Born in 1905, another daughter, Władysława, and in the margins a note that says she married Władysław Pilarz in 1932.

"Pilarz," says the priest offhandedly. "The name used to mean 'wood-cutter.'"

I continue searching my obituary book, discouraged that I will find no trace of my grandmother in these two miraculous pieces of history, tracing my finger down the columns, looking for Sugajno, looking for Bryszkiewski. Sud-denly a list of names appears with a carefully lettered heading, "Polegli na Woj-nie." These are the names of the soldiers from St. Martin's parish who died in

World War I. Among them is listed a Jan Bryszkiewski, son of a farmer. Died August 18, 1917, at the age of twenty-five. Buried in France. Is this the brother my grandmother told me died of mustard-gas poisoning at the hands of the Germans? She clasped her hands together when she told the story, perhaps remembering the young brother she left behind, dead just four years later. "How everyone cried," she said.

I continue to search, and a few pages later I strike gold again: Died in 1927 at the age of sixty-six, Jan Bryszkiewski of Sugajno, on August 22. Buried three days later in Boleszyn, leaving behind his wife, Franciszka. Below her name are listed their children: five boys first, then four girls. Here they are all named and numbered: (1) Albin, (2) Jan, (3) Teodor, (4) Franciszek, (5) Władysław, (6) Helena, (7) Wanda, (8) Nikodema, and (9) Władysława.

In front of me for the first time I see my grandmother's name written on a document in Poland. Of Władysława and Nikodema, she often spoke with sad regret that she could not see them. They were just little girls of eight and ten when their big sisters went off to America. I look in my little stash of photographs at the faces of Władysława and Franciszek—their names written on pictures they sent to America after the Second World War. Pictures of two who stayed behind and endured, her mouth turned down with sorrow, his profile hopeful with the promise of his adopted daughter's wedding and the possibility of a used suit coming to him from his sister in America.

"It says my great-grandfather is buried in the cemetery here in Boleszyn, but I looked at every stone. He's not there."

Father Jank says with confidence, "He is buried there, for sure, but in those days people did not buy these big gravestones like today. A wooden cross. It lasted maybe ten, twenty years, and that's it."

But there is more. In 1931 the death of Edmund Bryszkiewski of Sugajno is recorded—five and a half months old, the son of a farmer. His only listed parent is Władysława Bryszkiewska. Father Jank looks at the entry, perplexed for a moment. "Perhaps a child born out of wedlock," he observes casually. Then in 1933 we find the death of Władysław Bryszkiewski, fifth child of Franciszka and Jan, grandmother's brother, a *robotnik,* worker. Murdered at the age of twenty-five at a dance party at the home of Franciszka Mówinska, January 7. Buried eight days later.

"Would it have been in the newspaper?" I inquire.

"The newspapers didn't write about such things here in those days," he assures me, eager, I think, to get at his daily duties.

"Everybody has a story," I offer as I shake his hand and head for the door.

"Yes, that is surely the truth. Everybody has a story."

The Priest and the Ledger
—

Temporary Blindness

―――――

Running a hose over my trouble-some Maluch and wiping the miniature front window, I prepare for the one-hour drive to Toruń. I've made several short runs, and no warning light has come on. Maybe it has had all the repairs it needs for a while—or maybe to-day is the day it will misbehave.

Route 52 west is becoming familiar—the hill at Kurzętnik, the curves through Kowalewo Pomorskie. I don't worry too much about the speed trap in Brodnica, figuring that as long as they don't establish a junk trap, I'm safe. The car chugs along past the disco where it gagged, choked, and broke down a month ago in the middle of the night.

A few kilometers from my favorite parking lot off busy Szosa Lubicka Street, the little tin can heaves a sigh and suddenly the steering wheel isn't working right. Somebody behind me honks with irritation.

I putt forward with a white-knuckle grip on the wheel and glide toward the parking lot. The attendant waves me in and leads me to the nearest open space. Is it a flat tire? No, something is hanging just in front of the right rear tire. Looks to me like what one would call the rear suspension.

The new course of my day decided, I head for a taxi and my Toruń me-chanic, with whom I am beginning to develop a relationship. He seems not the least surprised to see me and smiles, as if to say, "I had a feeling you'd be back."

"Remember me, the American from Nowe Miasto with a Maluch?"

"I remember," he smirks. I explain what's wrong.

"Well, you can't drive it like that," he concludes. "I'll call the tow truck."

A few minutes later a jolly old man in an enormous flatbed truck calls to me from the street. "Are you the man with the broke-down car? Hop in."

I give him my best three lines of Polish small talk and fool him for a moment.

"You live in Toruń?"

"Nowe Miasto Lubawskie."

"Born there?"

"No," I laugh, flattered. "I am from the U.S.A."

"Oh, U.S.A.," he sings out. I give him a little of my story.

"And what kind of car is it that you have? Is that it?" he asks as we pull into the parking lot, pointing to a Mercedes.

"No, mine is the green Maluch," I correct him.

This strikes him as the most amusing thing he has heard in a long time. "Maluch!" he exclaims. "From the United States and came to Poland and drives a Maluch! Impossible. This is what you drive when you can't get anything better. Of course, we used to drive Maluchs, but we have real cars now! Mitsubishi, Ford, Mercedes." He pats the dashboard of the truck. "Mercedes-Benz, the best."

When we reach the parking lot, he is still smiling and laughing as he steps out of the truck to load the car with a hydraulic jack. He points to the big black Mercedes. "Ah, there! There, American! That is the car you should be driving." He looks at my Maluch, points, and chuckles.

Leaving my car behind, I jump in a taxi and head for the conservation department at Copernicus University. On the way we pass a seminary, and the driver points to a group of seminarians dressed in long black gowns with clerical collars. "Czarne szaty," he says a bit contemptuously, turning to look at me in the back seat. "Black gowns." He takes his hands from the wheel and runs his right index finger in and out of his left fist. "They are all screwing."

"Is that really true?" I ask.

"Of course, it's true. Who doesn't know a priest with children? They have their women, their men, they do what they want in there." He flashes me a lecherous, gold-toothed grin.

The director of the university's conservation department, an imposing, middle-aged blonde in a tan business suit, is again fooled by my accent, remarking to her colleague, "He apologizes for his Polish and speaks with no American accent." But the myth is soon shattered as they descend into high-speed jargon, and my face betrays my ignorance. "Do you understand?" she finally asks, looking into my eyes as if into a well.

At the end of the tour I meet Maria Śliwińska in her computer lab for advice on archives that would contain family records. We head out for dinner and talk about the issue of being an outsider. "I had the chance to live in America," she says, "but I would be always struggling there—to make money, to learn the language. Here I know I can do something with my life that matters to me and that will make a difference."

I mention the taxi driver's observations about the sex lives of priests. "I can't abide people who hear one thing and therefore know everything," she observes. "As if he knows what goes on in the seminary!"

By the time we head back to the mechanic for my car, it has begun to rain. By the time I drop her off, it's pouring. "Are you sure you don't want to stay here?" she offers, looking around my little car.

The ride home is treacherous. On the narrow, two-lane unlit road, semi-trailer trucks whip by, engulfing me in their wake, cars speed past me even though visibility is only a few feet. Headlights appear at the top of every hill like sunrises that break the horizon and flash their rays into my face. At times my spinning little toy tires seem like the desperate flailing of a drowning man. Finally I pull off at a *zajazd* to wait it out over a Coke. Two women and a man appear, and the four of us watch the rain and electrical show in the sky from the open café door.

The next day's sunshine calls for a stroll through the Rynek.

"Is there a *pogrzeb* today?" the woman in the market asks as she slices ham for me. It's a word I haven't learned yet, so I look confused and tell her I don't know what the word means.

"Pogrzeb, pogrzeb," she repeats in disbelief but is unable to translate it for me. We finish the sale, and the minute I step into the square I know what she has asked. The procession of mourners in black, carrying their bouquets wrapped in stiff cellophane, has made its way from the church down one side of the Rynek, its tail end visible, heading up Third of May Street.

I run back into the store. "Yes, yes," I tell the clerk. "There is a funeral today."

In Nowe Miasto, then, there is the church, and its power over the community is still strong. Fifty years of a system of government determined to undermine religion, in a country where nationalism and Catholicism have become one and the same, is fifty years that did more to strengthen religion than to squelch it.

"Will Adam attend his son's communion?" Pani Wituchowska wants to know. I know only that Filip is to make his First Holy Communion some time soon, but I cannot tell her what Adam will do since he has told me nothing except that "a human being is a machine for reproduction, simple biology. That much is clear."

"All of this carrying on about religion and meaning is nonsense and does nothing but pit people against one another over things that ought to bring people together," Adam says. Cultures apart, we have gone through so many of the same stages in our lives, connected yet disconnected, five thousand miles across the Atlantic.

What about the strength of the church in Nowe Miasto? What about its age and beauty? What about the cemeteries, so carefully tended and elaborately marked? "It's a lot of carrying on about nothing," Adam believes.

My own mother decided for herself that she did not want an elaborate funeral with an open coffin, and she did not want to be buried at all but rather cremated and her ashes scattered. It was her last swipe at a church she could never shed but with which she was angry and blamed herself for the anger. She could never seem to do anything right "in the eyes of the church."

Even Pani Wituchowska, who places the little metal cross she bought in Jerusalem in the front window of her wine shop along with pictures of the pope, says, "I don't necessarily go every Sunday. I like the church best when it is empty, and I can pray in my own way."

In his characteristic way Adam said, as we rose at 6 A.M. Saturday morning for his kayaking adventure, "Don't worry, it's nothing."

Fourteen hours later I'm sitting on the patio of a bar on Lake Lidzbarskie, my arms like noodles, barely able to hold a pen. My exhausted kayaking partner, Oliver Chilson, a second-career volunteer with the last Peace Corps contingent in Poland, is plotting his escape, a three-kilometer walk back to his home in Lidzbark.

For about two hours it was pleasant enough, Oliver telling me the Polish names of wildflowers along the bank, pointing out deadly nightshade and a man and a woman digging out wild irises for their front yard, where "they won't grow." Now and then we would pass Adam in his safari hat, paddling alone in his own kayak, lying back and sipping a beer. Where is this reputed girlfriend, I wondered.

Six hours later we were still paddling and still had the polluted water of Lidzbark to float through, a mill to carry our boats around, and the length of a lake to go. Poor Oliver at times found himself knee-deep in muck, besieged by hungry gnats, nearly stabbed as we paddled our way smack into fallen trees, and exhausted after eight straight hours of paddling—142 kilometers,

Temporary Blindness

—

embarking by bus from a secluded little village of cabins in the woods and paddling our way back against the wind after being dropped off on Lake Grądy.
The gnats loved the stinky stretch the best and seemed to find my face equally
appealing. I thought I would go mad until Oliver pointed out that cigarette
smoke did the trick, and I lit up.

One of Adam's good-natured, beer-drinking friends, built like a Chicago
Bear, saw us struggling over a fallen willow and practically lifted the kayak—
with me in it—out of the water and shoved it through the crotch of the tree
while I lay flat on the wet floor and Oliver balanced himself on a branch. He
did it all for a cigarette.

An ugly growling Dalmatian, so close on the shore I could see the tartar on
his teeth, seemed ready to leap for us. Oliver thwacked the mutt across the face
with his paddle to shut him up.

As we paddled up to the dock Adam rushed out to help. "How was it?"
he asks.

"Don't spoil his fun by complaining," Oliver murmured.

"Oh, I liked it very much. It was perhaps a tad too long for the first kayak
experience," I lie.

We gather around tables and tear into enormous helpings of *bigos,* saurkraut
and mushrooms, and deliciously fatty kiełbasa, Oliver making small talk with
his bizarre, American pronunciations. Now and then someone in the company
turns to me and asks me to repeat what he has said, as if to ask, "Why is he talking like that?"

The other kayakers aren't too tired to gather around a campfire and roast
more kiełbasa and tell stories. Ryszard and Grażyna arrive to nose out the news
from this motley group of adventurers, and we plot my escape back to Nowe
Miasto with them. Raindrops fall lightly through the pines.

"Jedzie boat" was a phrase that always brought gales of knowing laughter
from my family when I was just a little guy, before I went to school. The story
was that an immigrant relative (no one was sure exactly who) got his English
and his Polish mixed up, was standing by a river, and yelled, "There goes a
boat!" Half in Polish, half in English. The phrase struck a chord and seemed
to entertain everyone, no matter how many times it was repeated. I, of course,
didn't get it. "What's so funny?" I would ask, but no one seemed able to explain.

Adam and I chatter away in what has almost become our own English-
Polish mix. "I think it might be best if I skip out. Oliver has gone home, and
I don't think I want to paddle the kayak alone. I hope that's not a problem."
This boat has jedzied all it's going to.

CHAPTER 19
—

"No problem," he says.

The thirty-somethings are laughing and making jokes that go completely over my head, so Ryszard decides to tell one for me:

"Did you hear about the guy who'd had it up to here with his mother-in-law?" he asks, marking a line over the top of his head with his finger. "Yeah, he complains to his friend, 'What can I do to get rid of my mother-in-law? She's drivin' me crazy.' So the friend says, 'Buy her a car. Women are such lousy drivers she'll kill herself in no time.' So the guy goes out and buys his mother-in-law a Polonez, a rather low-performance Polish car. A few weeks later the friend asks, 'So how did it work? Did she kill herself yet?' 'No,' says the guy. 'What kind of car did you buy her?' asks the friend. 'A Polonez,' says the guy. 'Well, no wonder,' says the friend, 'you need something more powerful. Get her a Jaguar.' So a few more weeks go by, and the friend sees the guy and asks, 'So how did it go with the Jaguar?' 'Great!' says the guy. 'Ate her just like that.'" And Ryszard growls and makes a swipe with his hand like a jaw.

We leave Adam at the campfire with his son and head to my cabin so I can pack my things. Grażyna flops onto the freshly made bed and says it smells good. Ryszard is pouring beer as rain starts to fall hard. He breaks into a chorus of "Singin' in the Rain," laughing, proud of his knowledge of things American.

"Where did you pick up all this American culture?" I ask.

"When I was a teenager," he explains, "we fixed up a radio in the attic where we could pick up Voice of America and Radio Free Europe. They had the signals scrambled so you couldn't get broadcasts from abroad, but there were ways around that. We heard it all," he winks confidently and starts recalling stories for me about his parents during the war.

"My mother was sent to Germany to work for Göring," he says casually. "You know Reichs Marshal Hermann Göring. She worked on a farm for him. He told her when it was over that she could go where she wanted to go, and she said she wanted to come back here to Poland, to her home. 'You're not going to Poland, you know,' he told her, 'you will be going back to Russia.'"

In the morning it looks like rain, but Pani Kopiczyńska is already in the garden picking strawberries.

"I heard of a cow that was killed by gnats recently," she tells me when I complain about how they attacked me on the kayak. "Swarmed by so many, they got into her nose, and she couldn't breathe."

I guess I got off easy.

"What did your family do for you for Mother's Day?" I ask.

"Adam doesn't pay any attention to things like Mother's Day," she pouts. But her youngest son, Michał, "gave me my first granddaughter. Her name is Basia." She holds her head up high and wiggles it coquettishly from side to side.

In town, Grażyna and Ryszard are on the job as the square is prepared for the Marian music festival—she chats with a police officer, he with a priest. Some people head home from church; others linger and wait. I spot our neighbor. The blonde librarian dressed to kill with a big white purse and a man on her arm heads for the canopy reserved for honored guests, in front a row of gold tubular chairs from the Ratuszowa. Electronic equipment is hauled to the covered stage. I see more than one old woman on the arm of a grandson. I see a lady who cornered Oliver and me in church, then whispered and gasped over Matka Boska Łąkowska and the marvelous transfer of the statue from the old monastery on Grunwaldzka Street to the church. "She is covered now, but later she will be uncovered," she disclosed, breathless with anticipation, her eyes wide. "Is this not fantastic?"

A line of important people proceeds to the canopy from the church. Among them is Senator Alicja Grześkowiak, all the way from Warsaw. Archbishop Marian Przykucki marches beside her, his black robes punctuated by a hot-pink hat with a fuzzy tassel. All this ceremony is for Mary, the queen of Poland, and specifically for Mary, the queen of Nowe Miasto, whose image is safe inside the church. Before any dignitaries are introduced, a young priest tells the tale of her life inside the *klasztor* and her journey to a new church. Burmistrz Lendzion suavely does his mayoral duty with introductions.

There are perhaps three hundred people waiting, now and then nodding to one another stiffly. Men in brown, gray, and tan suits, women in high heels. The sky drops a bit of rain, and umbrellas pop open. Some people go home, and windows open, and heads appear all around the square. The singing begins with an off-key song about Matka Boska Częstochowska and the national icon's miraculous survival during the Swedish invasion of Poland, followed by "Ave Maria."

The rain falls harder. The archbishop is getting soaked as the water drains off the canopy onto his feet. People begin to scatter again, but the music goes on, and then the Blessed Mother intervenes and asks her son to hold off on the rain until her concert is over. He owes her, after all. "I brought you into this world to save me," she must have said, "but you run off with a bunch of men, live like a pauper, and then go and get yourself crucified." It's what a good Polish mother would say to her son.

All Those Good-Byes

When I was a kid, we were always saying good-bye to Auntie Mary, each time her husband's Air Force furlough was over and we found out where he was to be stationed next. Uncle Bogdan packed the car slowly the night before, their clothes stuffed into the set of Samsonite luggage they had received as a wedding present. I was five when they married and watched them come and go—from Utah, Texas, Germany, the Azores, and finally New Jersey—until I was in my teens. They always left early in the morning, and my grandmother, my mother, and I would stand dazed in the backyard, hugging and kissing as the children climbed into the car, too young to think of anything besides going for a ride. Then my mother in her housecoat started crying, for tears came to her without permission, whatever the occasion, happy or sad. Then Grandma, already dressed, would reluctantly get morose. Finally Aunt Mary's eyes would swell with tears no matter how much she tried to maintain her dignity. And then I, too, would cry as they headed down the driveway and onto Thirty-Two Mile Road.

Uncle Bogdan always seemed to patiently endure these parting rituals, but he never gave in to the drama. He had had separations of his own in Poland during the war, far more brutal.

Today I am thinking about the time when I will say good-bye to Nowe Miasto, trying to imagine what those days in 1913 were like in the Bryszkiewski *chałupa,* where my grandmother and her sister must have carefully considered what to take to America. How well did their Uncle Stanisław prepare them?

It's twenty minutes by car from Nowe Miasto, but how long was it by horse and cart? Surely three or four times as long. If my grandmother and her sister left Sugajno with their uncle at five in the morning, perhaps they would have been in Nowe Miasto in time for a train to Iława, then on to Poznań, Berlin, and Bremen by the end of the day. Surely they packed lunches, bread and sausage no doubt, perhaps tomatoes and cucumbers from the garden.

How their mother must have cried when they left, as my grandmother cried when Auntie Mary left, knowing that she must go, knowing like a child that each such departure is a little death, but knowing too that her own brother would take good care of them.

When I moved to Chicago, my mother cried every time I left for home. Standing on the porch of her little Hamtramck house, she said flatly, "Maybe this is the last time you'll see me," and her eyes moistened. She didn't live in the past; she lived instead entirely in the future, always anticipating the worst and predicting its arrival.

"Oh, mother," I pooh-poohed her, "every time could be the last time," until the day in November of 1996 when it was the last time I would ever see her standing on her own two feet, waving that familiar, tearful good-bye.

My grandmother never thought of her journey to America from "eastern Pomerania" as part of a "Great Migration," as it has subsequently been called, that would foster a new breed of Polish children who spoke English, married people of strange nationalities, moved away to live in far-flung parts of the world, and did not cry at each separation. Two young sisters in a family of nine could be spared to seek a better life where the streets were paved with gold.

In Sugajno this morning I stopped at the Bryszkiewski farm. Helena and her daughter-in-law Grażyna were pinning underwear on the clothesline when I pulled up in my little Maluch. They looked baffled at first, but then I told them I had been reading documents in the church in Boleszyn and wanted to tell Jan what I'd found.

"Good, good," Pani Helena says. "Jan went to see someone in the hospital, but we want to invite you back."

"It's been such a long time since you were here," says Grażyna, seating herself on the stoop. "You will come back, won't you?"

"I'll be back," I tell them and speed away to say good-byes before leaving for Bremen.

I stop at the Dom Kultury. Ryszard has something to show me. A book, *Mit Hitler in Polen* [With Hitler in Poland]. It's autographed by Adolf Hitler and raises my suspicions that many people in this town survived by cooperating with the conquering Germans in ways they would not be eager to admit today.

"Is this real?" Holding it, I expect some sort of burn. I examine the inky scribble. "Where did you find it?"

"We tested it with water," says Ryszard. "It's real ink, not a stamp. I found it in our attic."

Published in Munich in 1939, the book is a photographic chronicle of the German triumph over Poland. It shows the führer looking sincere and righteous, taking back these parts of Germany that were so unfairly handed to the Poles after the First World War. So many pictures I've never seen before. Full-face shots of the benevolent führer in glorious poses—looking through a periscope, studying maps, checking the bombed ruins of Polish military trains.

Ryszard pulls out more pictures, postcards of the Tannenberg Denkmal, a site he pointed out to me on the way to Olsztyn. "Hindenburg's funeral was in nearby Olsztynek," he explains. "The complex you see here was destroyed completely. It was dismantled and used to build communist party headquarters in Warsaw. Did you know there is still a communist party office in Nowe Miasto?" he adds. "They call themselves social democrats now, above the new Tiffany restaurant. I won't go there—to think or to eat."

Ryszard laughs and puts Prussian marching music on the CD player. "Only this music will do for such photographs!"

The next day I arrive at the train station in Iława an hour too early. "The tickets are not in the computer yet," says the clerk behind the glass. "Come back in half an hour."

So there's time—time to study the old steam engine that stands in the park outside the station. There's time to stop by the lake across the park and see two pure white swans floating across the water while a kayaker paddles his inflatable craft out of the reeds.

A glass-encased sign in the park welcomes arrivals with a map of Iława—in Polish, English, and German.

What did the train she rode in look like? Could the antique engine in Iława be the same one that pulled her passenger car out of Poland? I look out the window as my train pulls out and imagine what it must have been like for a shy, young farm girl to see her house disappear behind her forever, to see the country pass into Germany out the window, farm by farm by farm. Rickety wooden fences are still visible, old barns, the German-built stations—these things were all here then, the garden patches of city folks.

All Those Good-Byes
—

113

I must remember that she spoke German, that the transition to Germany was a gradual one, for there was no border. Technically she lived in Germany, studied German in school. There were no passport control officers on the train as there are here when we reach Frankfurt-an-der-Oder, officious in their brown uniforms, checking against a ledger. Did she see the prosperity grow as she headed west as we can now? The land is the same, nothing that says "Poland ends here." On a map of Poland in 1913 there are no international borders between Sugajno and Bremen. The characteristic brick train stations, school houses, and homes continue uninterrupted.

Berlin begins slowly, the tracks multiply. In the eastern section are the typical communist barracks, a cluster of graffiti-covered, old rail cars, then the construction begins to appear, and suddenly the entire city seems to be resurrecting itself. At the former main station in East Berlin a woman tells me in English as she cradles her grandson and soothes her granddaughter that the entire city is thriving, building everywhere. It certainly beats anything I've seen in Poland.

By the time we pull out of Berlin it is hot, too hot. I look for a place in the shade on the platform as I change trains. There are newer houses here; it's richer, cleaner. The brick stations and factories continue along the line, looking like the schoolhouse in Sugajno. None of what she saw here could have been too foreign to her, just more of the old country intensely Germanized. I wipe sweat away from my eyes and open the train window as she might have on her summer journey.

On the way to Hannover, some of the small brick stations with their stately peaks are as shabby and forlorn as the station in Nowe Miasto. At a place called Mieste there is another train station, in Oebisfelde more buildings with old German lettering, falling apart, a factory with multiple window frames collapsing like the old slaughterhouse in Nowe Miasto. Surely this was here in 1913. Perhaps she even glanced out the window and saw these windows as I am doing now.

"You are in luck," says the young man at the tourist information office in Bremen. "There is an exhibition at the museum in Bremerhaven."

This is where, I'm told, my grandmother would surely have left for the United States in 1913, one of some seven million who departed through Bremen and Bremerhaven between 1815 and 1914, making it the most important emigration point in all of Europe.

I board the train to Bremerhaven at the Hauptbahnhof, sitting across from a cocky young smoker who mutters something to the smiling, smoking blond woman to his right. Then he gets up, stepping on my foot, and staggers out of the compartment. She looks at me perplexed. I shrug my shoulders, "I don't understand."

"It's his problem," she says in perfect English.

In 1862 the train ride just from Bremen to Bremerhaven took two hours. There was also, I learn in the Morgenstern Museum, the Ruhleben station near Berlin, where every emigrant stopped for routine paper shuffling.

An exhibition includes a video that features the imagined journey of a Polish girl in 1907. "These were not good times for peasant farmers," the girl laments. In Galicia they were eating the seed grain intended for next year's crop. "It is a sin to sweep bread crumbs from the table to the floor," she says, hugging and kissing a loaf of bread. I spot a wooden rake on display exactly like the ones my grandfather made in Michigan and that I used as a child to rake up dry grass. "For bread, they went to America, for bread," as Pani Witu-chowska says.

But my grandmother did not travel in steerage as I once thought she had. The passenger record shows she traveled second class, and I remember her talking about sharing a cabin with her sister.

"The second-class passengers also went through processing at Ellis Island," says a museum staffer in perfect English. "It was only the first class that did not have to."

After making the trip from Nowe Miasto to Bremen in one day, I am be-ginning to doubt that anyone could have done so in 1913, as Andrzej Korecki suggested. There were places to stay in Bremerhaven. Perhaps they spent a night or more in one of those places. Perhaps they would not have been so con-fident as to head out on so tight a schedule and risk missing the boat, so to speak. They must have arrived early. How else could they have been the first entries in the ship's manifest?

The fictional Polish girl in the video says, "We Poles didn't understand a word the Germans said." Someone German must have written this script; my grandmother understood German well enough—and the forced Germaniza-tion that went with learning it. I remember her using a German word now and then—*Kartofel* instead of *ziemniak* for potato—and then correcting herself. "No, that's the German word."

A jolly museum guide shows a plan of the docks with little wooden boat shapes that can be fitted into spaces according to their size, a different dock for each size ship. At 177 meters the *Prinz Friedrich Wilhelm* would most likely have left from Kaiserhafen III, built in 1909.

All Those Good-Byes
—

115

But all of this was bombed during the war, the guide says, her face suddenly turning dour. Another video shows the destruction of Bremen and Bremerhaven, as she explains how residents tried to take cover. "Ninety-seven percent bombed," she says, shaking her head.

Along the old docks, the whole town looks postwar modern. I spot a lighthouse, built in 1854, and some small brick warehouses, the church spire in the distance, but little else from a hundred years ago except the sea air and a sparkling expanse of water beneath heavy dark clouds sliced by sunrays that bounce off the waves and into my eyes. The ocean seems to flow in rows, back and forth in opposite directions, like alternating rows of cardboard water curls on a stage. A cold wind blows across the raised walking path that hugs the sea.

In Bremen I walk the affluent streets, where friendly locals are eager to take my money, to answer my questions, smile, and proudly show off their English. Such a civilized place, this Germany of the twenty-first century. "Who won the war after all?" I wonder. Certainly not Poland. You had to be on the "wrong" side to be a winner in the postwar half-century. I walk the streets of Bremen and have everything in common with these people, even a German name—their fashion flair for black, their taste for middle-eastern food, their liberal politics. They do not gawk when black people walk by; it's not a big deal.

Back at the hotel I hear Polish chattering in the hall as maids scurry away to earn a few precious marks making German beds, no doubt grateful for the opportunity to take whatever money they can earn back home to Poland.

There is little more to see of my grandmother's journey, so I buy a ticket back to Poland. On the train we approach the border, and a Polish passport-control officer jerks open the compartment door and calls out, "Paszport!" He puts on his most officious face, the one that says, "I am doing my job, sir," and he checks and looks, checks and looks, pulls out a black spiral-bound list, checks and looks at my face, looks again. "Do you speak English?" I ask. No, he shakes his head. In my best Polish I ask, "What is in that book? Can you tell me what you are checking?"

"Nie dla państwa," he says, astonished to be asked. Not public information. No Polish person, it seems, would dream of asking such a question. Then he smiles and gives me an envious sort of "Good for you with your brassy American attitude" look.

Leaving Germany, I have a sense of "coming home" to Poland, to my land, my people, for better or worse. I order a Żywiec beer as we head for Gdańsk, woods and woods passing by the window, three men in camouflage pants barreling down the aisle. The train rattles over old tracks, the first-class compartment hot and dusty, now and then signs of repair and replacement along the route, men flinging picks at the ground. Inexplicably the train stops, then takes off again after a minute. Polish progress—at its own pace. We arrive late in Poznań, but the connecting train to Inowrocław will wait, says the conductor.

We all pile out with four minutes to change trains and no directions. I see a crossing straight over the rails and proceed, hesitate, proceed, and drop my luggage in the middle of the tracks. "Is this the train to Inowrocław or not?" I holler to the engineer.

"Yes! Yes!" he calls and waves.

I can tell which car is first class—only by the "1" on its side, and the smoking cars by who is smoking and how many "no smoking" signs have been crossed out with a dry marker. It is hotter than eighty degrees now. A young woman unfolds a Kleenex and lays it on the heat register at the bottom of the corridor wall in the aisle crammed with second-class passengers, where she sits tidily as if it were nothing odd at all.

The country passes by my window, lush and green with pines, birches, lindens, oaks, ramshackle farm buildings nestled in pastures and fields. The roads are like those to my Uncle Hank's house in Michigan, roads I traveled grudgingly as a seventeen-year-old. By that age, the family had agreed, it was time to get some work out of me. My uncle would pay me a decent wage to help pay for college, and I would work summers on his farm. Too afraid of heights and too unskilled to help him and his father-in-law build a new barn, I nevertheless was good for shoveling manure, cleaning, painting, and harvesting—especially all that heavy hay.

"We're gonna get another load in." "It's almost time for a second cutting." I dreaded those words, but I never knew what self-discipline was until I saw my uncle work—always twice as hard and quick and long as anything he ever asked me to do. And how he seemed to miss his father, the *dziadzia* I barely knew, and how he needed a son—but received instead a German father-in-law even more disciplined than he, an effeminate nephew, and five daughters.

The serious, inhuman architecture of the Soviets passes into view, no different from most postwar construction in the United States, always designed to look its best from a mile or more away. How out of fashion two world wars have made the Germans' sturdy brick buildings. Now everyone wants a new house that looks like a chalet in Zakopane.

Lush green landscapes sail by—fields of grain, forests for lumber, berries and mushrooms, even the brambles and fungi are edible.

All Those Good-Byes
—

"Nothing works," says the young man in the seat by the window, lifting his eyes in exasperation and waving his Marlboro toward the control panel above the compartment door.

"A year ago there was a better train from Berlin to Gdańsk," he adds, "through Świnoujście, but it's discontinued."

"Sebastian," he says, offering his hand. He could be a cousin, in his Adidas shoes, sweatpants and T-shirt, built like a football player, with a brush haircut and close-cropped beard. He wants to talk about Poland to somebody not from Poland. "These are strange times in this country," he says with all the wisdom of a quarter-century of living, eager to explain why so many things, from the trains to the banks, do not work right.

"I am afraid we Poles always want someone to blame—the Germans, the Russians, the Jews—but, you know, it's never me." He shakes his head in exaggerated denial. "Do you know what I mean? It's never me."

The Body of Christ

There's great clamor today in Nowe Miasto, the church at the center of it. Up and down the aisles, young birch trees from the woods, six-seven-eight feet high, are fastened to the pews with nails driven into the ancient wood. I shudder as if at the nails driven into the hands and feet of Christ.

In the windows of half the houses and stores along the route from home, little shrines have been set up on the parapets with holy pictures that seem to have been taken off the walls and set on doilies to display them to the world.

At least five thousand people, half the town, have dutifully lined up outside St. Thomas's, and they listen as the priest pleads with his "brothers and sisters" to live the life of Christ every day. All of the recent communicants, including Adam's son, sit in front on little benches of honor, in their communion finery. Music squawks from old clarinets and saxophones. People sing, and the sun climbs toward noon, toward the hottest day in a hundred years. Adam is among the missing.

An hour into it a young girl, faint and barely able to stand, is escorted away. It's been thirty-five years since I watched someone endure a church service long enough to pass out. "Don't look at me," this young girl seems to be saying, equal parts embarrassed by and proud of her delicate nature.

An old woman I passed wobbling her way down Narutowicza Street arrives in the middle of mass. Pencil thin, she shuffles forward on what looks like sheer will power to soak up some of the action. She stands for a short dose, weaving, and then leaves the hot crowd for the cool church. Another old woman, sturdier, although she wields a short crutch in each hand, elbows her way into the crowd and drops to her knees in the grass.

There is the constant ebb and flow of altar boys with incense, pairs of girls walking away, more altar boys with collection baskets. Communion takes forever again. The young priest in his gold vestments turns in circles to keep up with the hungry mouths hanging open above praying hands.

It's Corpus Christi—Body of Christ—a feast day invented by St. Juliana of Belgium and celebrated for the first time in 1261. Of course she was merely "an instrument in the hand of Divine Providence," according to the church, and her determination to see the holy day established was fueled by a vision of the church under the appearance of the full moon having one dark spot, which signified to her the absence of such a solemn holy day.

Nobody in Nowe Miasto thinks about Corpus Christi as an orphan nun's dream come true. Rather, it is a holy day of demonstration. If the church were a trade union, this would be a work stoppage and show of solidarity.

The procession that follows mass will take more than two hours for a walk that would ordinarily last about fifteen minutes. At each stop along the way, we spend ten minutes in prayer and veneration, bell ringing, kneeling, and a priest's soulful voice over a loudspeaker. One wonders how Christ managed the Sermon on the Mount without a PA system.

I spot Adam's friend Bogumił. "We are on the same schedule," he smiles, introducing me to his wife. This time both his young daughters are with him, wearing bright summer dresses and little straw hats decorated with ribbon. I watch the little girls endure this procession to the very end with no complaints, no whining. They have already learned that their behavior is a vital part of the success of the entire event. Perspiration drips off me, but the little girls do not complain about the heat.

"And with your spirit," the crowd chants at the first stop, somebody's house decorated as an altar with cloths and birch branches. The gold-enshrined Eucharist, which is being paraded under a canopy, is placed on the steps and venerated.

"Why this house?" I ask Bogumił.

"It has been selected. That's all. Each year someone's house along the route is selected," he explains.

"And why are people plucking branches from the birch trees?"

"It's for luck and good health for the coming year. You take a piece home and put it over your holy pictures, like on Palm Sunday."

CHAPTER 21

—

The second stop is the statue of St. Thomas in a little park across the street from the library. We stop, we venerate, the clarinets and saxophones blast. An altar boy helps the eldest priest take off his gold vestments, presumably to avoid the humiliating fate of dropping dead from heat stroke while venerating the Holy Eucharist.

"And with your spirit," the crowd calls out again. We head on to the cemetery, where a makeshift altar waits in front of the arched concrete entrance. Some marchers head for the shade; others, more devoted, kneel on the steamy asphalt of Grunwaldzka Street. It's been two hours, and it's over ninety degrees. This is the main road into Nowe Miasto, and it is closed. Three cars, just three, and one truck, wait patiently while two police officers hold them back. Meanwhile, the marchers fill Grunwaldzka with their devotion, they rise and kneel on cue, on the street, the sidewalks, nearby lawns. Matka Boska Łąkowska, her ceramic face sparkling in the sun, is elevated once again on her sedan chair as we head onward to the town square. Little girls throw flower petals onto the street wherever the holy statue and the Eucharist are headed. Marchers snatch branches from the altar for luck and good health.

The spectacle of Corpus Christi culminates on the Rynek, where an altar has been set up at the town office building. By now it is noon and the sun shows no mercy. Parishioners cluster under the Ratuszowa's umbrellas and shade trees, while a few mad-dog devotees kneel on the cobblestones and face the altar. Even the young communicants are clustered in the sliver of shade formed by City Hall.

On Kazimierza Wielkiego Street, Pani Wituchowska and Michał are standing in their own bit of shade at the front of the wine store. Pani is wearing a long dress and earrings, and her hair has been freshly hennaed, her face made up. I can see traces of the young woman in her *cywilny ślub* photograph, her face framed by her pearly earrings like the real pearl tiara she wore as a young bride.

Ryszard spots me and runs over. His mother leans out the window above us, her elbow on the parapet. "It was too hot for her to march today," he says.

Despite the all-pervasive Catholicness of Corpus Christi, the restaurants are open, lines form at the ice-cream windows, people break away and wander home. Only the most devout stick it out.

When I run home for a new roll of film, Adam and his kayaking friend Iwona are sitting on the couch in front of the television. "A long procession," he declares.

"Yes, Filip is still walking," I tell him as I dash out the door. I catch myself sounding like his mother, his wife, with my implied "And you should be there."

The Body of Christ

—

Later in the afternoon Pani Kopiczyńska drops by for her ritual of garden and flower watering. I hold the hose to the nozzle for her since the attachment has broken. "This is probably for nothing. I think it's going to rain," she concludes.

"Alina was here," she says with consternation. "She saw Adam with his new girlfriend. It was hard for her. She was upset to see it and know for herself that it is true, that their marriage is over. Poor Alina, alone with two children. And poor girlfriends. I know now that he has more than one. But do they?"

"It's his life," I advise uselessly.

"Yes, but poor children. Adam never around," she shakes her head, then quickly perks up. "But I will stick by him no matter what. I can accept what he does. I know he is a good man." She lowers her voice. "But his father has told me he cannot accept another woman in Alina's place. He loves her like a daughter."

Soon after Pani finishes her watering and departs, a storm swings in from the north in a fury, a pounding torrent that changes its mind after five minutes, returning the yard to utter stillness. The wet walnut tree outside my window droops in the sun's glare.

I love the way thunderstorms roll into Nowe Miasto from the Baltic Sea with sudden build-ups of cloud and darkness, then sprinkles, and all the trees hang still. The chickens hide themselves, and the waddling white ducks seem to wonder what all the fuss is about.

CHAPTER 21
—

CHAPTER 22

At Night by the River

J ust when I have concluded that this will be a quiet evening of reading, Ryszard calls to let me know that it is Noc Świętojańska, St. John's Eve, a night when desire cuts loose in the form of little floral boats bearing candles that will be sent down the Drwęca. "Get ready," he says, "I'm coming to get you now."

We rush to the scene, the bridge over the Drwęca at the end of Wodna Street, where a crowd has gathered. On the riverbank twenty floral "wreaths" are lined up and ready to set sail. In the folkloric past these candle wreaths were woven of flowers; today the tradition has been replaced with Styrofoam and lots of plastic, but the candles endure. Wherever the vessels drift ashore, the sender will find his or her future spouse.

At first it seems an event for children. They line up behind their little flower boats and hand them to an older man, who drops them into the water and shoves them off with a pole. Into the current they float, their candles flickering in the mist.

Young men light an enormous, wigwam-shaped bonfire; they skewer dozens of one-person-sized kiełbasa on long sticks and hold them over the flames. Beer appears in my hand. The Harmonia choir begins to sing—some fifty people, harmonizing in the grass on the riverbank, the director waving her arms emphatically while mouthing all the words.

The crowd is polite, applauding moderately at the end of each song, chatting in small groups. The ubiquitous white plastic chairs and tables as well as the beer umbrella have been set out, and there is little concern about turning a profit.

The choir concludes its concert, and the electronic entertainment begins; a band has set up on a rise in the ground and begins cranking out dance tunes unfamiliar to me. A few happy souls start strutting, most noticeable among them is one of the Harmonia singers, an imposing, white-haired woman in a floral skirt and loose-fitting blouse. She claps to the beat, gracefully swinging her heft and showing her appreciation to the musicians. An energetic young couple joins in, dancing a polkafied disco step and twirling like tops.

Behind us the little boats sail away to nobody knows where.

"Who floats these boats?" I ask Grażyna, "Is it just for the children?"

"No, no, all sorts of people make these little boats."

"Did you make one?" I ask.

She just smiles. "Come, come, we have other places to see."

We jump into the car and speed to Lake Gaj, where we drink beer while youngsters romp in the water, the boys pulling the girls in with their clothes on. Ryszard disappears into the woods and returns with three fine branches for roasting the kiełbasa he and Grażyna bought in a mom-and-pop grocery store along the way. The fire is spectacular, made all the more pleasing by the wet trees around it. A half-dozen teenagers, first the boys in their skimpy bathing suits, then the girls in their wet clothes, stop to dry and warm themselves. They chat amiably, not seeming to care that we are old folks.

Grażyna and I are feeding the flames when Ryszard calls from a clearing along the water. One of the lighted floaters is headed for shore, straight for him in fact, as if pulled by a magnet. We watch it sail in from far offshore, its candle struggling to stay lit, fire on water, the impossible combination that seems the very essence of hope in the face of all odds.

When we return to Nowe Miasto, there is more dancing, as Ryszard promised. "Chupaj szupaj" is what my grandmother used to say, clapping her hands. What does it mean? As near as Ryszard can explain, it was her way of saying, "Boogie down!"

Several men are staggering along the shore, so drunk they can barely see. "Here, hold this," one says to me and hands me a towel, while he readjusts the logs on the fire. I fear he is about to fall in, but minutes later he has dragged some poor woman out on the dance ground and is tripping the light fantastic. "I guess you looked like a towel rack," Ryszard laughs. "Or his mother," I say.

Grażyna soon wearies and Ryszard takes her home. I am mesmerized. "I'll meet you back here," he calls out.

I watch the bonfire as boys throw on more logs and roast still more kiełbasa. Two young men stand with their arms around one another, as no American men dare to stand and show affection.

"Let's go sit down," Ryszard says when he returns, and we venture over to the plastic lawn chairs, where the diehards are still full of life, gripping plastic cups. Vodka is poured. He introduces me, and soon the choir director and three other women are serenading me.

Alina, Adam's ex, appears and joins with her strong voice and trilling tongue. It's midnight now, and the band has stopped playing. "Yes, I sang for two years in the choir at the university in Toruń," she tells the other singers.

"Ah, you must join Harmonia," they all agree.

"I have two months off now," Alina confides, "a furlough, just like you, and I am very happy about it."

"What are you going to do with these months?"

"Maybe I'll go to America!" Alina laughs.

"Maybe we can trade places completely," I play along.

"What a great idea. I'll go to America and have your life, and you can stay here and have mine! I'll take your ticket and your credit card, and off I'll go!" She is gasping with laughter, and all the women at the table are egging her on.

Then the women want my story. What am I doing here? What was my grandmother's name? Between questions, they sing for me every Polish song I can name, about geese and ducks and red apples, so I can sing along—all except the national anthem, which would not be right for this evening by the river. One singer knows "My Bunny Lice Over De Ocean" and periodically belts out a few refrains in imitation English, smiling at me for approval.

The choir director throws her hands into the air, raising her head and jutting her chin forward theatrically. "The summer equinox is short, but the night is mine!" she shouts.

Soon these smiling faces are singing "For hissa jelly goot fellow, for hissa jelly goot fellow, for hissa jelly goot fellow, and sow sigh olive us. . . ."

The tipsiest of all of the singers reaches over and rubs my stomach and tells me her name is Ewa. Meanwhile, young men who have not drunk too much are snatching the chairs out from under us every time we stand up and stacking them in a van. They are ready to go home. Even the lone male choir member who has stuck by his colleagues has had enough. "Czas do domu," he says—it's time to go home—but the choir ladies are not ready for this midsummer night's dream to end.

Finally Alina gives in. Ryszard takes Ewa by the arm, she reaches for mine, and I offer mine to Alina, and we laugh our way across the bridge.

At Night by the River

—

"Where will you sleep tonight?" Pani Ewa croons.

Then Ryszard sweeps me off to his car and deposits me safely at home, the whole thing ended too soon. That is my lament, as it was my mother's and my grandmother's before me, and as many grandmothers as can be counted before her, no doubt. Too soon, too soon, from the mix of sadness and joy released.

Dinner with Madame and Her Son

ani Urszula Wituchowska's home is set across the top of her wine shop on Waryńskiego Street, filled with antiques—a hulking, wood dining-room set, a china cabinet loaded with crystal, a davenport built into a dark wood bookcase extending up the back into a framed version of the Last Supper.

Michał greets me downstairs and leads me up the austere corridor to a creaky flight of oft-painted brown stairs. I remembered to bring flowers, the Polish way, and to make them sweeter, a basket of gooseberries and black currants I picked in the rain in the Kopiczyński garden.

"Oh, Pan Pączek!" Pani Wituchowska exclaims, tilting her head. She has taken to calling me Mr. Doughnut, teasing me with the nickname I told her my grandmother gave her pudgy baby grandson. "I'm sure you looked like a doughnut stuffed with jelly," she giggles. "I was a little doughnut once, too."

She—the matriarch, the queen of this realm—shows me modestly and swiftly her kingdom. "And off the dining room is the bedroom." She flips on the light in the windowless room to show off the Biedermeier suite dressed in lacy antique linens. "And here a bathroom." A tiny corner next to the kitchen. "And here the living room." More antiques. "And here an extra room, where you would stay if you were an overnight guest. But it only sleeps one," she teases, picking up energy and giving me her characteristic grin and two-eyed wink.

We sit for a few minutes in the velvet armchairs near the davenport, me facing the piano over which hangs Pani's photograph, the one where she is bareshouldered, looking like Mary Astor in a publicity still.

"She was a beautiful girl, no?" Pani asks proudly, with no regret. She is wearing a silky, two-piece dress, the top in a print, the bottom in polka dots. As always, her hair has been freshly browned and her skin dusted with powder.

Pani encourages me to sit with Michał while she slips away to her secret kitchen, into which I have not been invited. Her son is more at ease tonight than the other times we've met. He's wearing a starched blue-and-white-striped, short-sleeved shirt and light brown pants with no belt. His wife and four-year-old son are at home in Toruń. We talk about travel—Jerusalem, Morocco, Spain. He wants to go to Egypt, but when I suggest prices are good now, he says, "None of those last-minute sales for me. They get you there on an unsafe charter plane, dump you off, and you are on your own."

We are summoned to the table. His mother calls softly from the kitchen, and Michał darts off and reappears with a platter of noodles and chopped carrots, arranged in servings around pieces of fried carp.

The rest of the meal proceeds under the direction of Pani Wituchowska in complete harmony with her son. Two or three words from the kitchen and he is up. A few words of reprimand from her son, and Pani changes the subject. There is another platter, more noodles, and meat roulades, one of veal and one of unusually moist beef.

A plate of turkey medallions, noodles, and mushrooms in cream arrives. Cold cuts. Little boiled sausages. Bread, tea, butter, horseradish, mustard, and little pastries, then talk and talk.

"Polish people love to eat," says Pani. "But this child," she nods toward her son, "would not eat a thing when he was little."

"Nor would I," I confide, "but look at us now, eating everything, beets, tomatoes. . . ." I know Pani does not like tomatoes, so I push the plate of them next to hers to make her laugh. "Uh-uh, don't like them. Doctor says I should eat them, but I just don't like them. They are for you," she pushes them toward me and laughs. "You be healthy."

Michał gets on a soapbox about abortion, so I fuel his fire with the church's stand on contraception. We reach a middle ground.

"I don't very much like abortions," I say, "but why are so many women pregnant who don't want to be?"

"There's no disagreement between us over contraception," he asserts after I rail at him as best I can about the absurdity of trying to tell people the only reason to have sex is to make a baby.

CHAPTER 23

—

He counters with a story about the absurd West sending contraceptives to Albania when people needed food. Then he is off on tolerance. "Tolerancja, fine. I don't accept what you do, but it is your right to do it. But now they want me to accept it, what do you call this, 'political correct,'" he says in English. "No. I am Catholic. Live next to someone who decides to renovate his apartment on Sunday while I am trying to hold a solemn meal on a Holy Day? No. It's natural for people to want to be around people who share the same values."

Michał is going on a pilgrimage to Częstochowa on Saturday, but his mother tells me she is not going because all the acceptable hotel rooms are booked. "He keeps telling me I must go, so there will be one more person there, one more to make it the best showing ever. But I just don't feel like going, and I'm not."

Michał opens a fifteen-year-old bottle of Hungarian wine and pours small amounts into crystal glasses. We toast to health: "Na zdrowie!"

Pani Wituchowska tells me her son is very smart. "They used to say we had *błękitna krew* in our veins," she brags—blue blood. "I think he got some of it."

I mention Ryszard Ulatowski and observe that "he and I are in the same business."

"He is really a carpenter you know, not a journalist," Michał notes contemptuously. "He writes local chat." But I do not recognize the word "carpenter" in Polish, so he looks it up for me in a dictionary he has brought along for the occasion.

"Oh, 'carpenter,' like St. Joseph," I trump him.

"Yes," Pani laughs with delight. "Ulatowski did the same work as St. Joseph."

I ask about Aleksander Kwaśniewski, president of Poland.

"Communist," says the mother. "Communist," says the son. "Once a communist, always a communist."

Ronald Reagan was a great American president, Michał opines, "tough on communists. Jimmy Carter, soft, let them do what they wanted."

And Bill Clinton? "I don't like people who lie," says Michał, "and he lied."

"Politicians tell people what they want to hear," I suggest.

"No, some have vision. They are leaders." He is getting a little agitated as he senses my liberal bent.

"You can see that I lean to the left. My family, we were always democrats. From Kennedy on," I admit.

"Kennedy was a good president," says Michał.

"But he did some unwise things in Cuba," I acknowledge.

"Yes, the Bay of Pigs. And what about Elían González?" asks Michał of the

Dinner with Madame and Her Son

—

little Cuban boy making headlines around the world for being washed ashore in Florida after his mother died escaping from Cuba.

"He should be with his father," I blurt out. Michał is really offended by that one.

"His father? His father? Such a father, who never even saw this son until he came to take him back."

"But would we keep any other son from any other father in the world if this were not Cuba?" I demand.

"To keep him from communist Cuba, it's worth it," Michał hollers. Do you know what he is going back to?"

"Yes, I do know. I was there. It was a beautiful place with big problems. But there are millions of children in poverty and worse all over the world. Should the United States take them from their fathers?" I demand.

"Cuba is terrible," he asserts. "It's right what the United States does to Cuba."

"And China? Is it better there? China is a favored trade partner. Does it make sense to you?" I argue.

"It makes sense to treat Castro as an enemy. You know what he did to people." Michał won't bend.

I look him straight in the eye because it makes him nervous. Tonight, however, he seems to be enjoying it, smirking back at me, happy to be showing his mother that this fumbling, bumbling American she has taken a shine to is not really all that bright.

"We never know how long we are going to live," his mother digresses. "It would be terrible if we did, for that would be all we would think about."

"God knows what he is doing," I agree, and I wish her *sto lat*—a hundred years. We toast again.

Pani brings out desserts. One is not enough. We must have cookies, a torte, cakes, sherbet glasses filled with meringue. There is more wine, but fearful that he must drive and might get caught under Poland's zero-tolerance, drunk-driving laws and lose his license and his legal practice, Michał the *notariusz* drinks nothing. So the bottle of banana liqueur is for his mother and me, and we have one shot and then another, and it's time to go to Lubawa.

We make departure noises and grab boots and umbrellas, for it has been raining for two days, and we are headed for a procession, something both mother and son have told me I must see. Michał brings the car from the garage to the front of the wine store. I am honored with the passenger seat; that way Michał can hold forth and I can soak it in. It is odd to see Pani Wituchowska take a back seat to her son, but she is comfortable there, dignified, confident in the walking shoes her son told her to wear and the raincoat just in case.

When we arrive, there are young people walking toward and coming from the church where Matka Boska Lipska has been displayed on a stage. She is another icon of indeterminate age, who resides in the church of St. Barbara in Lubawa and once a year is paraded across town to this little church, where she is prayed to, then conveyed back home in a procession.

Through the mud and down the path we go to the church, where there is room in the pews for all of us. Michał motions for me to sit between him and his mother, and we kneel around the small altar with its image of Mary as a dozen people with candles are walking, genuflecting each time they pass her image. The music on the stage outside changes to hard rock. I flash Michał a confused look. "To each his own music," he whispers in my ear and shrugs.

The mud forces cancellation of the procession through town. Instead the crowd begins the stations of the cross, genuflecting in the sloppy yard and repeating with the priest, "Pray for us. Pray for us. Pray for us."

We leave after the first two stations. "There will be people here all night for the vigil," says Michał as he gives his arm to his mother, and we make our way back to the car in the mud.

Michał says Vatican II pretty much ruined the Catholic mass. "But the priest had his back to the people, and who knew what he was really doing up there?" he laughs. "I am just conservative. What can I tell you?"

Meanwhile, thirty thousand Poles are headed for Rome on a national pilgrimage and for a special mass with Pope John Paul II, and the whole thing, according to Adam, my best nonpartisan advisor, is a big political show with Polish President Kwaśniewski joining Lech Wałęsa and the third candidate for president, Jerzy Buzek, for a celebration of the two-thousandth anniversary of the birth of Christ, which conveniently precedes the October presidential elections.

Here, however, we have had our own pilgrimage, and no airline tickets were required.

CHAPTER 24

In the Dark without the Son

"Come back in an hour—after the store closes," Pani Wituchowska ordered during our next chat in her wine shop, where I, umbrellaless, took shelter from the rain. "Ring the bell," she whispered conspiratorially, "I have important things to tell you."

Pani's doorbell is out of reach of little pranksters. When I ring it, I can hear at once her footsteps down the stairs. The door opens but no one is there. Pani is hiding coyly behind the door, winking and holding her hand to her mouth palm out. She is wearing a red-polka-dot smock over a plain brown dress; she shows me a pair of slippers, Michał's, that I can wear in place of my wet shoes.

The dinner table is set for two. "Oh, I have put together a few things. I always have food ready in case a guest arrives," she assures me, ducking into the kitchen.

"Please, please, go to the table. I'll bring soup," she calls. Michał has gone on his pilgrimage to Częstochowa.

It's a flavorful cream of cauliflower with dill and a little potato.

"I made it yesterday, and I made too much, good thing, so now we have some today. I like cauliflower; I hope you like it."

I make a fuss over the dishes and the furniture again, so I can hear Pani tell me stories about how they survived the war and the communists.

"The chandelier," she points to the heavy, brass light fixture with three glass globes above our heads, "belonged to my great-grandfather. I have it only because we hid it from the Russians."

"How do you hide such a big thing?"

She leans close to reveal the secret. Who knows, she may have to hide it again. "In the coal bin, under a ton of coal, right back here." She points out the window. "Only one of the glass pieces is not original. I broke it when I was a little girl. We had a new one made."

"In 1939," she begins, "there was a man who owned a photo shop on the corner there, where you turn to go to the church. During the Occupation, he hid in a chimney for a long time. He wanted to marry me. But there was a neighbor lady, older than he was, and she took care of him, fed him. He married her after the war. He was targeted, I remember, because before the war he had said to some Germans, 'Let Hitler come and paint my walls for me!' Hitler was once a wall painter, you know, and they didn't like that. They remembered. We Poles were smart alecks anyway, sure that England was coming to help us."

"I remember when the German soldiers first came. They entered the house and said our neighbor, too, was saying things he shouldn't say, and they took him away. This one SS man, a bachelor named Fritz, he already lived in Bratian. He said the neighbor lady had too many kids, but me he was going to marry. They forced Fritz into the German army, you see, and after the war he even came back for a while and tried to live here. He cleaned the streets, but they took him away and executed him. It happened to a lot of people after the war."

Pani Wituchowska tilts her head gently and muses, "My father was the kind of man who never said a bad word about anyone. Not the Jews, not the Germans, no one."

The next course is escallops of something that could be chicken or veal.

"Turkey," she says, "in egg and flour and breadcrumbs."

"And lots of butter," I tease.

"Oh, I know," she swings her head in guilt. "I'm not supposed to. But I eat it, and here I am."

Michał has called three times already to check on his mother. Pani keeps slowing things down, pouring more vodka and telling me I must stay until midnight. She hands me the phone, and Michał asks me if I've read Wergiliusz—Virgil.

Pani Wituchowska wants to tell me all about how it once was for her. How at her family's dinner parties people knew what fish knives were for. There was

In the Dark without the Son

cognac and cigars for the men afterward. Servants knew on which side to serve and from which to remove. We talk of many such things as I look at the remains of those days—delicate white china plates with a simple gold circle at their edges, floral patterned silverware, and little glass holders for mustard and sugar, a miniature spoon and ceramic pots for salt and pepper.

"Everything just so; I love to have everything just so. I think you know. I have felt, since the first day you walked into my store and we exchanged just a few words, that I have known you for a long time. But why is time going so fast now? Look, you'll be going home before long. Wine, more wine?" She pours a delicate half glass. "People just don't care about these things now in Nowe Miasto.

"I see how young people act. When I was young, we just didn't do these things. My husband, you know, never even saw me naked," she giggles. "Always I went into another room, then appeared in a dressing gown." She waves her arms around her body gracefully. "Now I see how people make love on television. No shyness, they do what is natural, what feels good. And I'll tell you this, if I were young now I would do the same. No question, I would do the same. I think I have missed a lot," she concludes.

"That was then and this is now," I try to tell her, pretty much in agreement that she apparently missed quite a bit. I try to tell her that it's never too late as long as one is alive. But it sounds lame.

"The doctor tells me I don't have such a bad body for a woman my age," she laughs, hand to hip, devilishly. "I had my son Caesarean section," she blurts out, "and with the sewing needle the doctor was pretty good—barely a scar!" For a moment she reminds me of my mother, who on my birthday could be counted on to recite, with her Polish-American accent, what we came to call "Da Birt Story," the details of my delivery and the anguish it caused her.

Anguish, however, is not Pani Wituchowska's style.

"I'll tell you plainly the kind of girl I was," she asserts. "When the Germans took over the hotel on the Rynek—it stood where Adam's two stores are now—before the Russians burned it all. There was a soldier, and, oh, he liked me; he offered me a basket of oranges. 'Wouldn't this be a nice thing to take home to your mother?' he said to me. But I knew what the snake wanted. 'I have all the oranges I need,' I told him. Of course, I had none, but I had seen what some of the other girls did for an orange. Upstairs to a room. Years and years later some of them were still living here, and, oh, how sorry they were. But he was very handsome, that soldier, very handsome."

Next Pani lays out cold cuts and little foil-wrapped triangles of cheese, like those served to me every morning at the OSIR hotel.

CHAPTER 24
—

"We always used to end with cheese, good cheese, blue cheese, hard cheese, then cognac. Look, I still have the kind my husband drank," Pani proclaims.

She jumps up and scurries to the china cabinet, but the door won't open, and she asks me to give it a try. We giggle and fuss, and finally she has the magic touch that makes the key turn. It's Martell she wants to show me. And cigars.

"They are fifteen years old, maybe no good," she says. But they still smell like tobacco, if a little dusty.

Pani points to the television atop her fine mahogany chest. She tunes in just in time for the pope's trembling message to Poles at the Vatican, just in time to see the presidential candidates make their way to him.

"I've been to Rome, I've been to the Holy Land, the pope is Polish, and I'm content," she says, and the television goes off.

"It was 1985, or was it '86? I got in trouble over a song. I remember sitting at the piano over there and singing "'Bo to jest U.S.A., to słynne U.S.A.'" she croons. "Just a song about freedom, just for singing about America, the security police came knocking on the door to correct me. That worm that came into my store. It was him, and that's why I did this"—she makes a spitting gesture to the floor—"and told him to get out."

Pani Wituchowska is never at a loss for words. "My husband was thirty years older than I, you know. Even the priest didn't want to marry us. But it was a good match. My husband was fifty-seven years old when Michał was born, and look how smart my son is!" she exclaims, laughing. "There is lots of time for you. And your children, if you have them later in life, will be smarter."

"I believe in tradition," she says emphatically. "The *pączek* doughnut is meant to be eaten on the day before Lent, not all year long, and that is that," she chuckles. "Everyone wants to live. Maybe I have twenty more years. Maybe not. But I'd like to think so. It will be hard on my son when I go. How he worries. 'Take your pills.' So when he's here I have to take them, but when he's gone, I don't. What can I say? I don't like them."

Suddenly Pani decides to take our blood pressure with a handy little contraption her son bought her. She straps it first to her arm, then to mine. Hers is a little high. Mine, after a second try, "is fine," Nurse Wituchowska announces.

"So now, I told you I had something special to tell you." Pani walks to her buffet and brings back two little packages.

"This is from Jerusalem. Now, when you get there, you will see these everywhere, it's just a souvenir, but this one is special. It was blessed at the Church of the Holy Sepulcher." It's four white crosses in each corner of a red cross, affixed with a little chain to hang it on the wall. It says "Jerusalem" across the center.

"I wasn't sure who to give this last one to. I didn't know anything about you and religion. But after we went to Lubawa, I could see that you are a good Catholic, a Catholic like me."

"Good enough, I hope, to be worthy of this gift," I reply.

"I don't go to mass every Sunday either, but I know in my heart. . . . It's the same with you in your heart," she smiles gently.

The other little package is a string of ten wooden beads and a cross. "A little rosary, one cycle. Say 'Our Fathers' when you are worried or troubled. Just pin it inside your jacket and hold on to it at such times. It will help you," she advises.

We sit quietly for a few minutes. I pour the Hungarian wine into the crystal glasses. Pani tells me her mother died peacefully at home. "Everyone in my family died at home. That is the way it should be. I remember my mother's last moments. She kept looking at something, straight ahead and far away. 'Mother, what are you looking at?' I remember asking her, and she said, 'Nothing, my dear, nothing.' And she was gone. My dear brother. It was his kidneys. But he looked so handsome until the day he died. He would say he was going to die soon, and I would say, 'Look in the mirror. Is this the face of someone dying?' We would have given anything, our house, for a new kidney, but in those days it just couldn't be done."

Thinking of my own mother and grandmother, I see that Pani Wituchowska is not wallowing; rather, she is relishing the miracle that once she had these people in her life. This is to be no weeping session even as we listen to a scratchy tape on her boom box set between two doily-covered armchairs, an ancient cassette of her brother scraping on a violin while she accompanies him on the piano. "Our only recording," she says, beaming.

Pani tells a story about a woman who left her husband and children for a younger man. "After he got what he wanted, he dumped her for a younger, prettier, thinner woman," she says, running her hands up and down her own figure.

"The women are the worse," she says. "No matter what the man does, they must stick by him. And to be caught cheating, you can't expect him to accept it." The woman must hold back or suffer the consequences; the man should hold back, too, but not suffer the consequences if he doesn't succeed. Nothing I can say will change her mind. It's the woman's responsibility.

"Fat women, no," she says, "men don't like this," and she makes sweeping hand motions over her belly as she leans back on the davenport, laughing. "They get on, and they fall off!"

"Jak muszę spaść, to z dobrego konia," she laughs. "If I have to fall off a horse, let it be a good one."

Pani remembers how her father was never the same after the Germans took the store away, and then he died in 1941, how they sang "Jeszcze Polska Nie Zginęła" to raise their spirits, how the banker across the street tried to co-operate but was shot anyway. "We kept thinking someone was going to help us, the English, every time there were planes we thought they might be American. But they never came, you know."

"Why is it that sometimes it is so difficult for me to make out what Pan Kopiczyński is saying," I inquire, "yet I understand almost everything you say to me?"

We throw down another vodka. "It's those teeth!" she says, covering her mouth out of guilt. "Those teeth are like a *szatkownica*"—a cabbage slicer. "He and Adam, just alike, no sex appeal whatsoever, skinny as string and all teeth. I couldn't get past those teeth." And now her shoulders are shaking as she tries to hold back the laughter.

A credenza door pops open exposing the stacked white china within— "like those teeth!" she hoots.

While Pani goes to the kitchen, I fix the door by moving the thumbtack she has stuck into the top.

"And I thought you were not handy," she teases when she returns to find the cupboard closed. "You're like a cat." She imitates me cautiously snooping around, "looking for a mouse."

Then she launches into a tirade about her audience with the pope. "The priest wanted to announce it at Sunday mass. Can you imagine? Everyone would have been so jealous. You think people are so good in this town, but they are not. How they would talk."

"What do you care what people say?"

"I have to live here," she replies.

"Adam says let them talk," I add. "And when people say something to me, I triple it. Do I have a girlfriend? No, I have three girlfriends." She seems intrigued by the logic.

Pani nervously takes another call from Michał and then runs up and down the stairs. "The champagne is no good, he says, so I have to go down to the store again." She returns with another bottle. "There must be champagne!" she sings. "And now tell me, what time of the day were you born?"

In the Dark without the Son
—

What time of day was I born? Suddenly it all makes sense, and I blurt out, "You think it's my birthday. It's not my birthday."

"What? O mój Boże, and all evening I've been waiting till midnight just to tell you 'Happy Birthday.'" For a moment Pani Wituchowska stares sheepishly at the floor. Why did I even tell her?

Then she laughs, and we have another vodka—"to your birthday"—and she presses "play" on the boom box and takes my arm so we can dance. When the song ends, she throws herself into an armchair and glances up at her photograph. "She was a beautiful girl, no?"

CHAPTER 25

The Underside of a Mushroom

"**P**anie Leonardzie! Panie Leonardzie!"
Pani Kopiczyńska calls from downstairs. Mister Leonard, she says. It's Sunday morning.

"I'm not dressed!" I yell.

"We are going to the woods. There may be mushrooms!" she sings back.

"Give me five minutes."

It's been raining off and on for three days, and this is the time we have been waiting for, a chance at the simple pleasure of picking wild mushrooms.

"I can't promise we'll find any, but I know a woman who has them even if we don't," Pani promises, and off we race, her twin sister in the back seat, Puma and Mysza, her sister's little terrier, in the back of the station wagon. She will make dinner for the whole family in a jiffy this afternoon. Meanwhile, "we have an hour or so," she says, to "breathe the fresh, moist air in the woods, too cold for mosquitoes and flies."

First, however, we must collect Pani's "mushroom insurance" on a little farm near Marzęcice. She explains that "these very, very poor people live there; they have to walk a long way to use a telephone; they find things in the woods to sell."

We drive and drive, down winding bumpy roads to a lane where a young girl rushes out of what looks like a shabby concrete shed in the middle of a small field surrounded by woods.

"What a mess that house is inside," Pani mutters. The girl is carrying a good-sized pail full of small yellowish mushrooms, dirty and mingled with pine needles.

"Oh, *kurki,* wonderful! Oh, look how many!" Pani exclaims to the girl as she pours the treasured chanterelles into a plastic bag. "Oh, but I said not to pick the little ones, to let them grow," she scolds, shaking her head in dismay. "But where do you find so many?"

"You have to ask my mother." The girl smiles shyly and brushes her straw-colored hair away from her face, which looks as if it needs a good scrubbing. She can't be any more than twenty and seems never to have traveled farther than the end of the lane. "Twenty złoty," she asks for—less than five dollars.

Soon the mother and her son walk up the lane to greet us. "Hello, hello," the woman says cheerfully, with a closed-mouth smile that probably hides a multitude of dental horrors. The woman's face is red and weathered, with deep wrinkles carved into her forehead and fanning from her eyes, like the crinkly underside of a mushroom, to her dusty, gray-brown hair. She is wearing rubber boots and an odd velvet jacket that looks as if it might have belonged to one of the Three Musketeers. She could be a hundred years old, but she walks with the gait of a young woodsman.

The son stands silent between the two women but reaches over to touch his sister's shoulder. She swats his hand away contemptuously, then smiles at Pani Kopiczyńska. The mother says mostly "yes" and "no" and "maybe," while Pani explains that I am an American who would like to pick mushrooms, not simply see them dumped from a bucket.

"We'll go, we'll go," the woman promises, her head bobbing up and down like the pate of a wooden puppet.

"She's a good woman, but she looks like Baba Jaga"—an old crone—Pani says as we drive away, shaking her head again, "and she is a woman not even in her fifties, to have such young children. And, oh God, how she smokes cigarettes."

"And a husband?" I ask.

"I have never heard of or seen a husband. But the son. . . . Once I bought a bucket of mushrooms. Later the daughter came to my house and told me her brother had taken the money and spent it on liquor. She wanted me to pay again. But I said I was sorry, I had already paid, and gave her five złoty for bus fare home."

We park in the woods, the dogs jump out, and down the lane we go, but we can find no mushrooms of our own. We look at every stump, in every damp leafy crevice. All we find are telltale signs of poking and prodding. "Someone has already been here," Pani says. "I could spend the rest of my life in the woods and never find the mushrooms that woman can find."

"How does she know?"

"She was born on this land. She just knows," Pani answers.

Pani Irena is making discoveries of her own and loses her usual blasé demeanor when she finds a particularly bountiful cluster of ripe *maliny*—wild raspberries. Soon we are all three lost in an orgy of picking and eating. At first Pani Kopiczyńska gives her berries to me, but soon she is herself eating, and there are so many and they are so sweet. "I think I will make raspberry juice," says Irena. "There is no taste like it, no smell. You take the cap off of the bottle, and the whole room smells like raspberries. You can't get that from the kind you buy in the store."

Here and there are tiny blueberries. We pick and eat; this unplanned bounty takes away our sense of responsibility for filling a container. "We'll come back," the twin sisters agree.

I hear the sweet, simple folk singing of Adam's favorite, the Saint Nicholas Orchestra, in my head: "Chodźmy chopy na malyny, chodźmy na malyny, kupa bab tam w malynach, skuś baba dziada, dziada skuś na malyny." Come on, fellows, let's go look for raspberries where the girls are. Grandma's looking for grandpa, but he's already looking for raspberries—just like this middle-aged nongrandpa, who can't think of anything he'd rather be doing than following the ladies.

All the way home Pani Kopiczyńska chatters away, and I miss half of what she is saying, but it doesn't deter her. She stops the car now and then to pick up beer bottles or plastic bags that the thoughtless have tossed into her beloved forest. She drops me off so I can walk home through the Rynek.

Lunch—which in Poland is always really dinner—is waiting for me downstairs when I get home. Adam rushes out, on his way to take care of another business matter in his wear-everywhere, tan linen sports jacket. Today his mother has left exactly the sort of meal my grandmother would have prepared and over which I would have whined, "Can't you ever *fry* anything?" Roasted croquettes of ground pork seasoned with onion, green beans and new potatoes, simmered together and flavored with handfuls of the wild mushrooms from Baba Jaga. I also taste vegeta, Pani Kopiczyńska's favorite quick spice—a mix of salt and other flavors I have yet to figure out. She has also made a salad of marinated fresh cucumbers and tomatoes with a little onion and sour cream. It's all quite delicious.

The Underside of a Mushroom
—

A double trailer truck full of caged turkeys rattles by my window; the birds look out at the world from the sides of the truck and struggle to keep their dignity as their plump, fluffy white bodies bounce and wiggle. The hostile neighbor to the west is painting his new front gate, and his tidy, front-yard garden looks healthy and lush, the lettuce ready daily, the cabbage heads swelling with green.

The church bells clang in the distance, and the old neighbor lady totters to the market. Three men wheel a bag of cement down the sidewalk on a flat wheelbarrow. The repairman arrives to fix the water pump, and Adam is talking quietly on the phone.

My phone rings, and it's Ryszard, beckoning me to the office so he can show me some special vodka. So into town I walk, faces passing, a young woman who resembles my mother in a 1936 photograph, her hair cropped, looking tough and defiant.

You can see in this town that some people are falling through the cracks— three young men making a spectacle of themselves trying to keep the drunkest among them standing—but you also get that sense of forward motion: Keep moving or you lose.

Ryszard and Grażyna are working like fiends to put the latest issue of the newspaper to bed before she leaves for vacation. Yet they still have time to entertain me.

"CDs for sale!" Ryszard yells, hanging up the phone. "Let's go!" he commands, like a floor captain marshalling a fire drill.

He leads us out the door and around the corner to someone's flat, where a woman greets us conspiratorially and takes us into a room where she has two large boxes of CDs. As we pick through them, a friendly and slightly tipsy man gives us a price: Nine CDs for one hundred and nineteen złoty. "Make it a hundred and ten," he says—twenty-four dollars—as I fumble for the correct amount, and he extends a calloused hand for me to shake.

Back at the office Ryszard follows me to the door to check his car. "Is it still there?" he jokes. "I don't have any insurance. A thousand złoty a year it would cost me. I don't have such money. O jeni kochani!" he exclaims. The last time I heard this euphemistic version of "dear God," it came from my grandmother's lips.

Early Sunday morning I hear Pani Kopiczyńska clacking about downstairs, but I run down to greet her before she can call up the stairs in her sweet, high-pitched voice, "Panie Leonardzie! Panie Leonardzie!"

She has found more kurki in the woods and can take me to them now. She didn't pick them, the better to show me exactly how and where, with determination and good eyes, one can find these delectable mushrooms.

So into the car we hop—I, always eager to follow someone as enthusiastic and energetic as she over something as simple as a walk in the woods. She is alone today, with Puma stuffed into the hatch and smelling like—well, like a wet dog.

We park the car along one of the lanes and head to the spot where she has located the little treasures. Pani is like a mushroom Geiger counter, and soon we are digging like two very genteel wild pigs at the spot where she has casually left a flattened beer can to mark the spot.

The little beauties are large and yellowish and buried deep in moss and surrounded by camouflage, yellowing birch leaves. Pani stuffs the beer can into her garbage bag and shows me how to pull the mushrooms out of the ground, clean the bottoms with a knife, and leave the tiniest ones, covered with leaves, for a future hunt.

These mushrooms will be as delicious as the bucketful we got from Baba Jaga.

The lanes in the woods are lined with blueberry bushes, and we pick handfuls and munch them as we walk, Pani telling me about an uncle who was taken to Siberia for labor after the war. "He was one of the lucky ones," she says. "He came back, but his health was ruined."

Pani has another plastic bag filled with garbage to unload in the woods, but she brings only decomposable kitchen waste—rinds, husks, and a gob of raspberry seeds from her jelly-making session over the weekend.

We head in different directions to look for more maliny, raspberries. What will I do back in Chicago, I wonder, without these woods to wander? Then I hear her calling, "Panie Leonardzie! Panie Leonardzie!"

She has discovered a grove of the little red delights and has converted the hollowed-out rind of half a muskmelon into a container that fits nicely into the palm of her hand. "We'll put only the best ones, the perfect ones in here, and you can take them home. The rest. . . ." And she makes a quick hand-to-mouth motion, smiling.

Then it's time to go home, for I have another distant cousin to meet at his home in nearby Kurzętnik.

I take along a six-pack, wondering if my empty-handedness has put off Marek's father, Jan Bryszkiewski. "Good day, and the first thing I have to ask you is if you drink beer," I call as I get out of the car in front of his hilltop house.

The Underside of a Mushroom

—

"Drink beer? Yes, of course!" he laughs, as if to say, "What kind of prude do you take me for?"

Inside, his wife has prepared coffee and brings cake and cookies to the coffee table in the living room, which is next to the kitchen and looks to have been conceived as a dining room, while the adjacent living room is home to a velveteen couch and a large console. The television stays on for the entire two hours of my visit, and I conclude that this must be a Bryszkiewski family habit. They rather effectively ignore it, at one point turning the volume down to nearly nothing.

I must meet his two little girls, ages six and three. "Pleased to meet you," they both say and shake my hand. It's been a long time since I've seen a three-year-old shake hands and speak formally to an adult. Then, with my notes and papers, we must establish the family connection, which, as it turns out, puts us in the same generation, although I am more than twenty years his senior. "Our great-grandfathers were brothers" is the simplest way to put it.

"It's funny," he says, and his wife, Jadwiga, nods in agreement. "Even I remember hearing about some distant aunts who went to America. But who thinks about such things? Someone else went to France, we always heard."

"I remember the old family home," Marek says. It was one of those typical wooden chałupki. I was quite small when it burned, probably about twenty-five years ago. But that farm is where Edmund Marklewicz lives today."

So how does a family farm end up in the hands of one cousin and not the other?

"I can't tell you for sure. His mother would have been a first cousin to your grandmother. She married a Marklewicz. She was one of the younger children. My grandfather went to live elsewhere, and she stayed at home. When she married, her husband wanted to stay on the farm. That is probably how it went until now, and her son is still there. We can go to see the farm if you like, although they have a new house there."

We make a date for the following Sunday, although I'm disappointed that this brings me no closer to my grandmother's brothers and sisters.

After a beer and a few nosey questions in my best Polish, Marek starts to talk.

"Was life better before or is it better now?" I want to know.

"Before," he says without hesitation. "Everybody had a job. You didn't have all these taxes out of control. You didn't have crime, people living on the streets. We have it all now."

"Wait," says his wife. "It depends on how you look at it. Before, we had money, we were comfortable, but there was nothing in the stores to buy. You had to stand in line all day when something like televisions were rumored to be available. Now the stores have everything, but we have no money to buy it."

"And I don't know from one day to another if I will have a job. I am in the kitchen cabinet business, and you can see in the kitchen, I cannot afford even to redo my own house."

I peer into the kitchen, with its decorative wooden cupboards and tiled floor, and it seems to me that there is something askew about the expectations rather than the kitchen itself.

"I was in Poland in 1981, and it was like traveling back in time. Everything has changed so," I offer.

"Yes, but my little girls, they don't remember those times. It will all be history to them," Marek asserts.

I begin to feel that either the logic or the language of this conversation is escaping me; yet they understand me, they welcome me.

"You have a very nice home," I tell them.

"Thank you. But we can't afford to finish it. We have to take everything in steps over a long time," says Marek.

"How about doing everything the way Americans do, on credit?"

"No, we do nothing on credit. We make a little extra, and then we can do something to the house. No credit."

Marek catches me staring at him and stares back and smiles. "Perhaps some family resemblance?" He does look a bit like me and like my cousins, and his little girls like my cousins' little girls, and so it seems odd to be sitting in the home of someone whose name you saw in a phone book, from a town you couldn't even find on a map a few months ago.

Then it's time to go home, where Pani Kopiczyńska may have left me dinner.

"Look outside," Adam calls from the kitchen as I drive up. "Para tęczy!"

He could be warning that a cloud of locusts is descending, for all I know, but before it is necessary to reach for my dictionary, I see to the northeast the brightest rainbows I have ever seen, a pair of them.

"The roof!" climber Adam says, and before I can say Wizard of Oz, we're up there—he, walking fearlessly on the wet tarred slope; me, out only to the waist from the attic entry he has flipped open.

It is a beautiful rainbow, seven colors, and a little farther to the north is another, dimmer echo of the first. We just stare.

The Underside of a Mushroom

—

"I wonder if they can see it in Iława," Adam muses.

"I think if we get in the car and try to get to the end of it, we won't ever find it."

"Jak Dorota," says Adam. Like Dorothy.

So we decide to take a walk into town to find the schedule for the week of street theater that is supposed to start tomorrow.

"When are you going to come to America?" I ask.

"Me? Come to America?" he replies as if the thought had never occurred to him.

Adam changes the subject. Tomorrow he must pick up his son from the hospital and help his former wife with some new living-room furniture she has purchased for her apartment. America can wait. So we walk downtown.

"I can remember," he says suddenly, pointing, "when this house and that house were still in ruins from the war. The bank there was only put up about twenty-five years ago. And now we have an automatic teller machine here and a new one on the Rynek. It's a revolution in Nowe Miasto!"

We stroll back home down Third of May Street, the cobblestones still slick from today's rain, a little shop near the corner displaying bronze-colored statues of two pseudo-Chinese men having their way with a woman, her butt pressed up against one on his knees, her face buried in the lap of the other on his back.

"A young guy owns that store; must be a novelty he picked up somewhere in his travels," Adam explains with a smile. "We don't have a sex shop—yet."

The Hunt for Hidden Treasure

n my way home I surprised the wicked neighbor of the west, who had hoisted his hulk up a ladder and was picking cherries from his tree, on our side of the fence. It was impossible not to say hello as I walked by. And so we started a conversation about how delicious the cherries are.

"Why don't you get a container, and I'll pick you some, too" he said.

I was about to go into shock. "For me? You don't have to do that."

"No, I'd be happy to. Get a container."

I headed to the house, and when I returned with a little basket, the neighbor lady had joined the scene and was staring up at her husband. Soon she was telling me how she makes *wiśniówka*—cherry liqueur.

Hurriedly, the neighbor on the ladder filled my basket with stemless cherries and handed it down to me. What a breakthrough in neighborly relations, I was thinking.

An hour later I looked out the window, and he was cutting every branch off the cherry tree that hung in our yard, beautiful fruit-bearing branches, many with red spots still dangling as he dragged them away. Adam explained later: "He's just goofy. He thinks now that the tree will grow entirely in his direction so he won't have to come into my yard again to pick."

Meanwhile, I am off to the Łydzińskis' for a meeting with Jan Miotk, the ninety-two-year-old custodian of the St. Thomas parish archives in Nowe Miasto.

Mieczysław has arranged a rendezvous with him, and we are killing time, waiting for his call. Urszula Łydzińska is happy today; she has a new job in the city offices as a regional medical administrator; she'll be making more money and can give up her old job.

"They'll have no trouble filling my position," she says. "There are so many people who need the work."

No sooner is the tea poured than Pan Miotk calls, and we must be off. He is waiting for us on Działyńskich Street. Mieczysław has never been to the archive either and doesn't want us to be late.

The old man greets us with a grin and a handshake, carrying a little black-patent-leather purse, something a young girl might have carried to a prom in Detroit in 1964. Inside are the keys to the archive. He leads us around a corner to a nondescript, cement-block barracks, up three flights of stairs, and, after much difficulty finding two keyholes in the unlit hallway, he admits us into a small room crammed with shelves, with a big book-and-photograph-covered desk under a window that looks out onto the church. There's a water spot on the ceiling directly over one of the shelving units.

"No water," says the custodian, "that's all fixed." Pan Miotk has the marvelous and infuriating nonchalance of a man who has lived almost a century and doesn't intend to be alarmed by anything. "Well, here it all is, take a look," he says, sitting in one of the three old chairs near the desk.

Mieczysław dives in, grabbing a book of parish records from 1875 to 1890 and setting me to work. "You may find listings from Sugajno here."

I do not, but I am more interested in our host than the record book, so I apologize for my bad Polish.

"Well, what happened, did you forget how to talk?" he says, trying to figure out my story.

"I was born in America. My mother was born in America. But my grandmother was born here, in Sugajno," I tell him.

"Oh, well, American. I speak German. I am Kashubian," he reveals, running his hand over his right ear, most of which is missing, "and when I was in school, we spoke only German. Polish was forbidden; only at home we spoke Polish. When I came to Nowe Miasto, it was already after the Second World War, 1946. During the war the Germans put me to work. In 1931 I was in school in Warsaw, then I went to Romania. It's a long story, but here I live now."

"You can remember the First World War?" I ask.

"Yes, of course, I was ten years old. But the First War, it went by like lightning. I remember the Germans came, and then it seemed as if the next day everyone went to work as usual. But they took one brother into the German army; they wanted to take another, but the war ended before they got him."

Mieczysław is letting out little gasps over the treasury of old books in our midst—local history from the nineteenth century, with pictures that he has never seen of castles and churches.

A photograph of the cemetery chapel is hanging near the books, and the old man tells us the little ruin near it is what's left of an older chapel that stood when the cemetery was Evangelical. It seems that after twenty years or so cemeteries were reused, and the wall fragment is the only sign that remains of the old occupants.

I find a Paulina Jurkiewicz listed in 1867, no doubt some distant relative, then start looking at some of what appear to be the oldest volumes, remarkable, leather-bound Latin tomes. I reach for one under the water spot and see that they were once soaked—and not so long ago. Inside, the pages are worm eaten.

Pan Miotk asks me for my business card and stuffs it into the little black purse.

Mieczysław pulls out enormous leather-bound volumes in Latin—*Sylveira Commentariorum in Textum Evangelicum*—dated 1665. His face lights up, then dims to horror over their condition.

He tells our host, "You could sell one of these books for $15,000 in the United States."

"By all means do it!" Pan Miotk replies. "We could do with some of that money. Let the book go."

"Wouldn't it be better if they were sent to Toruń?" I inquire, "to the conservation lab?"

"And we would never see them again," Mieczysław snaps. "No, it would be better if we found a proper place for them here."

We stop for a beer, and I goad Mieczysław into ordering golonka, pig hocks, so I can watch in disbelief as somebody else eats those hunks of fat and rind.

"Remarkable how those volumes lasted so long, and within just the last few years they suffered more damage than in the previous two hundred," Mieczysław laments.

"Has he ever told you what happened to his ear?" I ask, thinking it must be some horrible war story.

"Yes, a simple infection, not so very long ago, and a very bad doctor."

Women Dancing in Their Slips

I

t's one of those days to be treasured.
There is the market to go to. Potatoes are coming in, fresh horseradish that makes your eyes tear the minute you put it to the grater, blueberries scooped from big white plastic pails, cauliflower and cabbage in heads bigger than mine. It's impossible to resist these fresh fruits and vegetables when they are being sold for dimes and quarters by women and men who look like your grandparents. Impossible. And so maybe I won't eat all that I buy, but I have rings of kiełbasa simmering on the stove in a two-dollar bottle of Bulgarian wine from Pani Wituchowska's shop, carrots in the sink with their greens still attached, and new potatoes ready for steaming.

The one thing I have learned about Polish cooking is that food is rarely served "as is." You don't grill steaks or roast chickens and serve them looking like what they are. Meat must be served as a cutlet or a roulade or a schnitzel, coated or stuffed with egg and crumbs. Food is not good food unless it has been "prepared." The major exceptions are pig hocks—golonka—and, for special outdoor occasions, the entire pig.

When I stopped this morning to leave Pani Wituchowska some mushrooms and blueberries, she was chattering away in High German with a visitor from Dresden, by way of Iława, where with his wife he is working and living temporarily. He spoke even less Polish than I, but struggled with it valiantly, and we are able to talk. Before long, he gave me his card and urged me to visit him and his historic city.

"He is quite taken with the store," she said after he left. "He's been here three times and says he is coming again tomorrow."

"I don't think it's the store he is taken with," I observed.

I told her about Pan Miotk and the ruined state of the archives. She made a spitting gesture. "Have nothing to do with him. He's no good, a commie all the way. When my uncle was here, Father Mechlin, it wasn't like that, I can tell you. Those old books were taken care of."

Now at home I am waiting for Ryszard and Grażyna, the St. Nicholas Orchestra wailing from the CD player upstairs. With a savoy cabbage on the table, a beer in my belly, and friends on their way, I stare out the window at the wicked neighbor and his wife, and they remind me that my grandmother and mother both were quintessentially Polish women, investing their lives in their men, then waiting for the payoff—except in America there was none.

My mother, to her never-ending frustration, was always learning American ways—to budget, to make every penny count, to work nine hours a day with no "benefits," no vacations, no holidays, no sick days, no insurance, no retirement plan, while my grandmother put every piece of food in the house on the table every Sunday when her son came with his daughters to drive us to church.

"Who drank up all the milk?" my mother would yell. "What do you think I am, made of money?"

"I did!" my grandmother would snap, both of them knowing that Busia would never permit my glass to sit empty.

The worst thing you can do in Poland is have someone arrive at your home—a friend, a relative, a stranger—and have nothing to offer, a bare cupboard, the most dreaded of fates, to have not even a glass of milk to offer your grandchildren.

Through the window I see the neighbor lady feeding her chickens. The phone rings for Adam, then Ryszard calls and says he and Grażyna will be here in five minutes. The chickens peck and know that the neighbor has food, for which they will put their lives on the line. How odd to have no arms, wings instead, but wings that have nothing to do with freedom.

My guests scurry in and quickly settle around the table and start the Polish gobble, Ryszard turning his nose up at my kiełbasa spoiled with wine and garlic. We watch Adam's cousin-in-law park the company van in the garage, and my guests speculate about who he is and how he makes his money and where his new house is going up.

In the middle of the meal Adam walks in, and I sense that he is uncomfortable having guests in his home without an invitation from him. However, he says he is hungry and polishes off the plate I heap full for him. There is beer, plenty of beer.

Adam leaves as quickly as he came, in his new silver Mazda. My guests speculate about what is to become of his old Honda; then they get on a cell phone and huddle and plot. "Don't tell him I'm here," Grażyna whispers to Ryszard, while he is suave and abrupt. "Three minutes flat, that's all it took," he beams as he clicks off. I have no idea what they are up to.

We talk politics, and Grażyna says Lech Wałęsa has had his day and should retire.

Then Pani Kopiczyńska arrives with a smile on her face and a big, plastic shopping bag.

"Baba Jaga came through this time," she proclaims proudly. The bag is full of mushrooms, heavy white beauties with reddish caps, fragrant with forest and looking extraordinarily phallic, as we all smell them and feel them and exclaim over their beauty. Ryszard is beside himself with delight, and Pani puts aside a half dozen for me and fills a little bag for him.

"Leonard has made us some American food," says Ryszard.

"American food?" I protest, "I thought I had made you a real Polish dinner!"

From here it is time to pay a call on Janusz the mechanic for more Maluch repairs. Anna invites me in and places a steaming stuffed cabbage before me.

Janusz's eldest daughter, Kasia, says she enjoyed last night's little theatrical in the streets and in the woods, a bizarre performance that began a week of street theater brought to Nowe Miasto by a native, now with a theater in Gdańsk.

"Did you dance, too?"

"Oh, no," she answers shyly.

Their really big news is that they, like Pani Wituchowska and her son, have been to Licheń, where a new cathedral is nearing completion. "Wonderful, the largest church in Poland, the seventh largest in Europe," says Janusz. "You should go. It's beautiful, the cathedral, two smaller churches, the Way of the Cross in the form of a stone fortress, beautiful grounds. Everyone from Poland should see this." In fact, I read later, more than a million do annually, the next-most-visited site in the country after Częstochowa and the Black Madonna.

But I have been to Częstochowa, and it seems to me it more than suffices as a national shrine. "Why does Poland need such a big new cathedral when

CHAPTER 27
—

I have seen beautiful old churches that are neglected, half empty, like in Chełmno, and there is no money for them?" I inquire.

Janusz jumps to the cathedral's defense. "The priest, Eugeniusz Makulski, he wanted to build this cathedral, and the communists told him he could not; therefore he wanted to show them that it will be done and in this jubilee year! Isn't it the same in the United States? Don't you have plenty of old churches in Chicago without money? Didn't you build a new Częstochowa in Michigan?"

He's got me there. We did indeed.

As we walk to the Rynek for another evening of street theater, a visiting teenage American cousin joins us, darting out of one of the half-dozen barracks that sit between Janusz's house and the town center. She is in some breathless state of anxiety over a trifle, and her Polish family seems blasé about her dilemma. It is peculiar to hear her valley-girl style superimposed on Polish: "Co mam robić—whatever." But she has grown up bilingual, and of that I am envious.

The new theatrical is, as last time, late, so I walk over to the *Gazeta* office to see what light Ryszard and Grażyna can shed on a starting time. Instead I find that she has gone home, and there's a little note on the door saying he is upstairs—in a room with six others, including their coworker Anna, wearing a close-fitting, sleeveless floral dress that shows off her ample figure to its best advantage.

There are jars of paint and other art supplies lining every wall and heaped on the table, but they have been pushed aside to make room for vodka bottles. A boom box fills the room with Polish music. Anna decides it's time for me to dance, and so we cut a rug. "I don't know what to do to this song," I apologize.

"It's not a problem for me. I must do what you do," Anna teases, as we settle into a rhythm.

"That song is so old the Berlin Wall was still standing when they recorded it," Ryszard barks from the sidelines.

But the action outside is about to begin, and off we go. The lobby is crowded with a couple dozen young women in slips, with wildflower and weed wreaths on their heads, their faces sooted. "Smile," Ryszard says and snaps their picture. "Lovely, lovely," he says, shaking his head.

It's eleven at night when the parade finally begins through the Rynek. Janusz has given up and gone home, but his wife and daughters stick it out, waiting patiently outside the Ratuszowa restaurant, where the outdoor tables are still occupied by beer drinkers, two of whom Ryszard and I soon become. Janusz's wife does not drink alcohol.

The parade creeps around the corner and down the south side of the square, to the next corner and over the bridge to the bank of the Drwęca, where another ring of fire has been lit. Ribbons dangle from a sort of May pole, and the girls in slips start dancing around it, twisting the ribbons as they writhe and wiggle to the music of Kapela ze Wsi Warszawa, a group from Warsaw that sings the same plaintive folk songs as the St. Nicholas Orchestra.

The girls are dancing with wild abandon, shaking their behinds, and waving their arms, their bikini underpants clearly visible under their slips. Now and then they drag a boy from the crowd into the circle, but the boys are shy and hang back. After nearly an hour of erotic abandon, the pole is set on fire, there is a last outburst from the dancing girls, and the frolic is over.

Ryszard never wants an evening to end. "Chodźmy na maliny," he jokes, raising his eyebrows lecherously—"Let's go look for raspberries." Then he invites two young girls and the guy they are with to the *Gazeta* office for more beer, but they beg off, and he shows me the building over the bridge where once a honey factory stood, and next to it the house where the honey-factory owner lived, and it still stands. "I used to play here. There was a hole in the wall over there that I would climb through," he muses.

Back at the Ratuszowa it's nearly time to close, and all the chairs are upside down on the tables, but they have saved our beers, and we sit outside on a bench alongside the flower beds, and Ryszard tells me more.

"I think Grażyna is a little red," he says suddenly. "She likes Kwaśniewski. The younger they are, the less they remember, and soon they will be voting, people too young to remember what it was like under communism. I have no use for it. It was awful for me, I can tell you. One time an official came to Nowe Miasto to live, and he decided he wanted our house, just pointed at it and said he would have it. He almost got it, too, except for my father knowing who to talk to."

Ryszard points to his home above Alina's cosmetics shop, where he wants to raise the rent despite her pleas of poverty. "That is my wife's room, that's where she spends her time." This mysterious wife is no doubt there now, perhaps looking out at us, wondering why her husband is never home.

The next day we speed to Lubawa, twenty minutes away, to see the president of Poland. The turnout is good, three thousand people maybe, grabbing up photos being passed out by a slick-looking aide in a business suit. Security is heavy. They are checking for explosives under the tables in the restaurant where we are drinking a Pepsi and watching the action out the window.

People peer from second- and third-floor windows around the Rynek while a band plays "Hey, Jude," apropos of nothing. President Kwaśniewski's route is explained over a microphone on the grandstand, and people are asked to clear the way. Politely they move. The mayor passes our table, and Ryszard turns on the charm, his eyes darting left and right.

"We say there are three powers in Poland: the church, the government, and the press," Ryszard says proudly after the mayor pays him homage.

Outside, we are escorted to a special area reserved for the third power. A band marches to the grandstand. Elvis sings "Blue Suede Shoes" over the public-address system, while a woman with a long extension cord vacuums the blue platform carpet. A man in a green uniform marked "policja" leads an evil-looking wolf dog down the sidewalk past us.

A man at the mike holds up a three-year-old boy and says he is looking for his mother or his babcia. "Love Letters in the Sand" blares over the loudspeakers for no reason, followed by "Tutti-Frutti." Members of the little band fidget with their trumpets and saxophones and clarinets, waiting for their turn.

"Let's have a round of applause for the lady who vacuums for the president," someone in the crowd yells.

The security guards come around to us with their metal detectors. Ryszard seems to love the excitement, as a man in a suit with an insignia pin on the lapel examines his camera and rummages through his bag.

The sun is shining, and people are waiting patiently behind barricades of plastic tape, pressing against the temporary iron fence that has been erected around the speakers' platform.

The band plays "Aloha O'è" for no discernable reason. The press from Lubawa arrives, and Grażyna and Ryszard start muttering to one another. The black-and-yellow "Straż" police drink Pepsis and wait.

Finally the man arrives, Aleksander Kwaśniewski, in a white van preceded by wailing police cars and greeted by two women with bouquets. He makes his way down the sidewalk that has been kept clear for him, shaking hands and greeting the Lubawians who line the way.

At the microphone he is automatonic, surrounded by plainclothes security, beginning with a joke about the staging of the battle of Grunwald that is scheduled for this afternoon. "I heard an advance report on the radio that we won," he jokes, then moves on to education, investment. . . .

"And housing," someone in the crowd yells.

"And housing," mimics Kwaśniewski. The past five years have been progressive, he says, but he needs five more to really do the job. The crowd cheers, and people wave from windows.

"Commie," Ryszard says. "Wanted to throw everyone in jail."

"Some people ask, where is the fruit of the labor we have endured for these years?" says Kwaśniewski, then assures the crowd that investments and new factories are happening and will continue to happen. He descends to shake hands and sign pictures, and the sky clouds over. Leszek Miller, another leader of the Democratic Left Alliance, is behind him, also signing for the crowd.

"Wouldn't vote for him under any circumstances," says Ryszard in the car on the way back to Nowe Miasto. "He's not so bad," says Grażyna. It starts to pour, so hard that we can barely make out the presidential motorcade on its way to another rally in Iława.

To Grandmother's House We Go

I't's a sunny Sunday morning, and a hundred people are standing outside St. Thomas's for mass since there's no more room inside. A baby is crying, a young Gypsy girl is kneeling on the ground near the sidewalk, holding a sign: "I am very poor. My mother is lying in the hospital. Please help me." Everyone ignores her. But it is so sunny and cool that outside seems the right place to be, even if kneeling in the dirt.

I'm going to see the relatives in Sugajno today. Marek Bryszkiewski seems to have sensed that I want more out of his family than one visit, and he has precipitated a clan gathering.

I'm ready a little early. The beer is packed up for the men, chocolates for the women, chocolate bars for the little girls, and a plastic bag full of gołąbki that I made last night with that irresistible head of Savoy cabbage and meat I ground with an old grinder that belonged to Adam's grandmother. No one seems to like those green, outer cabbage leaves, just as we used to peel them off and toss them away when I was a kid. I cannot resist their chlorophyll richness, however, and I save those for myself.

Marek is waiting at the front door at the conclusion of my second try in my Maluch up the hill to his house. "I guess I still haven't learned the way to drive this thing," I explain.

The girls are dressed in their Sunday best, Marta scampering about and

Kinga putting her tights on. "Dziękuje bardzo," each says politely upon being presented with a chocolate bar.

Then we are off, with Marek racing ahead in his own Maluch to show me how it's done, no doubt. I try to keep up and pull out in front of a white Mazda in the process. The driver gives me the finger as he rams on the gas and passes.

Out to the farm we go, by a new route that takes us onto dirt roads and through Sugajenko, where we pull over to see a new Zakopane-style, Alpine house going up for "a retiree who wants peace and quiet," says Marek.

Jan is on the porch to greet us, and Helena and daughter-in-law Grażyna are just inside, making coffee and waving us through the kitchen and into the living room, where the coffee table has been set.

Before very long we are ready for another round of looking at photographs; this time the whole family seems intrigued by the old shoe box full of captured moments. And this time I am given a handful to copy and return. No matter how hard we look or how much I am able to get Jan to remember, it seems that Marek and I, living lives on opposite sides of the ocean, can go no further back in our family tree than our great-grandfathers, who were brothers. We don't have a single piece of paper that says they were, however, only the vague memories of a man barely ten years older than I.

"I do remember meeting cousin Franciszek, your grandmother's brother. He went to France to live, but I remember him coming back to visit now and then after the war. I saw him several times," Jan says.

He also remembers tales of how my grandmother's brother Władysław was murdered. "Yes, yes, it was at a party, I was told, and someone hit him over the head."

Jan's daughter, also named Grażyna, arrives with her husband, Mirosław, and their daughters Kamila and Dominika, and Marek's little girls are already introducing me as their uncle from America.

Compiling a family tree is not the point. I want to see where my grandmother was born, and they are certain now that they can show me.

"So let's go and see," Marek urges and takes off with his wife and kids staring and waving at me out the back window of their Maluch. Mirosław and Jan take me in another car, and soon we are bouncing down a dirt road and stopping to look at a grove of trees and lilac bushes.

"This is where my grandfather Wincenty lived," says Jan. "The house was there." He points to a clearing surrounded by trees.

Across the street lives Edmund Marklewicz and his wife, Leokadja. "Maybe he'll remember more since he is older."

Pani Leokadja comes out to greet us and soon ushers us into the house for coffee. Pan Edmund is lying on the sofa, his right hand in a glove, his face gaunt and deathly. When we enter the living room, though, he rises and offers tooth-less greetings filled with assurances that he is doing okay in spite of how lousy he feels.

Pan Edmund is ready to talk but cannot offer any clearer memories than his cousin Jan's. He doesn't know the names of his great-grandparents either. His wife serves coffee and a cherry gelatin cake. "I think it's a little too sour," she says, but it tastes like fresh cherries.

Edmund and Jan, cousins, light up. Jan, overweight and tapping his chest as he laughs and hacks; Edmund, skinny as the cigarette he is smoking. Edmund cannot tell me much about my family, but he is off on World War II and his early memories of life in Sugajno. He was taken away to work on a farm dur-ing the Occupation. Like so many people in Nowe Miasto, he remembers the German invasion as a rather smooth operation. "They thought this was Ger-many already, so they were very careful in the way they took it back."

We drive to a lane that is almost impassible in the mud, then down a hill, up a hill, as far as we can go, and then we park.

The others wait while Marek leads me through a wet wheat field and to-ward an apple tree heavy with fruit. "There, you can see where it was," he points.

There in a clearing, which was long ago someone's yard, is the best ruin I have seen in Poland yet, better than any castle or medieval wall, because this is the ruin of my grandmother's home. This is where she was born and where she ran as a little girl, just as little Kinga Bryszkiewska ran ahead of me mo-ments ago, calling back to me with her blond braids bouncing on her back.

"This was the house," Marek says, pointing. "I remember how it was, a typ-ical chałupa made of wood. It burned." And there is the stone foundation, a deep hole where once there was a cellar.

"Over there was a cow shed." We examine what is left of a crumbling foun-dation.

"And here, I remember, was a barn." We look over another foundation, a cement slab, with the remains of something like steps. The owner is someone named Stanisław Domżalski. They are not sure how he came to own it. They are not sure exactly how the Jan Bryszkiewski who lived there was related to them, but he was married to Anna and lies buried in the Boleszyn cemetery.

We follow the path home that my grandmother must have walked to school, for there it is ahead of us, the old schoolhouse just beyond Jan's farm.

I think it is perhaps time to go home, but the coffee table has been expanded and chairs put all around it, and dinner has been laid out, with my stuffed cabbages side by side with chicken and duck parts. There are galareta and potato salad and cold cuts and mushrooms that Grażyna the daughter-in-law has picked in the little woods on the farm. "They are *maślak,*" she says, "also known as *pępki,*" and they all laugh. It means "little belly buttons."

Daughter Teresa arrives with husband Jacek and son Michał, and the family gathering is almost complete except for their other son Paweł and daughters Agnieszka and Iwona. Agnieszka speaks English, has studied it in school, everyone agreeing that it is the thing to do for a better job, and they are sorry she is not here, so I could quiz her and see how she's doing.

Jan and Jacek are joking about the fish they almost caught, carp and wild *karaś*. Kinga is smiling and flirting and wants to sit on the arm of my chair.

While daughter Grażyna cuts Jan's hair, Mirosław tries his best to get through to me with complicated opinions about Polish history and politics, finally settling for some travel talk about sites we've seen in Poland, then outside Poland, and he tells a joke about Scotland: "This Scottish guy invites some guests for dinner, and the servant brings out bread and water. After a while the servant comes around and asks if it's time to bring out the chicken. 'No, not yet,' says the Scotsman. And the guests continue to eat their bread and drink the water. The servant comes out again and asks if it's time now to bring out the chicken, and the Scotsman looks at the diners and says, 'No, not yet.' When the servant asks a third time, the Scotsman sees that everyone is done with the bread and says, 'Okay, you can bring out the chicken, the crumbs are ready to be pecked up.'"

The next morning I am off again to Toruń. The idea of people digging through dusty archives looking for the names and dates of people whose sexual proclivities played some part in their presence on earth has always made me want to go right to sleep. I did not come to Poland to do genealogy; rather, I came to get to know "my grandmother's people." Until today, on the verge of giving up on all those brothers and sisters of my grandmother, I have avoided archives and "family tree" sheets and the endless digging and copying of the true genealogist. But Maria and Adam and Mieczysław have inspired me.

I walk the bridge across the Vistula River in Toruń early in the morning to get to the *archiwum państwowe*—public archives—tucked away in a former movie theater in a residential area of old, barrack-style apartments.

A fussy man in a green smock greets me at the door. Do I have an appointment? No. Am I here representing an agency of some sort? No. Well, fine, then, come this way, he says, and seats me in a very bare, very white reading room with eight very utilitarian tables, all of it put together in that communist-modern style that seems to have fallen into a time warp about 1958.

Soon, after an explosion of chattering and welcoming, I am put to work filling in some rather modest forms. Meanwhile, Pani Anna Chruściel is delivered to my table, for she speaks English. The first order of business is to get me a cup of coffee.

This is no ordinary archivist. This woman seems as enthusiastic about the preservation work she does now as she must have been when she started in the archive thirty years ago. Smiling like someone who has a wonderful secret to share, she soon snuggles next to me to help me make my way through the German documentation that awaits.

You've got to give it to the Germans who controlled West Prussia in the nineteenth century. They thought people's lives were important enough, for whatever reason, to keep precise records of them.

Pani Chruściel gives me a quick lesson in forms and phrases, and we settle into a pleasing mix of Polish and English that has the other two clients in the room looking at us in wonder. "The director of the archives isn't here today, and that is why I can sit with you and help," she confides, tearing through tough, old leather-bound volumes with such gusto that I fear she is going to rip out a page for me at any moment. A colleague comes over to bring more volumes. "This is the assistant director," she nods at her, "but she is my friend, so I can do this." I feel guilty, but we find our first record and she is possessed.

"Evangelical," she says, flipping pages, "Protestants, pass these by. Your people were Catholic, no? I see we even had some Jews living in this little village of Sugajno. Interesting, no?" She flips on.

"Do many Americans come here?"

"Americans, no, rarely Americans, and usually only Jewish. Our clients are German, mostly German. They have to come to Toruń to find their history."

I find an annotation slip of some sort in one of the volumes.

"Oh, the Mormons," she sighs. "We photocopied it all for the Mormons a few years ago for free. Now they *sell* it," she lowers her eyes and looks at me from under her brows.

She flips past more pages. We look for the family name, then the discoveries accumulate, the names of more ancestors, and always the town, Sugajno. It seems there was a Jan Bryszkiewski, the name of my grandmother's father and of the long lost cousin I saw over the weekend, living there for the entire nineteenth century, as far back as we can go.

Jan, my great-grandfather, was born July 1, 1861, "at Sugajno," the son of another Jan (who died June 5, 1896, at the age of seventy-three) and Marianna, nee Kozicka, Bryszkiewska (who died March 21, 1896, less than three months before her husband), and her parents were Jan Kozicki and the former Rozalia Kozlowska. So now I have been introduced to four great-great-grandparents. Farther in, we find that this Jan (or Johann as the German records most often refer to him) was the son of yet another Jan Bryszkiewski, whose wife was Anna Kulkowska, and now I know my great-great-great-grandparents. But that is not all. Pani finds my great-grandmother's birth record as well: Franciszka Jurkiewicz, born July 25, 1863, at Sugajno, the daughter of Franciszek Jurkiewicz and Barbara Szczygłowska, who was the daughter of Antoni Szczygłowski and the former Brygida Czaplinska; another set of great-great-great-grandparents revealed.

My great-grandparents' marriage record is the source of wondrous information. The happy couple's parents' names, their birth dates, their Catholicism, and that they both lived in Sugajno, the little-changed place where I walked only days ago, where I scooped up dirt from the ruins of their home. Jan was "a leaseholder," and they were married in January, 1888; all four of their parents were alive to see the wedding.

As my swift and enthusiastic partner uncovers the record of a second marriage for Barbara Szczygłowska, I remember my grandmother's voice, telling me about this notorious grandmother in her dugout house with her kettles outdoors over a fire and her many husbands, all of whom she outlived.

"I am married twice myself," Pani Chruściel says, "outlived them both. But only one child. Now I have breast cancer." She is not asking for pity and quickly moves on. "But I want to live, you know, and I am fine."

"You have deep roots in Sugajno," Pani tells me. "Back before this, who knows how long they lived there in that same place? There is no record."

The door opens, and our fussy friend ushers in a pack of chattering Germans. "My, my, it looks like International Day in the archive!" Pani Chruściel enthuses. "Oh, but they are only looking for information about bridges," she whispers in English.

We've been turning pages and taking notes for four hours. "I have to have a cigarette," Pani confides and breaks away for a few minutes. Then her mother calls on a mobile phone and wants to know what time she'll be home for dinner.

Before long, Pani finds the birth record of my grandmother's sister, Wanda, who sailed to America with her. "Born February 21, 1893."

"That's odd. She was younger than my grandmother, but my grandmother was born in 1894. She was nineteen, my grandmother twenty, when they sailed for America in 1913, according to the passenger list."

"These records are not wrong," she says, and to make matters more perplexing she finds my grandmother's birth record. "Born 30 August 1891."

"That's impossible. She was born September 6, and the year was 1894. That is what she told me. That is the birthday we celebrated every year. She turned twenty in 1913, and that is on the passenger record."

"What is on the passenger record is what she told them. These records are not wrong," Pani assures me.

My grandmother, my *Busia,* a liar? Yet, I am looking at her birth certificate. "Helena Bryszkiewska, born at Sugajno, 30 August 1891, the daughter of Jan Bryszkiewski and Franciszka Bryszkiewska, nee Jurkiewicz. Father unable to read and write." My grandmother never lied—but then, she was the sweet little old lady in the back seat who got pulled over by Canadian customs after they asked her to tell them where she was born. "I born in a Michigan," she fibbed, just to make the crossing from Michigan easier. After all, Uncle Hank told her she should. Instead, we got detained while they registered her as an "alien" and told her to carry an ID card for the rest of her life.

I suppose my grandmother could have taken a guess at her birth date for the Germans, too—just to have an answer, guessing that she was three years younger than she really was, just to get through the emigration line. Or was it something that just didn't matter? If this was a secret, if she knew that she was not born in 1894, it is a secret she took to her grave.

The hours pass; it's time to close. Pani has spent the whole day sitting with me with the exception of a cigarette break and a lunch break. I pay thirty złoty for photocopies of all of these vital records, about six dollars, and feel that a hint of something extra has been suggested by her attention. I am wrong. When I try to slip her ten dollars, she pulls her hands away and says, "No, oh no, I couldn't take anything. No, just give my regards to America!" And she dashes up a flight of stairs, hanging on to the railing and waving as if ascending the gangplank of an ocean liner.

"There may be more records, you know. They only come to Toruń after they reach a hundred years. These records came to us from Brzozie, and they still have from 1900 on."

I get out my map and see that it is not too far to Brzozie. And I still don't know when my great-grandmother died.

So many little things on my morning errand walk the next day seemed to say that nothing is as it seems. A hot fast car honking at an old man on a bike, the driver screaming, "Get out of the way!" At the cleaners they balked at my hundred-złoty bill, digging deep into their purses for change, exasperated. The new young woman behind the post-office glass rolled her eyes when I could not efficiently explain that my package contained ceramic cemetery portraits for a friend in New York, specially made for him in Brodnica. Even ever-patient Pan Kopiczyński's enthusiasm was low today, and though I got the usual firm handshake, he wasn't up for the ritual dramatic showing of the photos that is standard procedure before I pay.

Fired up by my success in Toruń, I get on the phone. First, to Stanisław Domżalski, the man who owns the land where the ruins of the old Brysz-kiewski house stand. Does he remember the Bryszkiewskis who lived there? No, no, only that they did, but after the war it was sold to the Pawinski fam-ily, and he bought it from them. There is still a daughter, Lila, living in Kosza-lin; perhaps she would remember, he says, or perhaps a family with the unlikely last name of Zero, living in Sugajno, perhaps the father remembers. In any case, I am welcome to walk on his land again and look at this place, he tells me kindly.

A call to the Zero residence yields zero results.

Spurred on by all this phone communication, I decide to try the other side of the family. Perhaps if I cannot find my grandmother's family, I can find her husband's. In the telephone book at the Nowe Miasto Telekomunikacja Pol-ska office, I have located a Danuta Brodacka in Biała Podlaska, a town halfway across Poland. Could it be the same cousin who wrote to her aunt and uncle in America forty years ago asking them for help? I carry a copy of her letter as well.

The phone book for the area looks like a guest list for a family reunion, all the Brodacki names in the United States, Polishized, like a parallel universe. I work up my nerve and pick up the telephone. When I tell her who I am, this Danuta Brodacka is intrigued by my call but tells me she is a Brodacki by mar-riage. Then I mention "Huszcza," the word written on a mysterious photo-graph I brought from home and end her doubt.

"Of course, of course, in Huszcza there will be many relatives," she says confidently. "I don't know the Brodacki family history. I will ask and find out for you," says this cheerful Danuta. She asks me to give her till Tuesday, and she will investigate.

CHAPTER 28
—

What Used to Be Polish

T o the market today for cauliflower, ripening now in enormous, clean white heads embraced by the greenest cabbagey leaves imaginable. The plums, too, are ripe. I ask the laughing farmer not to tear the tops off my carrots, so I can savor their fresh smell a bit longer.

On the way to the bank I pass an old woman walking, carefully escorted by a teenage boy. She looks so much like my grandmother—toothless, her wrinkled face encircled by a floral babushka—I want to stop her, hug her, and tell her I am home here with her. Alas, common sense gets the better of me.

"Some plums for you and a cauliflower," I offer as I enter the wine shop, but Pani Wituchowska has other things on her mind. There is a rose in a small vase in the window.

"Oh, that German," says Pani, half delighted and half disgusted. "He's been back every day! Saturday he brought me a rose, then it dried out, and he brought me another." Her eyes are twinkling, and she keeps lapsing into German, then correcting herself with pride at her fluency. "But he's overdoing it—always more, more, more," she protests, laughing, her hands creating an imaginary volcanic eruption. "But he is a nice man. He thought you were a relative to me."

"I think I'm a little jealous," I tease.

At such comments Pani merely laughs.

Oh, but the real story of the day is not the effusions of her German admirer. Today, Pani says, two men kissed in her store.

"Why, they were two very nice-looking, well-dressed men, as a matter of fact, from Switzerland, you know, where they make the clocks and watches," she explains.

"They were shopping for wine right over there," she points to the other portion of her L-shaped counter, "and they were talking just as nice as could be, and I turned around, and the shorter one looked up at the taller one with such admiring eyes and then gave him a kiss on the mouth. I asked them if they were brothers, and do you know what they told me?"

"No, what did they tell you?"

"They said, 'No, we are not brothers, we are married.' Well, I have never seen this before. Of course I heard about it, but I have never seen this before—two men."

"So now you have seen everything?" I bait her.

"Yes, I guess you could say I have," she laughs, "but I don't understand it. They offered me a box of candy. I know they were doing this everywhere they traveled because they reached into a big carton that held boxes of candy and pulled one out for me, but when I saw what they were doing, I reached here." She points to a box of Merci chocolates on the shelf behind her. "And I opened it up, and I offered it to them. I didn't want their chocolates anyway. Who knows, I might catch that disease," she shrugs with a half-laugh. "They had such a big beautiful car parked outside."

"I don't think you'll catch a disease from a box of Swiss chocolates," I assure her.

"That's not the point. They were so surprised when I offered them chocolates they didn't know what to say, but I think I was the first one to turn down their gift. I don't need people from Switzerland giving me chocolates. We have chocolate here, too. Switzerland was neutral during the war," she scoffs, "neutral, you know, meaning you make a lot of money while people die, without officially being on the side of their murderers.

"But kissing in public like that. I just don't like it. Two men," she pouts. "But really, women are the worst. I told you, they climb all over the men. And what is the man supposed to do?" She does a little imitation of a woman crawling all over a man.

"Do you think it's against God's natural law, two men?" I ask.

Pani pauses with that one. "No, no, maybe not. People are what they are. I told you we have lesbians here. Just not in public and not marching and carrying signs. It's not religion. People do what they want; they always have. Let them do it all in private. They had to kiss again on the way out the door! Enough already." Then that reminds Pani of the lovemaking she has seen on television. "I told you if I had only known the possibilities when I was young! But I was so virtuous. Untouched on my wedding night. And my husband did not jump all over me. Three weeks it was before it happened, and then three years before my son was born."

Pani Wituchowska remembers a time when she and her husband, before the war, went to the Moulin Rouge in Paris. "There was a handsome man, a very handsome man, came over and asked my husband if he could dance with me. He thought I was his daughter, you see. Usually my husband wasn't jealous, but this time he said no, that I already had this dance with him." She remembers a time when she played the piano for a group of soldiers. "Ty jesteś słońcem." She begins singing, "You are the sun." The tune is "It's Now or Never," and we sing it together in English and Polish and Italian, "O Sole Mio."

If I've implied that Pani Wituchowska gets all misty eyed and filled with self-pity when she tells her stories, that would be the opposite of how she is. Instead she is filled with laughter and joy and a kind of gratitude because she has had exactly the life she has had and no other.

I head back home with my string bag full of food from the open-air market, so I decide to make dinner for Pani Wituchowska. I call and ask if she is amenable. Yes, she says, a bit stunned when I propose to bring it all to her house.

Pani has been curious about my cooking, so I go home and simmer another kiełbasa with garlic in a bottle of her dark red wine from Bulgaria. The aroma fills the house. Those fresh carrots are calling for orange juice and a little grated peel. Since Pani's doctor says she must eat tomatoes, which she dislikes, I make a sauce with them, chopped and seeded.

When I get to her door, she chides me for getting my hair cut. "Where are your curls?" she demands.

Pani takes the food but stops on the way to the kitchen. "This is the first time a man has ever brought me dinner, but it's Friday, you know. Michał reminded me that I cannot eat this kiełbasa today." She sets all the food aside, pulls out two little stools from under the little scrubbed kitchen counter. "I'll save it all for tomorrow. For today I have made some potato pancakes. That is what I eat on Friday."

"I believe in tradition," she says, "even when the church itself no longer does."

Soon Pani is back to teasing me, off on another story graphically illustrated. This one is about a foolish, local married man who fell for a sexy younger

What Used to Be Polish
—

woman in his employ. She acts out the story, switching from role to role and laughing. The man, stiff and vulnerable, the woman with her skirt hiked up to the tops of her thighs. She mocks a sexy come-on by twisting her shoulders and unbuttoning a center button on her blouse. "And what is the man supposed to do?"

I, Pan Pączek, and Adam, Pan Sznurek—Mr. Doughnut and Mr. String—must be her new favorites, for with me she cannot make enough jokes about him; and with him, who knows?

Little Mysteries Unraveling

"Yes, they remember your grandfather. Was his wife named Helena? Did they have two children, Łucja and Stanisław?"

Danuta Brodacka has been asking questions for me in Biała Podlaska and Huszcza—and she's been getting answers.

"There was a Michał and there was a Piotr, who went to Canada," she says over the telephone. "There are many photographs."

"My grandfather's brothers?" I inquire.

"He had a brother Czesław?" she asks.

"Yes, I am sure he did," I confirm.

"Czesław had a son, and his son's wife is living in Huszcza. Their son lives there, too. They have a photograph of your grandparents with baby Łucja and little boy Stanisław" (my mother, Lucy, and my Uncle Stan).

Racing through my mind is the number of times my mother bemoaned the fact that there were no pictures of her as a child. The oldest ones we had were her First Holy Communion pictures at age eleven and another at about twelve, already looking like a young lady, shy and sad, beneath a straw, flapper-style hat with her sisters Mary and Agnes and brother Henry. Can it be this simple? Can you come looking almost a hundred years after your grandfather left, make a phone call, and find a picture of your mother that no one in America has ever seen?

"So if you would like to come to Biała Podlaska and meet your family, we would welcome you," says this warm and generous in-law. "The Danuta Brodacka whose letters you have lives in Sandomierz. They told me she used to write letters for Czesław, and they still have the letters they received in reply."

I am stunned, we make a tentative date, I promise to check the train schedules and call her back. So many questions, the most perplexing of all is how the connection was severed—and in my lifetime. I can only guess at the many reasons. I have to tell someone, so I call my Aunt Mary in New Jersey. Together we put together a few more pieces. My grandfather's brother Peter (Piotr) emigrated to Canada, she is sure. Another brother, Walter (Władysław), married a British woman and went to England. Their cousin Mike moved to Canada, too, and in those days you could clear and develop land there, and it was yours for practically nothing. They all Anglicized their first names. As she remembers it, there was a brother Chester (Czesław), who stayed behind in Poland.

My Uncle Bogdan has helped Mary understand the odd news that her mother was nearly three years older than we spent our lives believing, that name days and not birthdays were celebrated in Poland, and there was no annual "Now you are two, now you are three, now you are four" ritual. She is shocked that her grandparents were illiterate.

Aunt Mary also remembers her great uncle, Stanisław Jurkiewicz, who took the girls to America. "He was a talker," she recalls. "He loved to tell stories, and he was quite fat and would eat an entire chicken in one sitting."

"I don't know why everything was cut off the way it was," my aunt finally tells me. "I just don't remember what happened." Neither did my mother.

What I remember is that after her husband died, my grandmother fixated on her children and their weddings and their children, and most of all on me, and she could not look back. She had nothing to give back.

"It was supposed to be a quiet weekend, and look!" Grażyna says, back at the *Gazeta* office. She hands me the latest edition. A two-level coop collapsed on a turkey farm, and just when they thought that was the biggest story, a little boy drowned in the Drwęca, and Ryszard and Grażyna spent the weekend writing and talking to the grieving family. "Every year," Ryszard says, "every year somebody forgets how powerful that river can be."

"The mayor is going to look into the state of the church archives," says Ryszard, "but he'll have his job cut out for him." He sits down to write a story about the German children of extradited parents and grandparents who are in Nowe Miasto to learn about their history. "It's like Poles going to Vilnius," he acknowledges. "Everyone has to go east for history since the borders of Poland went west after the war."

"Nalej wódki," Grażyna mutters to Ryszard when I appear restless. "Pour him some vodka." She puts her nose back to the grindstone. Ryszard is throwing down shots, some plain, some mixed with orange juice, and I have never seen a happier man, though I have never seen either of them anything like inebriated.

"Do you know how wire was invented?" Ryszard asks, about to reveal a stereotype about what tightwads live in Kraków. "Two men from Kraków couldn't let go of ten *grosz*." He imitates two men pulling on the equivalent of a dime and stretching it between them. "That is how wire was invented."

Grażyna sits at her desk with paper spread everywhere, while Ryszard and I chortle and drink and forget what we are saying in midsentence.

Then into the office wanders the town bum, looking for bottles and cans and wanting to kiss Grażyna. He seems like a harmless lost soul. He announces that Tina Turner is coming to Sopot, and everyone is momentarily transfixed. Then they give him some cans and a shot of vodka and send him on his way. "I'm working," says Grażyna, pulling her hand away as he tries to plant his lips on it. Ryszard hides his trail with a spray can of air freshener.

"Whenever I am with you," Grażyna says to me with feigned suspicion, "he always seems to appear."

Ryszard launches into a story about his father and the priest he hid from the Nazis during the war. With great sadness and drama he announces, "This is something I have never told before. This is a big secret." He shakes his head in sorrow. "He had a child, you know, with my father's sister while he was hiding with the family."

"And what happened to the child?" I ask.

"Oh, he is living not far from here. We never see him." Ryszard says blithely. Then we are off on another topic. One of the office workers wants to know if I smoked marijuana in the sixties, and everyone is awed when I tell them I saw Janis Joplin in concert. "Ooo," they all gush at once.

Ryszard pulls out a photograph of a mushroom that weighed a kilo and had a cap thirty centimeters wide, found in the woods while I was gone. "But no wild mushrooms will ever appear in the stores or market," he says, "people keep them all for themselves."

"If you want to see what a girl really looks like, look at her mother at fifty," Ryszard says for no reason.

"Give him another vodka," Grażyna mutters with a smile, "and one for you."

Little Mysteries Unraveling
—

"Let him go," says Ryszard. "Madame is waiting."

When I arrive an hour and a half after the appointed time, Pani Wituchow-ska is ready to give me a good scolding. "Everything is cold," she grumbles with exaggerated exasperation.

"It wasn't my fault," I plead.

"My husband used to say, 'One must be punctual,' and an hour before we had to be anywhere, he was pacing at the front door. Humph," she lowers her shoulders in a dramatic pout.

"And I had to have not one, but two cognacs, while waiting so long," she winks and giggles, throwing herself back in her chair.

"So now that's enough of that. We eat. While I am getting everything warmed up, you wanted an old picture. Here." And she steps into the next room to fetch her envelopes of snapshots. "You look at these while I am in the kitchen."

And there she is again at sixteen, gazing into a bouquet, and during the war looking like a partisan in a tailored coat with her hair swept up, and in her wedding photo.

"All dead, except this one, this one, and this one," she points out, her arm around me, the better to see the photo, before leaving the room.

Dinner is another two courses; platters filled with carefully arranged servings of soft vegetables, potatoes, mushrooms, escallops of chicken, then beef roulades on the second platter. "Eat, eat," she urges, dashing back and forth from the kitchen. Finally she sits with me and sails into her favorite topics.

Adam, Pan Sznurek, she laughs, Mr. String: "The man just wants to be pampered and caressed by a woman, to lie there and be taken care of."

Her husband, the country gentleman: "Only days before he died, he stood shouting in the Rynek for an end to communism, then asked, 'Why don't these trees grow all the way to heaven?'"

Her son and constant advisor: "Such a smart man he turned out to be. He'll call at nine o'clock to check on me and see which boxes of candy sold this week and which didn't."

The war and the offers she had from the Germans.

The Russians and all that they took after the war.

Pan Świniarski: "He brought sex tapes over for me to watch once and broke the video cassette player trying to shove them in. A good man, good man, but talks like he has a mouthful of marbles."

"Maybe because he has no teeth?" I inquire.

"No, no, he talked that way when he had teeth," she assures me.

Her shop: "It doesn't make enough money to pay the electric bill, but for forty years we couldn't have this store, and now, by God, we are going to have it. I have been offered fourteen hundred złoty a month to rent it. More than my entire retirement pension, but I won't let it go."

Her cousin in Toruń: "His son is an opportunist and never visited his grand-mother when she was ill. I won't have the son in my house! Look at him, the little boy on his father's lap in my wedding picture." She hands me the photo-graph, a sweet child in knee pants.

"Couldn't it be the father's fault just a little bit?" I suggest.

"All this familiarity. Children calling their parents 'ty.' 'You, give me that; you, buy me that.' It's not for me. My son still never calls me 'ty'; I am 'mama' to him. No 'ty' for me, I am 'Madame.'"

Tonight, wine will not do for Madame. She is pouring vodka: two, three, then another shot. "Jak się Polacy rozchodzili, to jeszcze po jednym wypili," she says. "When Poles meet, there's always one more drink." Then there is brandy, and she is laughing and telling me how strong she can be and stroking my bare arm and tugging at my sleeve.

"My uncle, the priest, had hemorrhoids," she announces suddenly with glee. "They hurt so bad he couldn't sit. I just went right in there and took care of them," she says, making, to my shock, a sort of massaging-stuffing gesture with her hands. "The neighbor girl had such a cyst on her rump, she was al-ways sitting with one buttock up in the air. Finally I asked her if I could see what the problem was, and I took care of it. Such stuff you never saw. Doesn't bother me. Nursed my mother, my husband, my brother. Just seems normal and necessary to me."

"You could have been a good doctor. I don't think I could do such things so easily," I squirm.

"Oh, yes, a good doctor, a very good doctor. You would be under good care with me. Bathed, cleaned, fed." She goes into the kitchen to show me a cal-endar, the day her mother died: March 26, 1981. "It was the time of the Byd-goszcz incident, when they beat members of Solidarity. This has hung since the day she died. We stopped the clocks for a year, closed up the piano. In fact, the piano has not been tuned since."

Then we must have a course of sausages with mustard and then ice cream with triangles of wafer sticking out of it at fancy angles. "For such a meal you need a waiter," I suggest.

"Yes, a waiter, not a waitress. Women, I don't need a woman." She makes a soft spit to the side.

"Your tomatoes, I must tell you, I couldn't eat them. They were so spicy," she says.

Little Mysteries Unraveling

—

"That was so you wouldn't taste the tomatoes. You don't like them." I explain my fairly mild tomato sauce.

"No, can't do it. Your mushroom sauce in wine was good, but I had to chop up the mushrooms some more." And that is the end of her food critique. Nothing about my carrots. She is clearly not looking for a cook.

Now it's time to take my blood pressure, but the machine won't give us a proper reading. "Maybe I am not living," I suggest.

"Maybe you eat too much hot food. You know, they say a man who eats too much hot food, doesn't want, well, you know." She smiles and hides her face and rests her head on my shoulder.

It is past midnight now and time for me to go.

"We have a special confidence," Pani whispers. "You can tell me anything, and it's between us."

Pani swings herself in front of the piano, her energy reaching a new pitch. "I must play you this song, just to show you I can play." And she plays on the out-of-tune upright "It's Now or Never," but the words in Polish are "Słońcem to jesteś ty"—"You are the sun." And then a waltz, and afterward she pounds a single key that makes no sound. "You see, you see, it is so out of tune." One more time, and she is lifting her shoulders and looks up at her own portrait. "She was beautiful, no?" she gushes.

Yes, and she is beautiful, very much alive and warm and full of life and longing.

"You came along twenty years too late," she says. "Or maybe I should say you were born twenty years too late." It's time to say goodnight.

CHAPTER 30
—

What Took You So Long?

S unday morning feels like a good day for another drive through the linden canopy to the little wooden church in Boleszyn. As they have for a thousand summers, crops are ripening, the corn is tasseled. A week of intermittent rain seems to have washed everything clean, time for a fresh try at getting through to relatives in Sugajno. Speeding down this road I can run away from the approaching end of my little life in Poland. Time is running short.

I am too early, however. The mass is at ten thirty. At ten, not a car is in the lot, not a person in sight. So I pass the church and head for the cemetery. A group of people is leaving; a lone man heads in through the gates.

Perhaps one last look at the only Bryszkiewski grave I have found—Jan and Anna, with no birth or death dates, no record in the church archives. The same graves my mother and I saw in 1988 and concluded were those of my grandmother's brother and his wife. As I stand and look at the grave, it suddenly occurs to me that there are flowers on it. They are plastic and a bit faded and worse for the wear, but they surely have been here no longer than six months. I scold myself: Why haven't you been more aggressive? Why not just stand in the middle of town and yell "Bryszkiewski"? Why not ask the man walking here ten feet away from you?

So I work up my nerve and my Polish. By now I have told the I-am-an-American-my-grandmother-was-born-here story so many times that when I end with an apology for my bad Polish people invariably tell me, as this man does, "No, no, your Polish is excellent!"

"Do you happen to know anything about these people?" I ask, glancing down at the Bryszkiewski grave.

The man is somewhere in his sixties, sturdy and serious, checking a gravesite just across the path. He walks my way and glances at the flat tombstone covering the Bryszkiewski grave. "Yes, of course I know these people. They are relatives."

I can hardly believe my ears. "If they are your relatives, I may be your relative, too, for I am quite sure this is my grandmother's brother."

He smiles a generous, closed-mouth smile that changes his stern cemetery look to a warm, inquisitive gaze; his hand reaches for mine. "Teodor Wrzosek. Anna was my aunt, my father's sister. We must talk, we must talk," he says. "I was on my way to mass. Come, and afterward you can come to my house. It's next to the store around the corner." He seems as excited as I to have stumbled upon a relative from America.

"What a day. I never go to the cemetery, but for some reason today something said, 'Go!'" he exclaims.

"And the same with me. Maybe God was looking at us." I explain that I had all but given up on finding any more relatives, that finding the living Jan Bryszkiewski and his family was as far as I had gotten, and our relationship is quite distant.

"We'll figure it all out, I assure you," he says. "You are with family now."

Inside the church he stands in the vestibule with other solitary men. When I suggest that I would like to be a bit closer to the altar, he orders me to open the door to the choir loft and ascend the steep stairs for a better view. "Of course you can go up there. Go, go, it's not a problem."

Father Jank is hearing confessions in the open confessional, where a young woman kneels at his side and whispers into the wooden screen that separates her from the priest. Nine altar boys in lacey white tunics are readying the stage. The organ hums, and all around me voices emerge, and I am in the front row with a perfect view. On either side of me men pray, their large scrubbed hands clasped together in front of them.

How odd it seems—to have given up on relatives, to have come with just a handful of old photographs and a few old letters and be unable to put names to these faces. Can this man really just show up in the cemetery and be the key?

Father Jank's voice is gruff and strained today, as if his tongue were strapped to an anvil. The altar boys fight with their lace as they clang bells again for five minutes nonstop. The lesson from the gospels is the miracle of the loaves and fishes. The men to my sides nod and try not to look me in the eye during the gesture of peace that substitutes for the handshake of American churches. It seems comforting somehow to be in this little church, the gold-and-silver painted statues and woodwork gleaming all around, to be in a place that five minutes ago started to seem like somewhere I belonged.

After mass, Pan Wrzosek is waiting for me at the gate and sweeps me away before the two men nearby can ask who I am. I think he wants me to be his own private discovery, wants desperately for me to be a relative.

"But he is not your blood relative," his wife, Krystyna, insists to her disappointed husband who has already given me a tour of the store his son has run for three years, introduced me to his daughter-in-law, who tells me she had heard that I was talking to Pani Lubieniecka down the road some time back but didn't know who I was looking for. "Bryszkiewski, Bryszkiewski," her father-in-law says. "They should all have been able to tell him."

A box of old photographs appears at the table, and within minutes Teodor and Krystyna are both rattling off the names of every person in the old photos I'm carrying in my bag. We establish quickly that his father's sister Anna married my grandmother's brother Jan. "So we are not blood relatives, but you are among family. Their daughter lives in Gwiździny: Marianna. She is eighty years old. You can meet her. We'll take you this afternoon."

"Don't we have to call?" I ask.

He looks at me like I'm crazy and says, "She'll be home."

Pani Krystyna serves lunch—cheese, bread, cold cuts, herring. "On Sunday she does not cook," explains Pan Teodor. I am thinking of the young face in the old photograph, a face I have stared at for half a century without knowing who she was, a gentle face tilted to the right, with a teardrop earring dangling from the left ear, shoulders supporting the straps of a jumper with buttons down the center over a striped blouse with a bow. Her hair is pulled off her face in three finger waves and swept back behind her ears in a large bun across the back of her head. She is smiling modestly behind sad, gentle eyes. "Who is this woman?" I wondered as I packed these pictures for my trip to Poland. Now I am about to meet her. I could not have imagined that she was still alive.

Gwiździny is just east of the road I have taken now a dozen times between Nowe Miasto and Boleszyn. Pan Teodor is driving my Maluch and doing a better job of it than I. "Practice," he says, "we all drove these things." His wife is in the back seat.

We pull up to a row of some of the ugliest of the barrack-style housing I have yet seen in Poland. Gray, shabby cement blocks, their yards a patchwork of weedy gardens, guarded by three men sitting on the stoop. "Let me go in first," says Pan Teodor.

"She is not well," he says when he returns to the car. "Her daughter says she is having a hard time sitting up today. But we must come in. She says we must come in."

Then a young woman with dark curls framing her thin face approaches. "Jola," she says, smiling. "And what do I call you? Uncle? Cousin?" She plants three kisses on alternating sides of my face. "Welcome. Welcome. I could not imagine. . . ." She looks into my eyes.

"I saw you in *Gazeta Nowomiejska*. I remember now." She cannot stop talking. "Living in Nowe Miasto, looking for relatives. But they did not say 'Bryszkiewski' in the paper. If only they had said the name, I would have known. I never dreamed it was us you were looking for."

Jola ushers me into the living room. It's a tidy, clean little home with an enormous set of cabinets and a sort of entertainment center dominating the living room. On the couch lies an old lady, her swollen stomach and her legs covered with a blanket.

"Mama, sit up, come and meet your cousin from America," says Jola.

The old woman moans softly, but soon she is standing, holding her daughter's arm. There is no doubt, for Pani Marianna Szczygłowska's face is the face of the young girl, my grandmother's niece, in the picture, covered with fine lines and framed by a thick mat of white hair. She holds my face between her hands. "From America," she whispers. "Who could imagine I would meet you. It's so long, so long. I have forgotten everything." She seems to know she is about to be questioned.

I sit next to her on the sofa. She holds my hand. Jola stands next to her, putting pieces together. "You were here—in Boleszyn—a long time ago, in the cemetery, asking about Bryszkiewskis. It was you!" Jola exclaims.

"Yes," I tell her, "but how do you know? Twelve years ago my mother and I were here for an afternoon in Boleszyn, then Nowe Miasto, and then we had to go back to Warsaw. The two women my mother talked to in the cemetery seemed to be saying there were relatives living here, but some distance away. I thought I had found them when I found Jan Bryszkiewski."

"Pani Gabriela," Jola says to her mother, then turns to me. "It was Pani Gabriela. What's the matter with her? She should have told you his daughter lived just up the road." So I am given to understand that our stop in a taxi for a few minutes a dozen years ago made local news and is remembered even to this day.

CHAPTER 31

—

"What about this distant cousin Jan who lives in Sugajno? Do you know how many of his photos I've looked through trying to find you?" I tell them.

The families maintain no connection, says Jola. "Still, he too should have known." She shakes her head incredulously.

"Oh," Pani Marianna moans, pulling her leg toward her in pain. "Twelve years ago. You should have come twelve years ago. How good I felt. How I loved to talk. I could have met my cousin."

It is then I have to hold back the tears. How my mother too would have loved to meet this woman, her first cousin. How they would have talked. Born, as it turns out, in the same year, 1919. Her father Jan and my grandmother were brother and sister.

The memories come back to her in spurts. When I mention a name, she remembers. "But not Aunt Helena, not Wanda. I don't remember them. They were gone to America before I was born." Now and then she clutches my hand or touches my face, tells me I must call her *ciocia,* aunt, not Pani. She is such a gentle soul and in such pain.

Her family begins to arrive to meet this American cousin. Soon the room is filled with chatter and questions. My head spins. I cannot keep up. I try to take notes. I am so astonished I can barely remember anything, but the whole family is fascinated by the information I have dug up in Toruń and in the Bo leszyn rectory.

My new aunt's first memory of an uncle is the murder of my grandmother's brother Władysław at a party in 1933. She was fourteen. "It was a brawl, with more than a little alcohol making the rounds," she recalls. "He was engaged to a Dąbrowski girl. What I remember hearing is how she had a premonition that something was wrong. When they came to tell her, she had been pacing the floors, unable to sleep."

"What happened to the man who killed your uncle?" Jola says.

Ciocia Marianna thinks for a long time. "Nothing, I think, nothing. He hadn't meant to kill him; he didn't use his hands. Nothing I think. Only that no one would touch his hands after that; no one would shake his hand."

She remembers what she can of her aunts and uncles. Albin, he died long before the war. Teodor, she smiles, yes, Teodor. Nikodema died during the war. Janina, the bride in my old photographs, Uncle Franciszek's "orphan," was really his sister's daughter, whom he found living in squalor, sleeping in a pig pen. "He took her away, took care of her, made sure she had a good life and a proper wedding." Władysława, even the children know the story of Pilarz, her husband, "who wanted to be a farmer but didn't know anything about farming."

What Took You So Long?
—

Yes, Marianna remembers her grandparents' farm. Yes, it is the ruin I have been to see. Yes, I have my grandmother's brothers and sisters straight. But still we cannot establish who the Jan was who is supposed to have died in the First World War. She doesn't remember and is confused by the idea that there were two sons named Jan. No, her father was Jan. Then who was the Jan who died in the war? Perhaps it was really Albin. She cannot say.

More old pictures are brought forward, along with children for me to meet, the grandchildren, many now in their teens. The old photographs contain no pictures of my grandmother's brothers and sisters, no pictures of the old house. Marianna does not remember ever seeing the pictures I have brought with me. "They were sent to America."

We wonder as a group for a while why the connection was severed. I recall that after the war we were not rich, and my grandmother was perhaps ashamed that she did not have more to offer. "My earliest memory of relatives in Poland," I remember, "is sitting by the kitchen table watching a big box being packed with clothes and such."

"And I remember receiving the box," says Marianna. "You are right, we did wonder why, why there wasn't more, why they forgot about us. Those were hard times. We had so little."

"After my grandfather died, my grandmother seemed to think only of her children. She didn't want to look back," I try to explain, "and it took all of her life and most of her children's lives working hard so that their children, I and my twenty-two cousins, could have something today." My new relatives almost seem to disbelieve me when I tell them my mother never had a vacation day, holiday, or retirement pension in her entire working life.

Marianna groans and tries to adjust her leg. Her daughter Jadzia massages it for her and tells her she must walk. "The doctor says the less she walks, the worse the pain will be."

"But I can't. I can't," says the old woman. "I should go for the operation. I should go. I cannot live with this pain."

The operation would be hip replacement, they tell me. It costs a lot of money, says Jola, a lot of money, or you get in line and wait. How much money? They tell me 2,500 złoty—about $625. I am already thinking about how I can help, but the sons-in-law are whispering to me about her age, her health, the trauma of surgery, one day she wants it, the next she doesn't.

The sisters bring me photos of their grandfather's funeral, Jan Bryszkiewski, my grandmother's brother, in his casket outside the old house. He died in January, 1962. The mourners are all wrapped in coats and scarves, her brother

Franciszek among them, wearing circle-shaped black glasses. I was in junior high school. If she knew about it, my grandmother never said a word about her brother's death.

Marianna points to Franciszek. "Remember, in those days we were communists, whether we wanted it or not. Uncle Franciszek wanted it. He believed it was the best for laborers, and he was an organizer in the coal mines and a friend of Gomułka. I don't want to say it, but Ciocia Helena told him not to write to her anymore. She was afraid."

The odd uniform my grandmother's brother wore for the wedding photo in my briefcase, they tell me, was the uniform of a communist labor organizer, not a railroad conductor, as I once imagined. Franciszek and brother Teodor spent time in France in the mines, but no one can recall what became of Teodor. "As far as we know," Marianna says, "that is where he stayed and had a wife and children."

I ponder what I've just heard; it explains so much. Władysław Gomułka, first secretary of the Communist Party at the height of McCarthyism in America.

"Come on, let's go for a walk," I coax my new aunt. She manages a weak smile and doesn't say no. Arm in arm we walk toward her room. She is so tired.

The family urges me to go with them to Bratian to meet more family, Marianna's daughter Wiesia and husband and children. Cousin Jadzia's son Bartek rides in the car with me. He is sixteen and shy about English but is studying it in school and knows rather a lot. "But we never speak in school," he says. "We only write."

In Bratian I am swept into a family cookout—sausage, potato salad, bread, sweets. Wiesia greets me with silent awe. The men folk can't get enough of me. Somehow we manage conversations about politics, sex, and religion.

The Clinton sex scandal: "Nonsense. Who cares?" they tell me.

The Second World War: "What kind of justice is it that Germany, Japan, and Israel got all of America's money and Poland got communism?"

Life in Poland: "We are not rich people, but we get along. Who doesn't want to have more?"

I get a tour of the pigpen and a serving of smoked ham. "This is not bought in a store," says Jadzia's husband, Stefan. "Oink, oink," emanates from the shed behind him. Everyone is smiling and looking at me, and it's time for a photograph.

As the evening ends, rain is blowing in unexpectedly from the Baltic Sea, delivering cool breezes from Scandinavia.

Everyone in Poland, my new family no exception, seems to have read

What Took You So Long?
—

Bolesław Prus's classic novel *The Doll*. As I fall asleep trying to figure out a way to hold on to these new relations, I read, "The worst loneliness is not the one that surrounds a man, but the emptiness within himself."

"Now I understand," thinks Prus's doomed hero, Wokulski, "why visiting a church intensifies faith. Here everything is arranged so as to remind us of eternity."

A Young Man and His Needlepoint

⊶——⊷

"**Y**ou must meet Basia; you must come to Iława." When we ran out of time on Sunday, Cousin Jadzia Wiśniew-ska, Marianna's daughter, urged me not to stop meeting them, now that I had found my Bryszkiewski family. "No need to worry about when, just come. No need to make appointments."

"But I will call," I promise. My questions sorted out, names written down, and brain spinning a little less, I attend to my morning errands. Ryszard and Grażyna spot me on the sidewalk and pull over to ask me where I've been. "You missed the music on Sunday." I show them the picture of my mother's first cousin, Marianna, and tell them how Cousin Jola saw my picture in *Gazeta Nowomiejska* but never imagined it was her family I was looking for. "The name," Grażyna calls to me as I head out the door, "one of the three questions should have been your grandmother's name!"

Jadzia's son Waldek answers the phone. "Just come," he says. "Now is fine. We are here." I have the map his brother Bartek drew for me when we met at his grandmother's house.

Cousin Jadzia warned me that "we live in one of those blocks," but this one is even larger and uglier than her mother's in Gwiździny. Squeezed into a res-idential area full of houses that belonged to German families before World War II, when this town was beyond the Polish border, outside what was known as the Polish Corridor to the Baltic Sea.

Bartek is waiting for me in the parking lot. Gentle and soft spoken, all smiles, both shy and confident. "Better lock the car," he says. "You never know around here." He flashes a smile. He and Waldek both resemble their mother, with their square faces and toothy smiles.

The halls to the apartment are dirty, neglected, shabby. Graffiti greets me on the doorway to a lower level. On the other side of the brand-new, natural wood-paneled door is another world—small but cozy, clean and comfortable. Jadzia is working in the kitchen canning marmalade for winter.

I present them with a small confection; Jadzia slices it and places it on a plate with her own cakes, which are prettier and tastier than the store-bought gift. "You shouldn't have," she says. "I didn't want to come empty handed," I reply.

Jadzia shows me around the apartment. "It's small," she says. Two bed-rooms—one for mother and father, the other for the three boys. The eldest son is in the army now, and Waldek sits at a computer he has left with the family. He joins us at the table of sweets and coffee this smiling second cousin has laid out for me. "We love sweets here, but of course I am not supposed to eat them," Jadzia says. She is overweight and has high cholesterol. The task before us is for me to get everyone's name straight, but I want to dig a little deeper into what became of my grandmother's brothers and sisters. "For that we will see Basia; she's the oldest and has more pictures," says Jadzia.

Above the smaller of two sixties-style nylon couches in the living room, there is a cross-stitch of the face of Jesus. "You like it?" Jadzia asks. "Bartek made it. It's his hobby. He'll make you one. A present." She and Bartek take me back to the boys' room, where he shows me an identical cross-stitch half done.

"He was a little embarrassed, you know, because usually girls like to do this sort of thing." Jadzia never stops smiling, showing off several gold teeth, and I see my grandmother in her face—the smile Busia gave to me when I watched her pump the old treadle sewing machine and begged her to let me try, the smile she gave to me when I learned to hook rugs, the way she did.

It's a short walk across Iława to Basia Tafel's apartment in a slightly less bleak housing block. We settle into her living room with husband Stanisław, daughter Renata, and son-in-law Eugeniusz and their son Krystian and new baby daughter Wiktoria.

Basia looks like a younger, slightly rounder version of her mother, with a generous face and more gold teeth. We take to one another at once. She is ready to tell me stories.

Perhaps the most surprising one is how well she remembers her Uncle Franciszek, my grandmother's brother. He was married twice and emigrated to France for a period, where some of his children and grandchildren may still live, but she is not sure. He visited often when she was a child and had a retirement pension from France, Basia recalls. His first wife, Józefa, died in France. His second wife, Emilja (of grandma's old photos), had her children in France. Yes, he was an organizer in the coal mines in Wałbrzych and spent his last years there without his wife. Basia remembers that he had a hemorrhage and was in the hospital in Nowe Miasto for six weeks. They brought him coffee, and he recovered enough to return to Wałbrzych and live another five years until 1974, two years after his sister Helena died in America.

Basia repeats the story of the infamous murder of Władysław Bryszkiewski and adds to the tale her explanation of how he could possibly have been hit over the head with a goat, as I read the church record. A *koza,* she laughs, is also slang for a sawhorse. "It was a fight over a girl, everyone knew that. It is also true that nothing happened to the man who killed him; he didn't mean to kill him. He was sorry. But I remember that my grandfather, even though he was a kind man, could never forgive him and refused to shake his hand when he offered it. He had killed his brother, after all."

Basia also sets me straight about how my grandmother's sister Nikodema died. It was in childbirth, during the war, with her third child. Her husband, Piotrowicz was his name, deserted from the German army and grieved so much for his wife that he finally went into the attic and hanged himself. It was then that Nikodema's brother, Franciszek, took the daughters, Janina and Felicja to Wałbrzych and raised them as his own. Janina still lives there. She has pictures of her with her son, when they visited Iława not so many years ago. So the Janina Kułak, my grandmother's niece, whose wedding is described in the old letter in my briefcase, whose picture I carried with me from America, is alive and well and living along with two sons, Aleksander and Janusz.

My grandmother's brother Jan, Basia's grandfather, had seven children. The first was Jadwiga Igielska, born in 1917 and died in 1997, but she was her mother Anna's daughter from her first marriage. Her picture is also in my briefcase. They are all amazed when I pull it out. The next child was Marianna, their mother, then a son Jan, born in 1922 and died in 1993, they believe. He emigrated to Germany, where his three children live now. They have lost touch with them. The next son born was their Uncle Franciszek in 1923; he is the debonair young man in another photo in my bag, the young man named after his uncle, who wrote to his Uncle Antoni and Aunt Helena in America and sent them his wedding photo. He died a few years ago but had seven children who live somewhere near London. Anna was the next child, named after her mother and also in my old photograph. She was born in 1927 and died

A Young Man and His Needlepoint

—

of a heart attack in 1996. Next was Łucja, born in 1929, married a Mikuczeń-ski, and lives in Kurzętnik; they point her out in another old photo. The youngest was Feliksa, born in 1934, "just ten years older than I," says Basia. Feliksa is the sweet young girl with the communion candle in another photograph. She is now Feliksa Licznerska and lives in Nowe Miasto. I must meet her, they tell me.

Basia remembers when she and Feliksa waited for their fathers to come home after the war. Feliksa's father, Basia's grandfather, returned first, and when they both rushed up to Jan Bryszkiewski, Feliksa jealously told her to wait for her own father, Marianna's husband, Teofil, to return.

The house in Jan and Anna Bryszkiewski's funeral pictures was torn down, and the land purchased by Teodor Wrzosek's brother. It is not the house my grandmother was born in; rather, the other Bryszkiewski cousins were correct in the site they showed me, Basia confirms what her mother has told me.

Basia also remembers tales of her great-great-grandmother Basia, Barbara, who had not three but six husbands, outlived them all, and was famous for her tiny feet, "so small they would fit in the hole made by a fencepost."

"Both your father and grandfather fought in World War II?" I inquire.

"Yes, but my grandfather fought with Anders." General Władysław Anders led the Polish Second Corps in the Allied invasion of Italy. Her grandfather was with Anders while his son-in-law fought on the opposite side.

"Your mother's first cousins from America fought with the Allies, too," I tell her. "Great Aunt Helena sent two sons to fight in Europe, in the invasion of Italy."

We fall silent—eating, drinking, until it's time to go home.

In the morning the garden needs watering and weeding. A snail makes its way up the twelve cement steps to the garden, where the sunflowers have taken over. The snail is on number seven. This is the first one I have seen almost fully out of its shell, a bizarre creature, stretched out before and behind its muddy brown home. By snail standards it must be moving like lightning, antennae groping forward, a flat-bottomed tube mottled and bumpy and veiny. But it's getting there, it's getting there. And so am I.

Adam is game for going with me to the archives in Brzozie, where I've learned area records for the last hundred years are kept before they are sent to Toruń.

The archive is in a concrete office building, where a lone woman at her desk guards them. She smiles, says yes, indeed, she has these records, but can we come back tomorrow? She has to leave work early today.

"Can we look at them today and come back again Thursday?" I bargain.

CHAPTER 32

—

"Yes, yes," she says and offers tea and clears a table in an adjoining room.

There is something comforting about warm tea in a utilitarian room not overlit with fluorescence. Adam takes one stack of the old tomes, and I take another. Within ten minutes I have discovered that my grandmother's brother Teodor married Leokadja Zakrzewska in 1920, and on July 1, 1922, they had a son, who lived eleven days.

The German documents are full of careful notations—the subject's occupation, robotnik, worker, and so forth—and are a marvel of careful record keeping. Time passes too quickly and soon it's time to leave. But it's a sunny day, and Adam has time on his hands. We turn off the main road and park so we can climb a hill and visit the robbed grave of a German Freemason who died in 1915. We eat the sweet blackberries from the bushes that line the way up. Then Adam leads the way to two nearby Evangelical cemeteries.

"After the war," he says, "everything was taken as building material, the same as with the Jewish cemeteries. They even robbed the graves for jewelry and gold fillings."

The smaller of the cemeteries is nestled in a grove of trees with a rusted fence around it, in the middle of nowhere. But there are flowers on this grave, and the broken monument has been restored to its pedestal. Somebody else has been back here, too, looking.

A Young Man and His Needlepoint

—

Pilgrims

I

t's eight o'clock Wednesday morning, and pilgrims are leaving for their long walk to Częstochowa, the Shrine of the Black Madonna, the holiest site in Poland. Mass has ended, and dozens of people are gathered on Kóscielna Street, waiting to say good-bye. A very old woman in a gray suit, leaning on a cane and holding a younger woman's arm, waits patiently, a navy blue babushka twisted around her face.

The pilgrims are mostly young people, bearing small backpacks. The crowd lining the street and spilling into the Rynek is older, and now and then someone embraces a pilgrim and wishes him or her well: "Go with God."

Why are they doing this? "To give thanks to God for what she has," one says. "It's a form of penance, of atonement," says another.

One of the oldest pilgrims, a woman perhaps in her late forties, heads for the empty church for a last-minute prayer before falling in line behind the sign-carriers: Jubilee Year 2000, the Land of Lubawa, and Nowe Miasto Lubawskie Parish. A portable microphone is wheeled into place. Police guard the proceedings and stop cars for the pilgrims. Young men in yellow aprons straddle the marchers and clear the way. An announcement blares from the loudspeaker, the crowd cheers and waves, and the pilgrims begin to sing about Our Lady.

The church has taken over the town again, and the crowd loves it. Down

Third of May Street toward Lubawa Tower they head, left on Grunwaldzka toward the bridge over the Drwęca, their songs picking up gusto as they wave to more well-wishers. The Nowe Miasto group of about a hundred marchers leads the way; the Lubawa group follows, having marched to Nowe Miasto the night before. Pilgrims all along the way will join them every morning from the town where they spend the night, leading the march onward the next day. Next stop: Brodnica, about twenty miles away.

There's an odd exhilaration in the air. Several priests march with the group, all in their long black gowns and missionary hats—one looking somber and handsome, with a serious purpose, another silly and waving like a hand puppet, his gown too short, bare legs exposed.

I understand their happiness. I am on a pilgrimage of my own. Getting somewhere is far less important than having somewhere to go.

Now that I have located Cousin Feliksa Licznerska, everyone knows her. "Yes, says Pan Kopiczyński, of course. She lives across the bridge. Her maiden name was Bryszkiewska. She walks this way." And he tilts his head into his shoulder.

"She walks this way," I tell Ryszard. "Oh, yes," he says, recognizing her at once, shaking his head with trepidation. "There is some kind of pathology going on there that you won't care for," he warns. "I remember trying to buy a car from her a long time ago. Just as we returned to pay her and clinch the deal, she decided to raise the price. She thought we were cheating her. It was the price she asked!"

As it turns out, Feliksa lives less than a mile away on the second floor in the third of three of the ugliest block apartment buildings in Nowe Miasto. The stairwell is particularly shabby, dirty, and covered with years of stain and grime. A stylishly dressed young woman makes her way down the steps as I go up. A gruff and dirty, unshaven man, his gray hair pointing in every direction, answers the door with "We don't want any" written all over his face. But when I explain who I am, he softens a bit and asks me to come inside. He ushers me into the kitchen and seems to wake up and starts to recall his brother-in-law Franciszek's emigration to England. I cannot take my eyes off the filthy kitchen stove and the grease dripping down its sides and front, pots on the burners that look as if they are never washed from cooking to cooking.

"It got pretty bad there in England, too," he says proudly. "No jobs. Franciszek once said he was sorry he wasn't in Poland."

His wife is with her daughter, his son is on his way home. But it is getting too close to lunchtime, and I am afraid they will ask me to eat with them, so I

Pilgrims

—

offer to return in two hours, when he is sure she will be back. There are no phones. Pan Licznerski shuffles to the door in his slippers, his dirty baggy pants drooping from his behind, shirt half out and half in.

Even my mother, who did not have housekeeping on her mind in those last difficult years of her life, would want to report this kitchen "to da boarda healt," as she always threatened when she saw a dirty food facility.

I head for the Ratuszowa to regroup. It's crowded today. Even the town lesbians are out and about. Being the town anything here must be difficult, but being the town lesbians must be particularly onerous. They sit at the next table; the more butch of the two, in a blue running suit, slurps down a bowl of czarnina, duck blood soup, then pulls hefty drags from her cigarette. The other in knit sweater and open-toed shoes devours a plate of food. They pull bread from a cloth bag they brought with them and eat mostly in silence, the way long-time partners often do, as if everything has been said and now they are just waiting.

The restaurant today seems as much a dream, strange and difficult, as it did the first time I came here in the cold, and threw open the door on a wedding party. It is perhaps as strange and difficult as every American phenomenon my grandmother had to face her entire life and never got used to.

Perhaps it is a good thing these relatives appeared so late in my stay. I cannot say that it even makes sense to go back and look for more in that filthy kitchen. "A Whiter Shade of Pale" is still playing on the sound system, while the lives of these new relatives unroll before me, revealing lives not so different from those I left behind. I must return to see Marianna soon, to clear up more questions about her aunts and uncles.

When I return to Feliksa's apartment, a young man answers the door with a perplexed look on his face. He is Adam, her son. His father tells him to take me to see his mother. This Adam is perhaps twenty-five years old. He walks with his neck bent and his head tilted into his shoulder, just the way Pan Kopiczyński described his mother. He smiles weakly as I explain who I am.

He takes me down the road to a cheerful house with flowers and a shrine to the Blessed Mother in the front yard. Inside, the house has been broken up into apartments, communist style. The door opens onto a bright, clean kitchen, where an astonished woman in a floral apron stands stunned as her son explains that I am a cousin from America.

"Can it be possible? Yes, yes," she says, her eyes wide behind big, horn-rimmed glasses. "My father's sister Helena in America, and you her grandson!" She throws her arms around me and plants three kisses on my cheeks, then grips my hand, repeating, "Mój Boże, mój Boże." My God. My God.

CHAPTER 33
—

Her daughter Ewa Grala is equally stunned, and she smiles broadly and introduces me to her little Karolina and her husband Marcin. Feliksa insists immediately that she is not "Pani" to me but "Feliksa." She talks so fast that I cannot keep up, remembering in rapid succession every old relative she can think up. She tells me about her nine children and the one who died at birth. "It should have been ten!" Ryszard Bryszkiewski was born before she was married and is now forty-eight years old and lives somewhere near Działdowo. Then there are Irena, Krzysztof, Zyta, Mirosława, Andrzej, Renata, and Adam and Ewa, whom I have just met.

Ewa also knows me. She works at the Lewiatan grocery store, the very first one I went into when I arrived in Nowe Miasto. "I waited on you. Who would have thought? I was at the vegetable counter and sometimes working in front."

Ewa is tall and slender, with dark hair cut below her ears and a bright smile and aquiline face. She and her mother talk at the same time, while Marcin watches television, and baby Karolina, who has just learned to walk, touches everything in the room.

So for a couple of hours we sip tea, and Feliksa tries to remember. She blows smoke awkwardly after taking quick drags off her cigarette. Her gray hair is neatly combed and cropped below her ears, and in her face I can see the young girl in the old photograph, shy and tan and dressed in white, holding a communion candle. She reminds me of my mother, and I tell her how much my mother, her first cousin, would have liked to share a smoke with her and about our failed attempt to find relatives in 1988.

"What a shame," she says, and then she is off with stories of her children and her pregnancies, and I cannot keep up, so I smile and nod instead. "A Gypsy fortune-teller told me, when I was just a little girl, that someone in my family would return from far away. It was true, it was true." And she takes my hand.

"Oh, mother," Ewa says and asks me questions about what I am doing here, clearly amazed that this odd foreigner who wandered into her store turns out to be her cousin. "What should I call you? Cousin or uncle?" she asks with a big smile because of our age difference. Then she digs through old pictures and letters for information about other relatives. She comes up with an address for her Uncle Franciszek's son in England.

We agree that I must come back tomorrow and meet Łucja, the third of Jan's living children, in Kurzętnik. There are kisses at the gate, and Feliksa repeats, "Mój Boże, mój Boże."

Pilgrims
—

The Nowe Miasto Hillbillies

◆

On the way to Brzozie this morning I passed a horse-drawn wagon on the main road into Nowe Miasto, the grandfather holding the reins, a big-bosomed daughter at his side. In front of me, another Maluch chugged along, a grandpa at the wheel, chatting with a grandma in the passenger seat, her head barely visible above the seatback. Semitrailer trucks and snazzy new Mercedes lined up behind the couple in the wagon, unable to pass with two rattling Maluchs coming at them.

It was peaceful today in Brzozie, sitting in the little room next to Pani Longina Milewska—she asking if I wanted tea, I turning the brittle pages of the German record books, page after page, finding a marriage certificate for my grandmother's brother Albin.

In the next room Pani Milewska sits in her office while her radio plays "The Clarinet Polka," then "Yes, Sir, That's My Baby," then a Motown review. The trumpeter of Kraków plays his mournful tune at noon, transmitting from the tower of St. Mary's church. I hear the clacks of an old typewriter, and nothing seems so long ago anymore when you see the names of the dead repeated and suddenly connected before you.

Brother Albin Bryszkiewski married a woman named Weronika in 1911, before the First World War. Wincenty, grandfather to the Jan who lives today in Sugajno, was their witness. They seem to have had no children, so perhaps it was he who perished, recorded in the church records as another Jan. On

July 1, 1903, sister Nikodema was born. She married worker Jan Piotrowicz in 1926. Brother Władysław, who was to die a mere twenty-five years later at the hands of a jealous rival, was born December 28, 1907. Władysława, whose sad photo I carry in my bag, was born July 12, 1905. In 1933, Władysław Pilarz attested to the death of Władysław Bryszkiewski in Sugajno. Sister Władysława signed a birth certificate for her son, Edmund.

My grandmother's sisters' and brothers' lives unfold before me from these dusty old books that someone thought were important enough to save. So many questions I must collect to ask Marianna, the eldest surviving grandchild of this family.

Out of the blue, Pani Milewska asks me my family name, makes a phone call, and soon I am holding a picture of the Bryszkiewski family home, the one my grandmother left behind, the ruin of which I visited with distant cousins Marek and his father Jan. She tells me her birth name was Czaplinska, the same name as my great-great-grandmother, Brygida, mother of the infamous and multihusbanded Babcia Basia. For months I could not find relatives; now they turn up even in the records office.

"My parents worked the land around the house, maybe thirty years ago. The house was already a wreck then," she says. She introduces me to her son, Mariusz, who is a little boy in the photograph, playing next to his grandfather. The house is a shabby patchwork of brick in the German style, much like the house Cousin Jan now lives in.

I arrive at cousin Ewa Grala's house at the appointed hour. A girl of seven or eight is pushing little Karolina in a stroller. "My name is Patrycja. This is my cousin," she replies politely when I inquire.

"Where is Aunt Ewa today?" I ask.

"She is working,"

"Is grandma home?"

She runs to get her, while I push Karolina around the yard. Karolina is a sweet and fearless child and wants to climb out of the stroller and into my arms.

"Are we ready?" Feliksa calls as she appears at the back door wearing a smile and a pink knit top decorated with silver threads. "Listen, would you like to meet my daughter? She would like to come with us to her aunt's house. Would it be okay?"

I assure her that it will be fine, and we all fit in my little Maluch. The stroller gets the front seat, and my three new cousins squeeze into the back. Feliksa smiles and nods and chatters away. Patrycja helps her grandmother with the baby, and off we go.

Daughter Mirosława, my second cousin, lives right on the Rynek, above the jewelry store. She has the very apartment I imagined would be mine when I first came to Nowe Miasto. Inside, it's not as I pictured it, however. Past the small foyer is a tiny neglected kitchen, not as filthy as her father's but bleak and uninviting nevertheless.

In the living room is the seemingly requisite cabinet unit and television blasting. It stays on for the whole visit, while Feliksa's grandchildren appear faster than I can count them. The eldest, in his twenties, lingers to find out who I am. He is a tough-looking boy with acne scars and a tattoo on his forearm, but he smiles gently, as if relieved to have someone unusual in the house. Mirosława's sons are Rafał, Marcin, and Paweł.

Mirosława is even tougher than the sons and nephews in her charge. She scuffles around in her house slippers, breasts flopping inside an old yellow T-shirt. Every third utterance is a bark at one of the children—into the room or out the window at Patrycja, who has been left on the sidewalk with Karolina in the stroller. She and her mother speak to one another in clipped, aggressive tones. "Pick her up." "Put her down." "What are they doing?" "They are fine." Coffee appears, and I repeat for Mirosława the story of why I am here. She puffs on her cigarette and shoots barbs at her mother, then orders one of the children to sit, then to stand, then to go outside. Her two youngest sons are fascinated by me and try to remember what they know that is American. McDonald's comes to mind. Their mother complains about the cost of living and the lack of jobs. Her husband, she says, died a year ago, then she sucks her teeth and takes a drag on her cigarette. Her fallback expression is "No, no," said with her head bobbing affirmatively. Her coffee is dark and strong.

I suggest that it is time to go, and I ask to take a photograph. "I have to change clothes," says Mirosława, and I notice that behind me she is putting on a polyester blouse, then a pair of blue jeans under her skirt. While I try to look at Karolina, her aunt slips off her skirt, then walks over to shelves near the television and sprays something under her arms and around her neck.

Into the car we pile, grandma in the back seat, baby on her lap, her knees near her chin, Patrycja along for the ride. There is no room for the boys. "You stay home," their mother barks, and off they trot. Whatever it is Mirosława put under her arms is not working.

On the outskirts of Kurzętnik we march to another set of block apartments, grandma Feliksa with baby in her arms, Mirosława galumphing next to me, making affirmative motions and periodically saying, "No, no."

No one is home.

A woman is working in a lush flower garden behind these housing projects, while six others sit on benches near the backdoors. For all practical purposes this could be the projects in Chicago, except that here all of the tenants are white.

So here lives that lovely little girl in the old photograph, her face so digni-fied and full of hope, lined up with her mother, her sister Anna, now dead, and her handsome brother Jan, also dead. So this is what awaited her after the war. This fate is what her family pleaded for relief from. This squalid apart-ment building is where she must spend her declining years, with a daughter afflicted with *heinemedina*—polio.

I am not sure I want to go any farther, but Mirosława is in full swing now. She asks the neighbors if they know where her aunt Łucja has gone.

"She is at her son's house," says one.

"Her daughter is having an operation," says another.

"Yes, yes, an operation," says Feliksa. "Her daughter had an operation yes-terday."

"We'll find her, no, no," Mirosława assures me, huffing and puffing as she scurries toward another of the sitting ladies and asks, "Where does her son live?" The woman doesn't know. "Does anyone know where he lives?" she calls out.

"Over in the new area," says one, but she doesn't know where.

"We'll ask when we get there," Mirosława assures me and hustles her mother and the little girls into the car. Patrycja smiles at me docilely, stroking her little cousin's head. Then we're off again, Feliksa chattering in the back seat, Ka-rolina grabbing for my hair, and Mirosława twisting with agitation. "It won't be a problem," she assures me. "They haven't lived there very long."

I have the feeling that, carless and phoneless, she doesn't go much of any-where. Now I understand why the other relatives did not rush me off to meet this side of the family. By now I am not even sure I want to meet Łucja at all.

Now comes a series of jumps out of the car, sometimes when it is still mov-ing, during which Mirosława races up to someone, anyone, and asks for di-rections to her cousin's house, then jumps back into the car. I suggest that we might want to try another day, but she won't hear of it and is successful on only the third try. "You see," she says, nodding her head. "We're here, no, no."

A pretty young girl greets us at the front fence and ushers us past a lace cur-tain hanging over the back entrance like a mosquito net, then into the living room, where an old woman sits on the couch in a blue floral housedress, stock-ing slippers on her feet, her gray hair clipped off at the ears and bobby-pinned off her face, which is resting on her hand.

At first she says nothing when they tell her to stand and meet her cousin from America. She looks at me and seems to roll her eyes. But then her face

The Nowe Miasto Hillbillies

—

breaks into a smile, and she gives me a hug, her eyes fill with tears, and she says, "Oh, mój Boże. I can't believe it."

I pull out my pictures, and she smiles as she looks at herself nearly fifty years ago. It's hard to see that young girl in her face, but then it appears for me in a smile, in her eyes. She has had terrible problems with her teeth, she tells me, hiding her mouth with her hand, the way my grandmother sometimes did.

Łucja's husband, Tadeusz Mikuczeński, died eight years ago. Her daughter in the hospital is Agnieszka. Her son is Kazimierz. He and his wife have four children, Monika and Małgorzata, who are not here; Kamila, who greeted us; and Krzysztof, who is shy but whose eyes light up when they tell him I am American and a relative. "Truly?" he says, his mouth hanging open.

The family soon settles into conversation about Agnieszka and the house and how they haven't seen each other in a while. Now and then Feliksa smiles my way and tells her sister "he looks like Ignacy" and again about the Gypsy who told her I would appear.

Łucja does not have much to tell me, and nobody seems at all interested in family history, not even Kamila, who smiles politely when I show her documents I found in Brzozie.

Karolina is the center of attention, and everyone is kept busy chasing after her, calling out to her, and worrying aloud about her safety.

"Za nim gruby upadnie to chudy przepadnie," says Feliksa. What diminishes a fat man kills a skinny one.

We take a tour of the garden behind the house, where a guinea pig entertains everyone by crawling around in the dill.

These sisters—Feliksa, Łucja, and the eldest Marianna in Gwiździny—all remind me of my mother, their first cousin. She and Feliksa especially would have liked each other, with their smoking and their gift of gab. Marianna and Łucja too remind me of the way my mother fought so hard against infirmity in those last years and summed it up often for me in the same three words, in her Hamtramck accent at its best: "Dis ain't livin.'"

I drop off Mirosława and Patrycja at their apartment in the Rynek. Mirosława's sons play with my steering wheel, while Babcia Feliksa waits in the back seat with Karolina. It's early, but I have visited with these cousins for four hours and am ready to call it a day.

Ryszard and Grażyna appear as we are saying good-bye outside my car in the Rynek, with a petition they want me to sign. The *Gazeta* staff is organizing to protest the lack of action over the deaths of two people at a country music concert in Gdańsk.

"Come and have a beer with us," they urge.

CHAPTER 34
—

Mirosława won't sign the petition. "Oh, no, I don't sign things," she protests.

I must go home and write, I tell Ryszard, but I take Feliksa home and return quickly to the Ratuszowa, where they are gathered around a table with others from the Dom Kultury.

"I thought you were busy," says Grażyna.

"That's what I told them," I confess.

"I told you so," Ryszard says, reminding me of the "pathology" he diagnosed.

The other Dom Kultury workers invite us all for a kiełbasa grilling, but my friends have had enough of their coworkers as I have my new-found relatives, and we head to Pizza Duo. Grażyna is wearing cutoff shorts, and it's starting to get cold. She shivers a bit, and Ryszard uses her favorite word. There must always be *kara,* a penalty, he says, even for beauty.

They spread ketchup on their slices of vegetarian pizza with corn, and I try to explain that it is redundant, but they just laugh, and Ryszard makes a face because he has accidentally put an olive in his mouth. He eyes the room conspiratorially, as if a news scoop lurks under every table.

I try to explain Mirosława by telling them she was eager to please but is perhaps not the sharpest knife in the drawer. They laugh but clearly don't get it. No matter how hard I try to translate, the comparison elicits blank stares. They are looking for a double meaning, some irony. I realize that to make it work in Polish I must say wryly that she is by far the sharpest knife in the drawer. They laugh.

I regret maligning my new cousins, but I enjoy such sessions with these two enigmatic journalists. It gives me an opportunity to say things I've heard them say, like "Daj spokój," give me a break, to repeat things I learn or hear on the street in the afternoon and have them analyzed.

The next day I call the other side of the family, my grandfather's people, Danuta Brodacka, a relative, however distant, by marriage. "You didn't need to reserve a hotel room," she says. "We have room for you. Everyone wants to meet you."

When I offer to take a taxi to her house, she won't hear of it. "We live near the station. I have a car. I will meet you at the station. Please, I would be happy to do this." She wants to know how she will know me.

"The guy with the big suitcase." For I am on my way to another pilgrimage—to the Holy Land—the trip relatives here only dream of and Pani Wituchowska has already taken.

There is *barszcz* cooking on the stove, there are photographs to organize, and I know now that there must be so many "cousins" here in Poland that it would take me a lifetime to get to know them all. I know that even if I were born here, or if I moved here and started a new life, it would be no different from the one I have: seeing friends and family stay loyal or drift away as the years pass.

In the background on a CD, Kapela ze Wsi Warszawa, the group I listened to on the banks of the Drwęca, sings about bread, and the refrain "O jo joj jo, joj joj joj," just as my grandmother sang when she was overwhelmed, as she must once have called out in her strong young girl's voice when she ran and played here.

I have scooped up a few crumbs of that earth she walked and put them in a little bottle, and I have met fifty cousins in five days. I don't want to do anything today but sit in my room and read and write and look at old photographs and listen to music.

I had seen no one here cry until yesterday, until this cousin Łucja, who shares my mother's name, stood to walk with me for a look at the back yard. She took my arm, and I know for a minute she wanted to believe that this man who had appeared out of nowhere was someone she could hold on to, someone she could tell about a lifetime of loss.

"My daughter was two years old when it happened. A normal, healthy two-year-old one day, and the next day she couldn't walk," and it still hurt to tell me what she saw. "I had no more children after that," she sighed.

CHAPTER 34

—

The Other Side of the Family

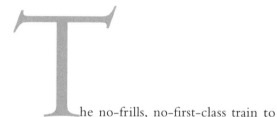

The no-frills, no-first-class train to Biała Podlaska chugs along. I've no time to waste now that I understand it's entirely possible to find my relatives in Poland. It feels different here, flatter, no sign of the German-style brick schools and train stations and post offices of Pomorze. Everyone seems to look more like my grandfather than my grandmother. Or is it my imagination? No, there is a man with a scythe at the railroad crossing; he looks just like him, dusty and worn, with a determined, lipless smile.

"That part of Poland is another world," Ryszard warned me. "Another region and near Russia, so you must be careful."

The train pulls into the station, and I see them right away—Danuta Brodacka and her daughter Monika, even though there are dozens of people crowding the platform in Biała Podlaska on this sunny August afternoon. She's a cheerful woman, built solid, with cropped brown hair, a strong jaw and smile. She spots me as well and extends her hand.

"Yes, yes, it is me," she says and introduces her daughter, a quiet young woman in her early twenties who hangs back but is also all smiles. "Welcome to Biała Podlaska," she says confidently.

"Not a lot of reason for tourists to come here," says Danuta, "but we will show you everything there is to see. You are with friends now even if we cannot figure out how we are family," she laughs.

Danuta takes charge right away. I tell her I have a room at the Capitol Hotel. She insists I should not be in a hotel at all, "but if you must, here is the Merkury, so close to the station, and from here we live just that way. We could walk." So the clerk at the reception desk calls the Capitol and switches me to the Merkury; then off we go in my noncousin's borrowed car.

Their house is a Soviet-style block with a beauty parlor on the first floor, which they rent out. Inside, it's cozy and homey—a big dining room with a television in the corner blaring "Xena," with the omnipresent narrator explaining her every move in Polish.

Her son is Adam; he is fourteen. He greets me with some curiosity. "He has studied English," says Danuta. But he is shy about speaking it. "My husband is in Austria working," she tells me. "I am sorry you won't be able to meet him. We are expecting him to call tonight or tomorrow."

The small sofa in this complicated family room is made of a familiar, red-flame-print material that was on pillows on my couch in Detroit twenty-five years ago. The drapes are gold crushed velvet. It looks like an efficient home, an iron on the window sill, a work table in the kitchen, a dining room with a cloth-covered table and four chairs, stereo, and a modular desk, where presumably homework gets done. Luscious smells float in from the kitchen down the hall.

"You don't have to worry about anything," Danuta tells me. "I have it figured out, and I will take you to Huszcza." She wants no money for gas, no dinner out, nothing I can offer. "We have everything here. Now be at home and eat." Adam and Monika start bringing food to the table, and a feast begins. Chicken soup, roast beef in gravy, potatoes, cabbage salad. . . .

Danuta tends the table until her brood of three is fed. Then she stealthily serves herself. Our lunch conversation is the story of how she found the phoneless relatives in Huszcza by knocking on doors and asking. The children dutifully clear the table with a practiced "thank you, mother" out loud before they rise.

Danuta and I drive to Huszcza alone. She explains that the car is borrowed from a good friend, and tomorrow another car will be borrowed in exchange for house-sitting. "I am lucky to have such good friends," she explains. Along the way the wooden houses stand out. "The old Russian influence," says Danuta, "and here"—she points to a block of tenements—"the new Russian influence. We are very close to the border with Belarus, you know."

Huszcza is a collection of old wooden houses and communist block stores with a new church towering over it all. It's bigger than Sugajno, more like Boleszyn. Danuta has a little trouble finding the Brodacki house again. "Look for the very blue tin roof," she says, "and you, too, can wonder why they would paint a roof such a color."

Soon we spot it, the front yard overgrown with bushes and flowers, the fence closed at the head of a driveway that leads to the barnyard, where chickens peck and a stout young woman and an older, suspicious-looking woman stare at us. Danuta calls to them, and they call back. The older woman eyes me seriously.

"Would you like to meet your American cousin?" Danuta asks.

She approaches me, her expression more quizzical. When I say a few words in Polish, she breaks into a grin. They both shake my hand.

"I am Antoni Brodacki's grandson," I declare, as if giving my credentials to immigration authorities. "His brother was Czesław."

Her weathered face broadens with a smile. She shakes her head in disbelief. The young woman at her side looks dumbstruck but breaks into a welcoming smile, adjusts her baggy T-shirt, and we head for the back door. The older woman begins to chatter in a scratchy, high-pitched voice that never stops for the entire visit. She can't believe it. Who would have thought? And then she is off, speaking a mile a minute about relatives I cannot keep track of.

"So come in, come in, we'll talk, we'll look at pictures," she says. Her name is Helena Brodacka, the same as my grandmother's married name. Her husband was Ludwik, eldest son of Czesław, my grandfather's brother. She has many old pictures to show and ushers us into a small sitting room with two giant couches facing one another and in proximity to the television. Her kitchen looks like a museum or a movie set, with a small refrigerator and a wood stove in the anteroom one must pass through from the back door in order to reach the sitting room and kitchen.

The house seems in a time warp. The living room also holds a gigantic credenza with drawers and shelves and glass doors, an expensive antique back in America, I tell them. They are not impressed. It's a place to hide old pictures and hold woodcarvings and knickknacks. Pani Helena brings apple cake and coffee. Her daughter-in-law, Beata, smiles blankly and now and then notices that her son Michał is running in every direction. Danuta is facilitating with ease; already she has learned how to talk to me, slowly, deliberately. "One voice at a time," she tells them, then tries to calm Pani Helena, who can't stop talking simultaneously about twenty relatives on all sides of the family.

The apple cake is delicious, just like Pani Kopicyzńska's.

Pani Helena grabs pictures one after the other, spouting names breathlessly and filling any pauses in her spiel with placeholders like "i tego"—"and that." Finally Danuta begs her to slow down for my sake, which she does for a few

The Other Side of the Family

—

minutes. Her son enters the room in his dirty coveralls and plaid shirt, his very blond hair pulled away from his face in a short ponytail. He reminds me at once of my mother's twin brothers, my uncles Joe and John.

"Mirosław," he says softly, politely, and shakes my hand. He takes his little boy in his arms and sits on the couch across from me. His mother is barefoot and sitting at my feet now, digging through the paper box of pictures, then her son takes over the hunt. What they find is astonishing to me.

She places in my hand a sepia photograph of my grandparents with two children, the baby in my grandfather's arms is my mother, the little boy my uncle Stanley. On the back of the photo is written in my grandfather's hand:

Beloved Relatives, Antoni Brodacki and his family, of whom was made this photograph, 15 March 1920. We send our love. Helena, my wife, is 26 years old. Stanisław is five, 7 April. Łucja is one year on the third of April. Learning to walk. As a memento, we send you, my dear relatives, my whole family in this photograph so you can see how we all look now. Dear relatives, please write and tell what day and month I was born, because I do not know, and I need to know as I grow older in this foreign country.

Maybe because I have never seen anything in my grandfather's hand, never saw a picture of my grandmother as a young mother with only two children, my grandfather holding my mother so proudly, I read this message over and over. And it saddens me that I cannot call my mother and tell her that at last I have found that baby picture she longed for. Maybe it is such a powerful picture because it confirms what I suspected about my grandmother's birth certificate. Neither of them knew when their birthdays were. My grandparents were married August 12, 1917.

Soon there are more pictures—my great-grandparents with their children, father Józef and mother Antonina—and I realize that he was writing to his parents, and the photo of the old couple I brought with me are my great-grandparents, and the simple notation on the back makes sense, "Zusia died December 13, 1948." My grandfather's sister, Zuzanna, died a year after I was born, just three years before my grandfather.

There are new versions of the unknown faces I carried with me from America in my briefcase. Mirosław's father was Ludwik; his father was Czesław, one of my grandfather's brothers. Czesław died in 1970; his widow was Michalina; their son followed him mysteriously in the same year. They skip over the details, but Danuta looks askance at me. Ludwik had a brother, Jan, who died a few years ago.

Helena recalls that my grandfather's sister had a daughter named Apolonia, who married a man named Rudzka and lives in Biała Podlaska, and that her own mother married the father of Czesław's wife Michalina. I begin to wonder how many generations it takes for people in a Polish village to start marrying their relatives over and over again.

Helena tries to clear things up by explaining that she was Ludwik's second wife. To make things more confusing, his first wife was also named Helena. She also died young, leaving two children, a son Marian and a daughter Danuta, she being the Danuta Brodacka, now Kołton, who wrote the letter I carry in my briefcase. My new friend Danuta soon deciphers the postmark—15 April 1965—much later than I imagined. My grandmother apparently never answered it. From his second Helena, Ludwik also left an older son, Sławomir, and a daughter, Bożena, who is a nun. Mirosław was five when his father died; Bożena two and a half. And that is all they want to say about that; Danuta casts me a sidelong glance.

Little Michał is sticking his fingers in the box; his daddy tells him to stop twice, then hauls him into the vestibule and gives him a smack, just as my grandfather would have. The baby wails but is hustled off, out of earshot.

Now there are more pictures, and Helena affirming identities in the Polish way, "*No* Piotr, *no* Józef, *no* father, *no* brother, *no* living, *no* dead," all the while nodding yes. "Let's take it slowly and one thing at a time," Danuta urges, delighted by my excitement. We exchange glances as Helena rattles on. Here is your grandfather's brother, Władysław, the one in the Polish army uniform. He married Bronisława and emigrated to England (there's a letter with a return address in Leicester) and had four children, one named Edward. On his photograph to my grandfather in August of 1919 he wrote, "Dear brother, I am very happy that you are married. I am twenty-two years old and have to serve in the army. I don't know when I will be married." Here is Piotr, the younger brother, whose photo I carry, with the inscription to my grandfather, "I am sending you this photo, so you will remember that I am your real brother." They think he went to Canada, but my relatives do not know if he had children. There is a picture of a young woman with my great-grandparents, sister Zuzanna, but they cannot tell me how she died. And there are letters from the brother in England.

There is a photograph of my grandfather with his cousin, Mike Brodacki, in Canada. On the back he calls him his brother.

There is my godparents' wedding photo. Grandfather refers to his son John as "one of the twins" and introduces another Helena into the family in 1948.

There is another with his sons Henry and John again, in 1949, in front of the other twin's—Joe's—house on Thirty-Two Mile Road. John at twenty-nine, Hank at twenty-one.

There is his brother Piotr with four children surrounding him.

There are grandpa and grandma together in 1946, this time with Hank and Joe.

There is Stan with his daughter Margaret; on the back is written: "My oldest son, and in his arms his daughter, my granddaughter, year 1949. He fought the Germans and married a German. I'll write later."

"You resemble Marian," Helena says suddenly and pulls out a twenty-year-old picture of him, and it looks like a twenty-year-old picture of me. We did, after all, have the same great-grandfather.

They also remember that there was a Michał Brodacki, Mike, the cousin who moved to Canada. I remember looking at pictures of him in the 1950s. There is a photo of him in their box and on the back his cousins again call him a brother. "They talked that way when they were close cousins," Danuta says, and I think of Adam Kopiczyński and his cousin Ewa, whom he called his sister, and perhaps that explains Piotr's comment about being a "real brother."

It's time to say good-bye. My head is spinning as we head out the door and into the yard. Helena is so excited she can't remember a thing and asks me if I was born in Poland. Her son corrects her impatiently.

"Do you see that tree?" asks Mirosław, pointing to a tall oak. "Władysław planted it before he left for England." There is an enormous woodpile near the barn, a very old tractor parked beneath the oak, and the butts of grunting pigs visible inside the shed.

"This looks like my grandmother's backyard," I tell them, and they smile at that, all of them.

"And where is the house my grandfather was born in?" I ask.

"Here! Here!" Helena screeches. "But it has been rebuilt. During the war it burned."

"What happened?"

"The neighbors were hiding Jews. The Germans found out and burned down their house. They were all shot. Our house was close by, and the fire spread. So what you see now was all rebuilt after the war."

The three of them wave good-bye, looking for all the world like serfs waiting for the Middle Ages to end. Behind them, their hut of worn, unpainted timber, the frameless windows oozing foam insulation.

"The windows are not finished," explains Pani Helena.

"When I get the money . . . ," says Mirosław.

CHAPTER 35

—

"Do you want to go to America with me?" I ask little Michał in his grandmother's arms.

"Nie," he snips, in that way babies have of rejecting a stranger.

"Lepsze swoje błoto niż w Ameryce złoto," Helena cackles. Better your own mud here than gold in America.

Danuta's daughter and son seem to wake up when we return to Biała Podlaska, and their mother is full of talk about relatives and how we are going to find out more. She calls "the real Danuta" and leaves a message on her answering machine. It seems she was just fifteen when she wrote to my grandmother for her grandfather Czesław.

Meanwhile, the table is again loaded with food: chicken breasts, cold cuts, beets, bread, noodles, and at last vodka.

"We're not driving anymore," says Danuta, and the kids open up more about how they have studied English for years and never speak it, how English is so hard "with all those tenses."

I assure them that they are fine with past, present, and future and can save most of the rest for when they are fluent. They seem relieved but still refuse to speak.

Danuta is warmed by the vodka and laughs at my assessment of English learning in Poland. "Kids study seven years here, go to America, and cannot say a word. Senseless," she agrees.

When Danuta tells Adam to go upstairs and watch the other television, he says it is more fun to watch it here and doesn't want to leave. Yet, he seems addicted to the thing, as if the background droning made sense of everything.

In the morning Danuta wants to show me the town. Monika is making potato dumplings. We conclude that somewhere there is a family connection between us, but what does it matter? "Your friends you choose!" Twice God smiled at me in my search for family, I tell her: once in the cemetery in Boleszyn and again when my finger landed on her name in the Telekomunikacja Polska phone book.

The Other Side of the Family

—

A Father and His Daughter

———◆———

Ludwik Kowieski is ninety-four years old. Danuta has been raving about him since I first arrived in Biała Podlaska. "This man you must meet," she said, when she told me the story of looking for my relatives. "He is full of life and stories. Perfect for an interview." Danuta is starting to talk like a journalist and wants to make sure that I meet her nomination for the top celebrity of Huszcza.

We chug into town in Danuta's fifty-dollar German car, her standby when there's none to borrow. It runs like a tank, with that indestructible feel of the old, stick-shift Chevy Nova I drove for years back in the States. We cruise up and down the road while Danuta tries to remember the exact house. "That's it," she says finally, pointing to another chałupa similar to the one where my cousin lives but without the blue roof.

We knock on the back door, and a woman answers. She appears to be about eighty years old, in a print dress and contrasting print apron and clunky rubber boots. Her crinkly red face is framed by a voile babushka, her mouth wide with a shy smile.

"We are here to see your husband," Danuta asserts in a clear voice, a little too loud.

"My husband?" The old woman looks perplexed. "Oh, no, not my husband, you must mean my father." She has the swollen hands of a man twice her size, the hands of a man who tends his own hogs and cows and chickens daily.

Danuta and I cast wide-eyed glances in each other's direction. I know what she is thinking. My God, if the daughter looks this old, how can we possibly be here to speak to her father?

The daughter ushers us into the kitchen and invites us to sit on a pair of wooden stools. The old woman settles herself on a stool by the cupboard, where a tray of buns and two loaves of bread sit cooling. Pan Kowieski, meanwhile, shuffles out from behind a drape, leaning on a cane, wearing a matted, print sweater, sandals, and socks. His full head of hair and reasonably complete set of teeth leave him looking not a day older than his daughter. He smiles as we introduce ourselves, seeming a bit flattered that someone wants to hear from him. His daughter tells him to take a seat, and he obeys.

Danuta begins by asking about their work on the farm. "He's got his, and I've got mine," says the daughter. They banter back and forth in clipped phrases, often talking over one another. Danuta tries to slow them down for me, but I suddenly remember that I have my tape recorder in my bag and discreetly flip it on. They seem barely to notice.

The old man says he remembers Michał Brodacki's wedding—he was in fact best man. Mike Brodacki, my grandfather's brotherlike cousin who emigrated to Canada. "Sure, they built a house. His sister Franciszka lived down the road, but she died. Your great-grandfather Józef and Michał's father were brothers." He cannot quite remember my grandfather, but then he was only seven when he left for America.

"Why did Michał go to America?" I inquire.

"For bread," Pan Kowieski replies. "He was looking for a better life, and he seems to have found it."

"Ludwik Brodacki drank," says the daughter bluntly. Danuta slices at her neck with the outside edge of her hand, the universal sign for a drunk. "Czesław was a good man," says the old lady of my grandfather's brother, "a good man." I can visualize him in the photograph his grandson gave me, sitting with his wife and two grandchildren proudly at his side. "But Ludwik drank," she repeats, shaking her head, "and he hit his wife."

I ask Pan Kowieski to tell me his first memories of Huszcza, and he begins with life under Russian occupation before World War I. I'm mesmerized, looking into the grisly face of a man who remembers this place as it was when my grandfather still lived here almost ninety years ago. He runs a hand through his full head of hair, still not entirely gray, then leans his weight forward with both hands on his cane.

"I was too young to be in the war," he explains, "but I remember the Armia Krajowa, the home army. When the Germans came, we took twenty-five

A Father and His Daughter

—

wagons and went to Warsaw with dried fish for the Armia Krajowa. I went to Warsaw in the wagon, and I couldn't stand the stink." He was a boy of twelve.

He remembers something called *Cud nad Wisłą*—the miracle on the Vistula River. "When we went to Warsaw, so many Bolsheviks had been killed by the Poles that there was a hill of dead Russians and another hill of carbines. The Bolshevik captain had told everyone he was going to Warsaw to drink tea, so confident he was that they would win the city. But they retreated to Vilnius."

Then Pan Kowieski's daughter is eager to remember World War II and a Jewish woman named Leah, who comes to mind as if she had seen her yesterday, yet this is a memory from 1943, when the area was at the center of mass murder committed by German Reserve Battalion 101.

"Leah was a neighbor girl," she remembers. "She was arrogant and always telling us what to do. She came here once on Saturday and told me I better stop sweeping the floor with a broom on the Sabbath, or soon they'd be sweeping Polish heads off that floor!"

"Leah went to Belarus on the Bug River. But she was killed in the field. So many were killed," says the old woman.

Danuta tries to slow them down. "Who was killed? What happened?"

"Nobody liked them very much," Pan Kowieski volunteers. "Leah had a brother named Abraham. Her father was a shoe repairman. He overcharged."

"He was a lousy shoe repairman," says the daughter, "and they were very poor. People would pay him with food sometimes. Once somebody paid him with a rock covered with a few potatoes. He fixed shoes today and tomorrow they tore again. 'Co ty cholera chcesz,'" she curses by invoking cholera, as if talking about someone who left town just last week.

"Zelda was his wife's name," they agree simultaneously, mother of Leah. "Zelda was at our house once when the Germans came," says Pan Kowieski. "It was October. They came to the house and said 'Good day' to her, and I said she was deaf and dumb. We were hiding ham. I told them that she was my mother, and she didn't hear or speak. I had just killed a pig, and they were looking for food. They even offered to pay." Later they came again, and a *szpieg*— a spy—ratted on her, he says matter-of-factly, "and they came to her house, took her into the field, and shot her. They killed them all. It was twenty armed Germans on bicycles."

Pan Kowieski continues without a note of self-pity. "Another time the Germans came and wanted to know who had pigs. I had eight, so we hid seven of them, and then snow fell, and there was no trace of their tracks. The neighbors verified our story, telling them that there was just this one pig for two families. My wife had put feed on the floor of the hiding place so the pigs would be quiet." They ramble on about the horrible times, and I am lost.

"What was the best time in Poland?" I ask. The daughter doesn't hesitate. "Now is the best time for him," she chuckles, nodding toward her father. "He gets his rent, doesn't have to work, a pension of seven hundred fifty złoty a month." Less than two hundred dollars.

"Before the Second World War it wasn't that great," says Pan Kowieski. There was nothing but gentry in Poland, and the rest were dirt poor." This is the glorious age that Pani Wituchowska in her wine shop in Nowe Miasto longs for.

"Edward Gierek," says Kowieski, "he gave pensions to farmers. I voted for him! Za komuny kradli wszystko. The fascists and communists, they were the worst thieves."

His daughter starts to explain the problems with the new Poland. "They want to pay us thirty złoty for ten liters of milk. You have to pay that for a bottle of water! It costs more than that for a bottle of beer! We bought a television on credit, and we had to pay for it with three months worth of milk."

For all her grumbling, however, the old woman says she likes her life. Her hands are swollen from work, the fingers muscled, calloused, and reddened. She takes care of her own hogs still and chickens and cows, all the daily chores of farm life. In the corner behind her father is the old ceramic wood stove where the bread and buns on the counter were baked. An old valance of gold crushed velvet decorates the arch to the room behind her.

When the sun is going down, we say good-bye. The old parent and child are still full of energy, but they have work to do.

Danuta stops the car at a small Jewish cemetery outside town. The tombstones are all gone, but the gate remains—cast iron, with a star of David. It swings back and forth on loose hinges. We walk the grounds and wonder.

Back at home, Danuta and Monika haul out another enormous meal and a bottle of vodka. "Will you have some?" I ask Danuta as she thumps the bottle in front of me.

"Yes, of course I will," she assures me.

"Then I will, too," I reply, and we toast to Pan Kowieski and his daughter.

"Let me help you with the tape," Danuta suggests, after we have downed two shots apiece and eaten our fill of herring with onion, cold meats, smoked turkey, Monika's potato dumplings, and tea with honey. "I can explain to you what they are saying when we come to parts you don't understand."

We down another vodka, as Monika and Adam kibitz from the couch while

A Father and His Daughter
—

they watch television. Danuta points out that I am constantly saying "Tak, tak" throughout the tape. "Now listen to you laughing," she teases. "You didn't understand what they were talking about, did you? Did you? And there you are laughing and saying 'Yes, yes' like a duck." Another vodka and a few more 'tak, taks,' and we're both laughing so hard we're crying. The old man and the old woman continue on the tape, unabated by their contradictions of one another, unfazed by my quacking.

The next day my new family walks me to the train station in Biała Podlaska so they can wave good-bye from the platform. "The real Danuta" never returned our call. The new Danuta packs cake and an apple for the trip to Warsaw, where "prices are crazy." She holds out her hand in a "buddy" gesture, then pulls me to her for three kisses. Then I get three from Monika, and Adam has no reservations, three from him, too.

"It's going to be sad now without you," Danuta calls up to the window when I have boarded. "All this excitement for three days. But you are coming back. You will write, won't you?"

CHAPTER 37

Waiting

"Proszę Pana!" a voice calls from across the street as I pass the Lubawa gate, heading for the Rynek to see what Pani Wituchowska and Ryszard and Grażyna have been up to while I was away in Biała Podlaska and then Jerusalem. "Please, mister," literally, but more like "Excuse me, sir," still in the formal Polish way to which I have become accustomed. It's Pan Kopiczyński dashing out of his photo shop and running down the street behind me as I make deliveries from a bag of souvenir crosses and rosaries from the Holy Land.

"Your relative, the cousin from Gwiździny," he says when he catches up with me, his face unsmiling, "I was talking to a man, I don't remember his name. He said she is in the hospital, and it is very serious."

My bag of crosses suddenly seems trivial. It has been little more than a week since my lucky walk in the Boleszyn cemetery led me to the family I longed to find. Now, as Pan Kopiczyński talks, I cannot stop thinking of Marianna's face, the young woman in those old photographs, and the way she looked the same to me, her gentle smile, her hand patting the side of my face. "From America, all the way from America, I never thought I would live to see you."

"It must be Marianna," I tell him.

"The man said you would know," Pan Kopiczyński says gravely. "There is something else," he adds. "I remember now, the funeral of Jan Bryszkiewski, your grandmother's brother; I took the photograph you brought in for me to copy. I was very young, just starting out. I stared at that picture, and it looked familiar, and then I realized that I had taken it. I remember going out to Sugajno to their farm. For your sake, I wish I had remembered sooner."

Pani Wituchowska welcomes me with a wide grin and a long, drawn-out, "O, o, o, Pan Pączek!" I know she is happy to see me.

"Almost, almost," she can hardly wait to tell me. "We almost met you at the airport! Michał thought of it. They have the best ice cream in Warsaw, he said, real Italian ice cream, and so he said we should drive to Warsaw for ice cream and while we are there pick you up at the airport. He asked me when you were due back, but I didn't know for sure, so we called the airport, but they said you were not on the Saturday flight from Israel. But can you imagine if you had gotten off the plane, and we were standing there waiting for you? Can you?" Pani covers her mouth with glee.

"By one day, off by one day," I lament. Yes, it would have been marvelous.

Pani is brimming with other news and insists that tomorrow we must spend the evening catching up. "So much went on when you were gone. We had a terrible storm with huge hailstones; I tried to save them in the freezer, but they didn't keep. Then I had a little concert in the store here."

"A concert in the store?" Ah, her tape.

"Yes, a piano concert, all sorts of people were here. Adam was here, and you should have seen his eyes pop wide open when he heard me play."

There is more news. "My Swiss friends have been sending me postcards. They want to take me out for dinner, and Pan Kopiczyński tells me I should just go."

"My mother's cousin, the eldest, is very ill and in the hospital," I tell her.

"And what is wrong?"

"She just seems to have stopped wanting to live. She was in great pain when I met her. Her daughters told me that since her husband died, she has withdrawn more and more, and now. . . ."

"Yes, yes, it is often that way," Pani Wituchowska says wisely. "Some of us know when it's time."

I am filled with regret. Oh, how Marianna and my mother—first cousins—would have loved one another in another time and another place.

"I have something to tell you about Sznurek," Pani laughs. "This will really shock you. But you have to wait until tomorrow, dinner, six thirty, and don't tell me you have to go off to Kwidzyn with Adam! Oh, I think I regret the day you walked into this store," she says, shaking her head.

I know what she means. Why get close to others only to have them taken away—as they inevitably are.

CHAPTER 37

—

"You really should have been a priest," Pani Wituchowska says suddenly. "Yes, I think it would have been the best for you."

"And had I been born here, it would have happened, I've no doubt," I assure her.

"All right, I'll tell you now. Adam and Alina were in Germany with the children while you were gone. Did he tell you? If they reconcile, and she moves back home, there won't be room for you, so you know there is a room for you here," she teases, delighted at the prospect that I'll be evicted and have to throw myself on her mercy.

At *Gazeta Nowomiejska* Ryszard and Grażyna are tired from a hard day's work but happy with their rosary and cross souvenirs, which look somehow tacky to me now.

It is still light when I pass by the entrance to the cinema in the old Evangelical church. A tough-talking woman is sitting on a bench, drunk, beating her chest, and explaining herself to a man towering over her.

"Wujek! Wujek!" I hear behind me, and then little Paweł is walking alongside me. "Where are you going, uncle?"

I hear Pani Wituchowska telling me to stay away from these children, to be careful because "they are just not nice people." But this is a seven-year-old boy, and I am suddenly Father Flanagan.

He sticks like glue, unaware that he has a great-aunt in the hospital readying herself to die.

"What are you going to do this evening?" I ask

"Nothing. Walk around."

"Where is your mother?"

"She said she was going for a walk."

"Where is your big brother?"

"Playing cards in the living room."

"Do you like to read?"

"Yes, lots of different stuff."

"Is the library open?"

"No, it's probably closed tonight."

He has walked me half way home, now and then looking up at me with a big, dirty-toothed grin, running his hands through his dusty blond hair.

"Uncle."

"Yes, Paweł."

"Can you give me a few grosz?"

"Are you asking me for money?"

"Yes."

Waiting

—

"Why?"

"Maybe for some ice cream?"

"It is not a good thing to ask people for money. When I was a little boy, I could never ask people for money. I like to talk to you, but I don't want you to ask me for money."

He walks along beside me, and I feel sure he is going to follow me right into the house, and I will have to be even harder on him.

"Uncle," he says, hands in the pockets of his raggedy blue pants, "I am sorry I asked you for money." Then he tags along beside me until we pass under the railroad trestle, where I cross the street, and he suddenly stops.

"Uncle. I have to turn around now. Good-bye."

So I walk back home and call Marianna's daughter, Jola, but she is not home, and her husband tries to explain. "Yes, she is in the hospital in Iława; her condition is not good."

I call her daughter Basia, and she patiently and with great resignation tells me that during my week away in the Holy Land her mother stopped talking, stopped eating. "She is near death. She cannot live long like this."

"Perhaps you will see her one more time," she suggests, "tomorrow if you like." I have a blessed cross of olive wood from Jerusalem to take her.

In front of the lyceum, Cousin Feliksa is sitting on a bench with Karolina in a buggy, little Patrycja tending to her. She rattles on incoherently about her sister in the hospital and asks me when I am leaving. She smiles gently and peers up at me with her head tilted to the right. "Come and see us again," she says.

At Pan Kopiczyński's photo shop I drop off the photos I took of smiling Marianna barely two weeks ago to make copies for her daughters.

"Dinner is ruined again," Pani Wituchowska teases, then rolls her eyes and says, "Mój Boże"—"My God"—when I tell her I have been talking to Feliksa and her wayward grandchildren. "Wujek! Wujek!" she mocks, "Uncle! Uncle!"

CHAPTER 37

—

The Vigil

No one is crying. Jadzia, Marianna's second daughter, welcomes me into her home in the Soviet block house in Iława. Waldek is leaving for work. Bartek is in the little room with his cousins, Jola's daughters, and the computer, making up an e-mail chain letter that he hopes will beef up his collection of used telephone cards from around the world.

Cousin Jadzia pulls cold cuts from the refrigerator and lays out sandwich fixings. There is turkey soup on the stove, and she jokes that it is an ugly gray color. But it's delicious.

Bartek walks me to the hospital, a newly remodeled building just a couple blocks from the apartment. Marianna's eldest daughter, Basia, and her husband are already there with Jola, the youngest daughter. The fourth daughter, Wiesia, is missing.

We have to put on blue paper booties, available for one złoty from a dispenser by the front door. The corridors are clean, sterile white, trimmed in pale blue and gray.

I have not visited anyone in a hospital since my mother died four years ago. Can it really be that long? Now I am going to see a woman I barely know, a woman who smiled gently at me just a couple weeks ago and asked what took me so long, a woman whose picture I stared at for so many years before learning her name, a cousin my mother might have loved like a sister had the ladies in the cemetery twelve years ago just pointed us in the right direction.

"The doctors say it is only a matter of time," Jola whispers, holding my arm. Her mother is lying on the bed, but she is struggling—against the needle in her arm, against being in the hospital.

"Andzia, Andzia," she calls out for her younger sister.

"She told me she thinks about her all the time now," Jola says. "Just the week before she came to the hospital, she called out at night, 'Andzia, are you in heaven? I am on the way.'"

Basia tries to hold her mother's flailing right arm, then she sponges her brow. But Marianna is not at ease; she is struggling, her eyes closed, protesting the fact that she is here, lying on these white sheets.

"Krystyna and Ignacy Igielski are here to visit my mother," says Basia over the telephone. "Why don't you come and meet him, the man in my grandfather's funeral photograph."

Ignacy is Marianna's nephew, his mother was Jan's stepdaughter, Jadwiga Igielska. His reputation precedes him, the multimarried, debonair lover. His cousins smile at the mention of his name. It's a lot to live up to, and of course he doesn't.

He is sitting on the couch in Basia's living room when I arrive, his blondynka, Krystyna, by his side. She is a hard-smoking, puffy-faced young woman who looks like she's seen her share of trouble. He has the tired look of a man past his prime. At first it's hard to imagine how this frightened, round-faced, rather slight man could ever have been young and wild. But there he is, tall and intense in that old photograph, his hair dark, his eyes alert.

Jola is at the hospital with her mother, so there is time for Jadzia and Basia to offer me cakes and coffee, for me to meet the last of Basia's daughters, Brygida, who resembles yet another cousin in America. We also have time for a walk with Renata, pushing the baby stroller. There'll be no talking with Marianna today, however, no coaxing memories from her.

We walk back to the hospital reluctantly, resisting the future we know must come.

At first Marianna is restful, then she begins swinging her arm with the intravenous needle taped to it, then her cries begin, angry calls, angry pained moans that sound like she is demanding something that will not come, perhaps an end to her misery. Her eyes are closed, and though her daughters stroke her head and moisten her lips with balm, her discomfort grows.

Ignacy and Krystyna turn their sad faces to me and talk about how difficult it is to see her this way. I tell them how difficult it is to meet someone for the first time, to hear her stories, so lucid and clear, and two weeks later to find her here.

Marianna's stomach is bloated. Jola says the doctors are talking about bone cancer. I wonder, why only now when only days ago she was walking and talking about a hip replacement? I can barely understand the rudiments of what is going on in medical terms, but I can see two loving daughters standing by helplessly as their mother nears death. "They don't know how long she can continue like this. They want us to move her to a hospice in Lubawa. But it's so far away," says Jola.

"It won't be long," Basia whispers wisely.

Marianna is restless again, and her daughters try to comfort her, but it is as if she is saying, "Let me go, let me go." Her family and I stand there in our blue one-złoty paper booties.

A nurse comes in and moistens the old woman's mouth as if she were a baby, but this only makes her wave her arms and call out, "Mój Jezu, mój Jezu!"

"It's her job," says Basia, nodding toward the nurse. She's not expecting sympathy. "Every day the nurse hears these cries."

It's too soon for mourning. Marianna is still alive, and Jola talks of X-rays and bone cancer and a hospice.

It is time for me to leave the room, but I can hear Marianna's agony down the sterile hall, her screams echoing off the walls, as if asking why it must be this way. How like birth death is; for many, it hurts so much there seems no bearing it.

There is the wait until tomorrow to see what the doctors say, and they will go on testing and guessing until the end, as they should. I must accept, with Marianna, this suffering woman I met only weeks ago, that it is time to go. She told me so herself. My mother, her cousin born in the same year, whom Marianna will never know, told me that it was time for her to go as well, but I could not accept it. Marianna's daughters seem wiser. They know the time comes.

Basia's husband, Stanisław, and Ignacy leave the room after me, and the door is closed, but we can still hear the screams.

In other rooms other women are getting well, digging through baskets brought by relatives or lying still, toothless mouths gaping, chests rising and falling. Then the screams from room three fade away.

Back at Jadzia's apartment, we have more tea and coffee and cake. Bartek has a present for me and shyly hands me a needlepoint face of Jesus in black thread.

Jola needs a ride home, and her daughters Żaneta and Karolina ride in the back seat of the Maluch, which coughs and sputters its way to Gwiździny. "I am glad you are here, Leonard," she murmurs, the youngest child, about to be orphaned.

Whether or Not It's Time

"No problem," Adam told me when I said I would like to make a farewell dinner for the special people who have helped me most during my little life in Poland. "No problem," as he says to everything, even the worst problem.

So today it's time to clean the house, to pull down the spider webs in the hall, to mop the floors, and pull out the table for dinner tomorrow. Adam retreats to his bedroom. I must go to the open-air market.

It is only now, in trying to arrange a small gathering in my own honor, that I realize what a small town this really is. Wituchowska doesn't like Laskowski. Ulatowski doesn't like Łydziński. Grażyna Jonowska won't be comfortable with Michał Wituchowski. Urszula Łydzińska has a grudge against Alina Kopicyzńska over the job she didn't get at the lyceum, and Alina doesn't want to be a guest in her own home.

So I split the group in two, half on Wednesday, half on Thursday. Pani Kopicyzńska agrees to bake a cake and advises me on menu and table décor.

"Panie Leonardzie," she says. "You should just invite everyone you want and let them do whatever they want. If they don't want to come, they don't have to come." It's good advice, but I have already decided, so she helps me write invitations and plan the food: kiełbasa, meatballs, potatoes, carrots, peppers with pineapple—at Pani Kopicyzńska's insistence—and her cake for dessert.

On the day of the first farewell, I have mixed the meat for the meatballs when she marches in, her familiar wooden clompers flopping at fifty miles per hour on the tile floors. She has two cakes and a sheet of apple and plum cobbler, sets them down, and proceeds to taste my raw meat mix. "Not enough salt." And she dumps in a few tablespoons of vegeta.

Taste, taste. More vegeta. Clomp, clomp, clomp. I give up and start setting the table.

Now Pani runs out to the garden and comes back with strawberries to decorate the top of her cake. "These late ones continue all through autumn. The plants cost a lot to buy, but we found them," she brags.

Pani has also decided we need to stuff a zucchini. She peels her garden find, scoops out the seeds, and fills the cavity with a quarter of my meatball mix. More vegeta, and into a pan, the one I was going to use to fry meatballs.

Pani moves back to the strawberries, pouring her red galareta all over the top of the cake until it drips onto the floor. Bam, bam, bam. All done.

"Don't fry the meatballs in that pan," she orders. "The dill is too old. I'll bring fresh. Don't soak those potatoes in cold water; you lose vitamins."

"What happens when you boil them?"

"That, too, so you should use the water for sauce."

Clomp, clomp, clomp.

The first of my two good-bye dinners is already a disaster. And it gets worse as each guest arrives. There are to be eight of us altogether.

Ryszard and Grażyna pull frantically into the driveway. She's wearing a baggy, red T-shirt. "That should go beautifully with the full-length gown Pani Wituchowska will no doubt show up in," I think.

She leaves Ryszard behind and speeds back up the driveway. He's wearing some sort of country work clothes and a vest with a chain hanging out of it.

He and Pani Kopiczyńska get along just fine, but then Pani Wituchowska and Michał pull up. She is indeed dressed to the nines, as if for the opera, in a long, navy blue dress and her famous coral necklace and pearl earrings, her hair freshly bronzed. I realize that she is the genuine article, that she has preserved this way of life through sixty years of war and communism, and she is only truly at home with formality.

I kiss her hand. She expects it. It's been raining all day, she observes. "Heaven is crying because you are leaving." I begin to wish that I had never brought together this combination of people, strangers who never see one another ordinarily and do not wish to. I begin to wish I'd gone to the hospital instead to be with Marianna, the real reason heaven is crying.

Michał drives the car home, and we chat and drink wine while we wait for him. Pan Kopiczyński will be late, his wife says. Grażyna will be late, too, says

Ryszard. We wait awkwardly, and I do not know how to say the small pleasantries that would bring these people together.

Pani Kopiczyńska has changed into a skirt and sandals, but she still looks like a servant girl next to Pani Wituchowska. She starts hauling food onto the table. All at once. So much for courses.

The dinner passes in a blur. There is nonstop chatter from Pani Wituchowska, nonstop arrogance from her son, and periodically he checks in with me to see why I am not talking. "I don't understand half of what you are saying" is all I can tell him. But he holds forth anyway. And off into politics he goes, proud as anything that he knows all about the upcoming American presidential election. He is fascinated by the fact that Al Gore's running mate is Jewish.

"It would be better if he were a woman, perhaps a black woman," I say with a straight face.

"Better yet if she had AIDS," says my friend the notariusz, jumping at the bait. No one is amused.

The phone rings, but by the time I get to it, the ringing has stopped.

Pani Wituchowska is still talking, and the phone rings again, and again I cannot get to my room fast enough, so I move the phone closer. I expect it will ring again. I thank all my guests with an awkward speech in Polish that Adam helped me write last night, thank them for letting me be their guest and opening up another world to me.

Everyone stares blankly, then with what looks like pity, as if to say, "You poor, lost, tongue twisted creature."

When the telephone finally rings again, it's Jola, calling to tell me her mother has died. "How she did suffer, but now it is over," she says gently, holding back her tears. "This is very hard, but I will have to be okay."

Dinner continues, but I cannot concentrate. No one passes food around. No one seems very hungry. The only obvious thing is how foolish and awkward this group of people seems. I have forgotten how to say anything of consequence. I just want it to end. Finally it does, as awkwardly as it began, with Ryszard, thank God, rising to announce he must work tomorrow.

Adam takes the Wituchowskis home, and when he returns, I tell him I understand now why no one in this group has ever socialized with anyone else in this group.

"She just talked too much," he says of Madame Wituchowska, as if that explains everything. "Perhaps she was the most nervous of all."

Yes. But it's more than that. It's the delicate distances that people maintain between one another, the positions of comfort they assume, and the chaos an intruder, looking for his family, can cause.

Whether or Not It's Time

—

The Last Act

 have said good-bye all day, thinking I should have taken Pani Wituchowska up on her offer to buy a house for me. I want to stay here forever. "This is where you belong," she said. It feels that way.

Pani Wituchowska gave me a big hug, and my bag fell awkwardly off my shoulder and onto hers, twisting our arms together.

Ryszard said he would drive me to the station. And now that the time is near, I don't want this life to end. What is the point of befriending people only to lose them? It feels not like going home but like going under water.

I keep hearing Jola's voice on the telephone. It doesn't matter when it comes, I told her, it is always too soon. Too soon for your mother to be gone. "I only just met her. I should have come sooner. I should have. . . ." She cut me off, "No, no. You should be grateful you met her. You came just in time. That is what you must remember."

But how does it happen that I meet this long lost cousin Marianna only to lose her less than a month later? The last dinner party passed quickly. Janusz and Anna, Mieczysław and Urszula brought roses and kissed me good-bye, all four of them. Dinner conversation was lively; I kept up with much of it as I served the leftovers from yesterday—in courses.

They asked me what I liked and didn't like about Poland. I smiled and told them clumsily that the only things I didn't like were the flies in the house because there were no screens and people hovering next to me like flies and looking at my business in bank lines and in the post office and in train stations.

When they asked me what I liked, I could only say, "the people." Without people, what is a country but a piece of ground? In the end it's always the little things you remember about people. The formal and quiet way Mieczysław makes his wishes known, the bossy way Janusz asserts his views, Adam's disdain for all problems.

I gazed across the table at my new friends.

"Oh, if my grandmother could see me sitting here," I told them.

"She does see you. She does," Urszula said.

In the morning, my last day in Nowe Miasto, the sense of drowning gets worse. Music doesn't help. I dress for the funeral, while Adam putters and gathers items for his weekend camping expedition. What have I learned? When drowning, do not kick. Oh, but I do not want to leave this place, these hard-won friends made in another language.

A loudspeaker blares outside my window from the lyceum, welcoming the kids back to school. The sun is shining, women with bags head for the market. The horse clip-clops by, pulling a cart of wood. Children are all dressed up.

I combine the roses my friends have given me into a bouquet for the cemetery. Pani Kopiczyńska advises me not to take containers of leftover food as I had planned. "It will be strange. They will not expect you to come with armloads of food. Just take yourself. The flowers. It's enough." I hug her and, surprised, she hugs me back. "No tears, no tears," she insists.

Adam says good-bye swiftly, with a hug. "You'll be back," he says. "No problem."

What I'll remember most about Marianna's funeral is its ordinariness.

No cars are parked in front of the block house where she lived with Jola and Andrzej, where I met her just weeks ago for that one long talk so many years overdue. The cleared road to the church is a sign of what is to come.

Pani was right when she advised me not to take food. I would have looked like a fool. No one is thinking of food.

Jola greets me with three kind kisses and tells me to park around the corner, behind the building. There, three men in white shirts and gloves wait near a blue van with "Pogrzeb" written on it—funeral.

The little apartment where I first met these cousins is crowded with now-familiar faces: Stefan, Stanisław, Ludwik, Andrzej, the sons-in-law, all shake my hand.

"Such a short time ago we stood here, and you met her," Stefan says and shakes his head.

The Last Act

—

Marianna's body is laid out in a wooden coffin on two stools where the coffee table stood, where I laid out my photos and letters and she looked at them with tears in her eyes, "mój Boże, mój Boże," thanking God that she met me.

"Doesn't look like my mother," Jola whispers. No, it does not, the eyes forced shut, worse the mouth caved in and frozen, a mocking reminder of the uselessness of the body without life.

Bartek forces a smile as he moves ahead of me nearer his grandmother with his brother Waldek. Basia greets me with three kisses and the four grieving daughters assume their places nearest their mother's head.

Sister Feliksa enters and takes her place on the couch facing the coffin. Then sister Łucja arrives, head in a babushka, looking puffy and ill, toothless. Feliksa follows loudly, proudly, her head tilted, fingering her beads, as another old woman leads the rosary.

I reach into my suit pocket and find a rosary that has been there since my own mother's funeral.

The room is full of faith, but it's hot and the rosary long. Jadzia looks at her mother's face and weeps. Jola adjusts a wisp of hair and the rosary and prayer book in her mother's hands. Stefan is wiping sweat from his brow. Andrzej drapes a piece of paper over a spot in the window where the sun is poking through. The rosary chant and rhythm are soothing, but I feel so hot I must take off my jacket or faint.

Jadzia cries for her mother most. Wiesia sheds silent tears beside her. They must sit down, and the couch behind them is cleared, the lit candle moved. Basia, the eldest, seems most at peace, most resigned to life without her mother.

When the rosary is done, Stefan's voice rises above the others as the singing begins. He wipes tears away. Then Feliksa leads into another song; her voice too is clear and strong, the room is filled with the voices of those who loved Marianna.

Small gestures, a word here and there, and I am made to feel a part of the family—long lost but never too late, never an interloper.

My thoughts are of my own mother. How the loss of parents changes us forever. How Feliksa resembles her. How she suffered long and often alone. How terrified I was of her coming death, too frightened to comfort her when she was certain the end was near, when she was scared. It's the fear that is the hardest to take, not the suffering, not the anger. Anger makes life easier.

"What's happening to me?" my mother once pleaded in a doctor's office when he said her clogged arteries made her "a walking stick of dynamite." Who isn't? I wonder.

CHAPTER 40

—

The songs go on, a third, a fourth, a fifth, a moment of silence, a sixth.

There is whispering, and a path is cleared for the priest, who enters with great bluster, a fat man in black vestments with silver sparkles down the front. His words are few—just a blessing and a sprinkle of holy water. The skinny assistant behind him responds, and the family says "Amen." Then one by one we file by Marianna, most touching her on the hands as I do when it is my turn, some gently kissing her forehead.

Then we wait outside with our bouquets of flowers wrapped in crinkly cellophane until the coffin appears, with its lid closed now and showing the crude carvings all around the side, like the folk boxes for sale in souvenir shops. Marianna's granddaughter Edyta gives me three kisses, she and her sisters looking so much like my cousins at home, family.

And now I am part of this funeral procession, so like all the ones I have watched in Nowe Miasto during my short life in Poland. A word from Basia and I know where to stand. Stefan is beside me as we begin the long walk. Jadzia tells me stories about where the daughters lived in Gwiździny when they were first married, before all these grandchildren walking nearest the blue van carrying their grandmother's body to church.

"The bell is not very impressive," Krystyna comments. "You can barely hear it. Our church in Zalewo has a loud bell, beautiful."

Inside the church she asks me if I can change a large bill for the collection basket. I forget the word for "change" and tell her, "No, I have a plane to catch." She looks at me as if I have a screw loose, but we figure out the misunderstanding and smile. When the plate comes around, she peeks at my handful of money and points to ten złoty and whispers, "Just that one will do." Ignacy flashes a handsome grin.

The mass is long, the priest comforting the family by telling them what a good Catholic Marianna was. Outside, a bus waits to transport members of the family for whom the walk to the cemetery is too long.

I must leave. The train to Warsaw is due. Ryszard and Grażyna will be waiting to take me to the station in Iława.

"Please tell them all that I am grateful for their hospitality. Tell them I had to catch a train," I whisper to Ignacy and Krystyna. They nod, and their eyes fill with tears.

I jump in my car, pass the cemetery on my way, where they will all be standing in a little while. The opening in the earth awaits.

At Adam's house, my friends are waiting. I am late. There is no time for talk or lingering. I leave my Maluch in the driveway, the only payment Adam will accept for my many months' room and board.

The Last Act

—

The train pulls into the station as we arrive, and we haul my luggage aboard in a rush. Tears are rolling down Grażyna's cheeks. Ryszard smiles bravely. Why does anything ever end?

The villages and barracks and lovely green fields and patches of woods and water pass quickly as my express train presses toward Warsaw.

Nearly ninety years ago my grandmother made a decision as well—to leave this town for a new and strange place where the streets would be paved with gold. When she made her decision, mine was made, too. And now, for me, czas do domu. It's time to go home.

Epilogue

———◆———

A few weeks after I left Nowe Miasto Lubawskie and returned to the United States, my phone rang. "Would you like to speak to your cousin from Poland?" a man asked in broken English. A woman came to the phone and said in Polish, "I am Danuta, Czesław Brodacki's granddaughter."

"I am Antoni Brodacki's grandson. Where are you?" I asked, thinking perhaps Sandomierz, where I had left messages on her answering machine more than a month before.

"I'm in Chicago," she said. "My brother in Huszcza wrote to me. When you met him, he did not know I was here."

We met the next day. I showed Danuta the letter she had written as a young girl to my grandmother. She was astonished that it had survived and that I had carried it with me back to Poland, across the ocean at almost the same time she was on her way to America.

Later that same week, based on a memory from my Aunt Mary, I called Canadian directory assistance for Prince Albert, Saskatchewan, and on the first try located a granddaughter of Piotr Brodacki, Antoni's "real brother." Astonished, Bonnie Cloak told me her grandfather died in 1975 and that she had recently embarked on a genealogy quest of her own.

A few weeks later I received an e-mail message from Wałbrzych. Marianna's family had contacted Janusz Kułak, who wrote to tell me that his mother, my grandmother's niece, would like to meet me, and so would he.

Janina Kułak died before I could return to Poland. When I finally met her son, he presented me with a cross from his mother. She had asked him to tell me that she was sorry she could not meet this grandson of her Aunt Helena, to whom she had sent her wedding picture, one of the photographs I carried with me during my short life in Poland.

Janusz and I spent some time together in Kraków, regretting that our mothers, first cousins and the daughters of sisters, had never met. I visited him and his family in Wałbrzych, where he took me to his mother's grave and to her Uncle Franciszek's grave, my grandmother's kind brother, who became Janina's father and grandfather to Janusz.

As I watched from my window in the Hotel Pod Różą, the trumpeter of Kraków played his mournful tune, and I dreamed of a family reunion here in this ancient city, with enough relatives to fill the entire Sukiennice—cousins from America, all of the grandchildren of Helena Bryszkiewska and Antoni Brodacki, and all the grandchildren of their brothers and sisters, from France and Germany and England, Canada and Australia, not separated by language but understanding one another's stories. What a gathering that would be.

When I was a child, it must often have seemed to my grandmother that I was lost, always looking for something, for I remember her asking many times, "What are you looking for?" and then she would pause and add, "Yesterday?"

Perhaps I was looking for yesterday. I would like to tell her that I have found it, and, having done so, I understand that, known or unknown, it is the past that brought me here, and every moment matters.

Index

Index
—

Index

—

233